SEAN PENN

A BIOGRAPHY

SEAN PENN

A BIOGRAPHY

NICK JOHNSTONE

OMNIBUS PRESS
LONDON · NEW YORK · SYDNEY

Exclusive Distributors
Book Sales Limited,
8/9 Frith Street,
London W1V 5TZ, UK.

Music Sales Corporation,
257 Park Avenue South,
New York, NY 10010, USA.

The Five Mile Press,
22 Summit Road,
Noble Park,
Victoria 3174, Australia.

To the Music Trade only:
Music Sales Limited,
8/9 Frith Street,
London W1V 5TZ, UK.

Photo credits: Front & back cover: Rex Features.
All other pictures LFI & Rex.

Typeset by Galleon Typesetting, Ipswich
Printed by Creative Print & Design (Wales), Ebbw Vale

A catalogue record for this book is available from the British Library.

www.omnibuspress.com

Contents

Acknowledgements

I would like to thank my agent Tanja Howarth for all of her support (both professional and personal) while I was writing this book. I would like to thank Chris Charlesworth and everyone at Omnibus Press for supporting this project. I would also like to extend my thanks to the following: my parents; the William Morris Agency in Los Angeles; H & M; the Cinema Book Shop; Keith Badman; Teena Apeles; Michael "Cloven Hooves" Bonner; Serge Carlito the Email Fiend; and my wife, Anna, who never once complained when I turned our home into a continuous Sean Penn festival.

Author's Foreword

This book was originally intended to consist of three parts: a biographical section, a section on Sean Penn's work as an actor and a section on his directorial output. As a matter of course I contacted Penn's agent to request an interview with Penn himself. I wanted to talk to him at length about his deeply personal outings as a writer and director (*The Indian Runner* and *The Crossing Guard*) and hopefully gain some insight into his acting method. Moreover, in light of the fact that he has been dogged with a reputation as a hellraiser and all-round bad boy since his stormy marriage to Madonna, I wanted to give him the opportunity to set the record straight and offer his own take on all those infamous stories, most of which were undoubtedly overblown by the press. However, my request for an interview proved unsuccessful, and I have therefore opted for a straightforward chronological account of Penn's turbulent personal life and passionate, serious work as an actor, writer, director and producer.

Although many questions were raised during the writing of this book that only Sean Penn would be able to answer, I believe this is the most definitive study of the man that anyone – other than Penn himself – could write.

Introduction

It's all a dream. Freddy Gale's dream. He's standing in a car park. He sees a father and a daughter. The little girl runs and leaps into her father's arms. It all plays out in slow motion. The father sweeps his little girl into the air while Freddy Gale watches. He smiles, but only for a split second. The smile vanishes as quickly as it came, followed by a stab of pain. His daughter is long since dead. She was mown down by a drunk driver.

The above is an account of a scene from *The Crossing Guard*, a film written and directed by Sean Penn. I often like to watch that scene several times in a row. I study it hard, feel the hairs on the back of my neck stand up, rewind the tape, watch it again. The way in which Freddy Gale reacts to his daughter's death causes a rift between him and his wife that soon becomes a chasm that cannot be filled. They split up. He's left with an anger that has nowhere to go; wherever he goes, he sees loss. His life is a blur of strippers, one-night stands and alcohol. He never lets go of his daughter. She's still there, running towards him, leaping into his arms. But it's all a dream.

For me, this scene sums up what Sean Penn's work is all about: emotions. Documenting emotions, discovering emotions, hiding from emotions, the inability to express emotions, painful emotions, lost emotions, an absence of emotions. I've always imagined Sean Penn to be one of those people who ploughs through life, breaking things along the way and more often than not hurting himself in the process. In his rare interviews he talks at length about the relationships between men, in particular the relationships between either brothers or sons and fathers. He believes in his art: acting, writing, directing. He believes in his family and friends. Perhaps most important of all, he believes in love.

First there was Marlon Brando and James Dean. Then there was Jack Nicholson and Dustin Hoffman. Later came Robert De Niro, Al Pacino, John Savage, John Cazales, Robert Duvall, Ed Harris, Christopher

1

Walken and Harvey Keitel. Finally there was Sean Penn and Gary Oldman. All of these actors share or shared a total commitment to acting; watching them at work, the audience is masterfully steered into a suspension of disbelief. These actors bring characters and their contextual stories alive. De Niro or Brando or Sean Penn are able to make the characters they play compellingly 'real', demanding the audience's involvement with the story. Watching a film with Sean Penn in it, its easy to forget that you are actually watching a film featuring the actor Sean Penn. The man himself vanishes when he's in front of a camera. He changes, transforms, becomes someone else.

This style of acting is most frequently referred to as 'method acting', often to the chagrin of its practitioners. Foster Hirsch, in his book *A Method To Their Madness*, describes such an approach to acting as follows: "The Method is not playing yourself. The Method helps you to observe, to see life, to look outside yourself." For Hirsch, those who became known for method acting from the Seventies onwards brought a refreshing diversity of approach to their roles: "Actors like Brando, De Niro, Hoffman and Robert Duvall seem always to challenge the criticism that the Method actor merely cultivates a neurotic persona which he transports from role to role. These actors exult in the chance to wear different kinds of clothes, to hide behind make-up, to alter the way they move and sound." As an example, Hirsch takes Robert Duvall – who would act with Penn in *Colors*, highlighting Duvall's ability to reinvent himself utterly for each new role, "moving from the faceless retainer in *The Godfather* to the demented warmonger in *Apocalypse Now* – for these actors, impersonation and self-transformation are positive values".

As part of their *modus operandi*, the so-called method actors research a part with great intensity and attention to detail in order to 'become', in as comprehensive a sense as possible, the character they're playing. The method is the bridge between actor and character. For instance, when playing troubled cab driver Travis Bickle in Martin Scorsese's *Taxi Driver*, Robert De Niro famously spent several months driving a New York cab, in order to understand a taxi driver's working life. Penn brings the same hands-on approach to his acting. He spent time with the Los Angeles anti-gang teams to play a cop in *Colors* and enrolled at a military academy for his part as a cadet in *Taps*. He learned Mandarin for *Shanghai Surprise* and studied his real-life character for the true story of

The Falcon And The Snowman. His role in *At Close Range* required intensive gym work as well as bleached hair. Other body adornments acquired in the name of art include two tattoos: one for his role as a gang member in *Bad Boys*, the other for his portrayal of a deranged American army sergeant in *Casualties of War*. Penn has also brought his own real-life experiences to bear on the roles he has played. He had almost a decade's worth of surfing experience to bring to the role of a stoned surfer in *Fast Times At Ridgemont High* and drew on his habit of drinking at an Irish bar in New York's Hell's Kitchen for his role as an undercover Irish-American cop in *State of Grace*. His performance as a death row inmate in *Dead Man Walking* was undoubtedly informed by his own much-publicised spell in jail in 1987, while his teenage ambitions to be a lawyer no doubt contributed towards his preparation for the role of a cocaine-addled lawyer in *Carlito's Way*.

This unflinching commitment to each part stems from Penn's respect for what he often calls 'the work' and a system of values learned from his role model, Robert De Niro. Even though Penn clearly uses elements of the classic Method acting style, he has repeatedly dismissed the tag of 'Method Actor'. "I would say I'm an actor who has a method," he told *Film Comment* in 1991, "more than I would say I'm a Method actor". This is typical of Penn, though – he dislikes analysis of his work, preferring to let the work speak for itself. He doesn't like to question his performance once the work is complete and prefers to leave the persona behind on the last day of a film's shoot. Early on, he was notorious for assuming his character's personality traits to such a degree that he would only answer to his character's name while working on a film. This intense work ethic earned him the tag 'Sean De Niro' during the shoot of his first feature film, *Taps*. By the time he was acting in *Racing With The Moon*, Penn was renowned for even leaving answering machine messages under his character's name. This exhaustive attention to the art of acting was bound to take its toll at some point; such dedication to the part necessarily takes its toll on the actor. When Penn publicly announced that he was retiring from acting in 1990, his fans and admirers deplored the decision, protesting that it was a criminal waste of talent. After all, this was the man that critics had labelled the best actor of his generation.

The decision to retire from acting came hot on the heels of Penn's divorce from Madonna. In retrospect, it seems that at the time Penn was trying to get out of the public eye and start a new life. He had been hounded continuously by photographers and reporters throughout the couple's stormy relationship. This constant invasion of privacy was too much for Penn, who married Madonna when he was only 24. The pop superstar was used to the attention but for Penn, a reportedly shy man, it was too much. The greater the intrusion, the more violent his reaction to it and soon Sean Penn was more famous for punching out photographers than he was for turning out excellent acting performances. The public spectacle that the marriage became took its toll; Penn sought solace in alcohol and fought to protect his privacy. As Madonna commented later, "Sean will fight for privacy. He wants to protect me . . . as inefficient as his methods may be, he sticks with what he believes in." She also complained that, "The press would make up the most awful things that we had never done, fights that we never had. Then sometimes we would have a fight and we'd read about it and it would be almost spooky, like they'd predicted it or they'd bugged our phones or they were listening to our conversations. It can be very scary if you let it get to you."

By the time the couple divorced in 1989, Penn was sick both of being in the public spotlight and of acting. Some time later, during an interview for the Bravo TV series *Inside The Actors Studio,* he revealed that he found himself staring at too many hotel room ceilings and asking himself what in the hell he was doing with his life. Acting was no longer fun. It had become a tortuous process. The degree of emotional investment that he threw into each role was wearing him out and when the films met with harsh reviews and even worse box-office performances, Penn was deeply hurt. He put so much of himself into films like *At Close Range* that he expected success and recognition in return.

Sean Penn has consistently shunned the type of big-budget films that peers such as Nicolas Cage, Charlie Sheen, Jennifer Jason Leigh, Rob Lowe, Michael J. Fox, Emilio Estevez, Tom Cruise and Demi Moore have acted in. If you flick through his filmography, you won't find anything overly commercial. There's no *Single White Female*, no *About Last Night*, no *Face/Off*, no *Indecent Proposal*, no *Wall Street*, no *Stakeout*, no *Top Gun*. Sean Penn isn't interested in making films that go hand in hand with a soft drink and a monster box of popcorn. He's interested in the kind of films that are considered offbeat, eccentric, raw, unusual. Above all, he's interested in realism at all costs and realism is something that often gets left outside a cinema when an audience takes to its seats. Most cinema-goers want simply to be entertained, to be taken away from 'real' life, dealt fantasy and escapism, shown things that don't happen in their everyday lives. These are not the qualities that Sean Penn seeks when he's looking for a new project to get involved with. It's no surprise that some of his mentors through the years have been stubbornly idiosyncratic figures such as Dennis Hopper, Marlon Brando, Jack Nicholson, Harry Dean Stanton, actor/director John Cassavetes and writer Charles Bukowski. They all speak a stubbornly non-conformist language; and so does Sean Penn.

After his so-called retirement from acting, Penn wrote and directed a powerful film called *The Indian Runner* that was set in Nebraska during the late 1960s. The grainy qualities of the film, and the emotional truths that the script riffed on, were backed up by Penn's obvious willingness to let his actors work their magic. This staunchly anti-narrative film, which dealt with the troubled relationship between two brothers, caused many critics to compare the film with John Cassavetes' independently made masterpieces. When *The Indian Runner* was released, it bombed – according to the IMDB website – and failed to gross more than $150,000. This return on an $11-million budget wrecked Penn's fantasies of working full time as a director and quitting acting altogether. Unexpectedly, he bounced back from the disappointment by returning to acting. His first acting job in three years saw Penn play a sleazy lawyer in Brian De Palma's *Carlito's Way*, a performance that won him endless praise when the film was released. Although this was heartening for Penn, his motives for doing the film had nothing to do with nursing a wounded ego. He wanted to work with Al Pacino and he wanted the cash. Penn had invested a lot of money in *The Indian Runner* that he never saw again. He also needed to bankroll money for his second film as writer/director, *The Crossing Guard*. However, even though his friend Jack Nicholson starred in the film, it didn't fare much better than *The Indian Runner* with the paying public. The anti-narrative approach was still there, perhaps less antagonistically than in *The Indian Runner*, as was a determined quest to pursue emotional honesty at all costs. However, when the film finished its brief run at American cinemas, it had only grossed – according to IMDB – a miserable $832,000.

Once again, Penn's feelings were hurt. As if to rub salt into the wounds, his performance as a death row inmate in *Dead Man Walking* was rapturously received. This time he didn't just receive praise from film critics – he was also nominated for an Academy Award® in the Best Actor category. Penn didn't win the award. It went to his friend Nicolas Cage for his role as an alcoholic in *Leaving Las Vegas*.

On the night of the awards ceremony in March 1996, Penn wasn't in the audience. He was with his partner, the actress Robin Wright. The couple, who had fallen in love after working together on *State of Grace* in late 1989, had been through some stormy periods. Although they had had two children together, they had never married and for most of 1995 they were separated. When Wright was taken into hospital on the night of the Academy Awards® for an emergency gall bladder operation, Penn rushed to be by her side. They were reportedly reunited immediately after she came round from the anaesthetic and haven't been apart since.

The two were married in April 1996 and Penn saw the event as an opportunity to put his wild days behind him. To do so required a radical rethink of the way he had been leading his life, to cut down on the booze, and accept the responsibilities that he now had as a partner and father. After Wright was car-jacked near the couple's Los Angeles home, they moved to Marin County, outside San Francisco.

The stabilising influence of family life opened a new chapter in Penn's turbulent life. He returned to acting with a renewed vigour, committing himself to a series of left-of-centre projects. He played small cameo roles in Robert Downey Senior's *Hugo Pool* and Erin Dignam's superb mood piece *Loved*, and jumped in at the last moment when Oliver Stone found himself without an actor for *U Turn*'s lead male part. He was taken up on his offer to act in any Terrence Malick film for one dollar and found himself spending several months on location in Australia shooting the acclaimed director's third film, *The Thin Red Line*.

Penn's two most committed parts were debts that he had to clear. When Nick Cassavetes decided to direct *She's So Lovely*, a script written some ten years earlier by his father, since deceased, Penn felt that he simply had to be involved. Not only had he taken part in acting groups at John Cassavetes' house that helped the writer/director flesh out his script, he had also been asked by John Cassavetes if he wanted to star in the film, should it get off the ground. However, things ground to a halt when John Cassavetes died from cirrhosis of the liver in 1989.

Veteran Hal Ashby took over the reins on the project, but died himself soon afterwards, and Penn spent a brief period trying to get financing in order to direct it himself. However, his stubborn insistence on wanting to shoot the film in black and white rendered his efforts to get backing impossible. When John Cassavetes' son exhumed the project Penn, feeling as though he owed his late friend, committed to the project, but not before he persuaded Nick Cassavetes to cast him opposite Robin Wright. The astonishing performance that Penn gives in the film won him the Best Actor prize when the film was premiered at the Cannes Film Festival in 1997.

The second debt to clear harked back to Penn's involvement in the production of David Rabe's play *Hurlyburly* that was staged in Los Angeles in 1988. Rabe and director Anthony Drazan had re-worked the play for the big screen. Penn committed to the project, but on two conditions. One, that Robin Wright also had a part in the film and two, that the film was relocated from the Hollywood Hills to the Oakland Hills, near to the Penn family's home in Marin County. Penn and Wright wanted to be near their children during filming. His manic performance in the film won Sean Penn the Best Actor prize at the Venice Film Festival in 1998.

Three more film parts were slotted in around *Hurlyburly*. The first was David Fincher's *The Game*, a film about the relationship between two brothers – something that surely sparked Penn's interest – which pitted Penn against Michael Douglas. The second was Philip Haas' *Up At The Villa*, a period piece set in Tuscany in the 1930s, which presented a different, lighter side to Penn. The third project was Woody Allen's *Sweet and Lowdown*.

This barrage of edgy, powerful work put Sean Penn's name back on the acting map. He was no longer seen as an actor who had walked away from his talent and profession. Instead, he was regarded as an older, even better actor who was ready to return to doing what he did best. His face, which had become noticeably more mature from 1996 on, added a new depth to his acting style, the older features lending his roles a poignancy that was previously hard to attain because of his fresh-faced, youthful visage. The parts he was now taking were all chosen because they fitted Penn's new ethic. He was only interested in acting in serious films. *The Game* is an exception; the other films are all driven by loose, rambling narratives that attempt to examine the complexity of human emotions. None of these films have obvious plots and all of them are decidedly offbeat. However, his return to acting does not signal an end to Penn's ambitions as a director. Even as I write, Penn is shooting his third directorial effort *The Pledge* which, like *The Crossing Guard*, stars Jack Nicholson. The key difference this time is that the film is not based on a Sean Penn screenplay.

ONE

The Uncommon Thought
On A Common Matter

When Sean Justin Penn was born on August 17, 1959, his fate was already partly determined by the kind of life he was born into. Penn's story is not another of those rags-to-riches American dream sagas. He doesn't have an underprivileged background that explains his hunger for a life spent in the public eye. Sean Penn grew up in a wealthy, comfortable environment: his parents were both heavily involved in the TV, film and theatre industries.

By the time Sean Penn's father Leo died in 1998, he had directed over 400 hours of TV. He had started out as an actor before moving over to direct TV shows and made-for-TV films. Penn's mother, Eileen Ryan, has been an actress since she was a young woman. Even as recently as 1998, she could still be seen acting on prime-time TV in shows such as *ER* and *Ally McBeal*. At the time of writing, she can be seen at cinemas across the world in Paul Thomas Anderson's much-acclaimed film *Magnolia*.

Leo Penn was born in 1921. He studied drama at UCLA, but after graduation his plans to teach were put on hold when the Second World War broke out. Penn was drafted and served as a Bombardier in the U.S. army. When the war ended, he returned to Los Angeles and decided that he wanted to act instead of teach.

After some theatre work, he managed to get three off-stage breaks. The first, in 1948, saw him act in an episode of The Philco Television Playhouse called 'Justice And Mr Pleznik'. His second break provided him with a foot in Hollywood's back door: he landed a part in a film called *Not Wanted*, which was directed by Elmer Clifton. Leo Penn

9

acted alongside Sally Forrest, Keefe Brasselle and Dorothy Adams. The film – based on the story of an unwed woman's dangerous involvement with a jazz musician – was released in 1949. Leo Penn's third and final break saw him land a part in another film – *The Undercover Man* – which was directed by Joseph H. Lewis and was also released in 1949. This thriller told the story of secret service men trying to nail a mobster boss on a tax-related technicality. This time Leo Penn's co-stars were Glenn Ford, Nina Foch, James Whitmore, Barry Kelley and Howard St John.

Just as Leo Penn's career seemed to really be taking off, Senator John McCarthy's anti-Communist witch-hunts began in the United States and the entertainment business became a hotbed of deception and double-crossing. The industry's employees were all put under pressure to 'name' anyone they knew who might be sympathetic to Communism. Leo Penn was one of the many who found himself accused of being a Communist. Once he had been named, Penn was blacklisted from the entertainment industry and found himself unable to work in TV or film. Unable to give up his love of acting, he left Los Angeles for New York. There, he assumed an alias and found work in the theatre, successfully performing in a series of plays before his blacklisted status caught up with him. Unfortunately, as soon as his alias scheme was smoked out, he found himself unable to work as an actor.

In an interview with *Rolling Stone* magazine in 1996, Penn revealed: "Being blacklisted hit my father pretty hard in terms of momentum. And my parents had my brother Michael to support. Luckily my mother could get some TV gigs. My father didn't talk much about it but I remember Elia Kazan was shooting a movie once on the beach at the bottom of our hill. I'd heard about Kazan because he had named names. And there he was at the bottom of our hill. Very strange."

By 1955, the heinous witch-hunts were over and Leo Penn was able to cross over from acting to directing, a move that his son Sean would also make later on. He made his debut as a director on several episodes of the TV show *Gunsmoke* and the brief taste of life behind the camera was enough for Penn to want to abandon acting for the director's chair. However, at the time a shortage of directing jobs meant that he had no choice but to continue to act in plays, including *Cat On A Hot Tin Roof* and *Of Mice And Men* in New York.

When Jason Robards dropped out of a production of Eugene

O'Neill's *The Iceman Cometh*, Leo Penn stepped in to take his place. It was during rehearsals for the play that Leo met an actress called Eileen Ryan; the two were instantly drawn to one another. However, when they left the Circle And Square theatre in New York City after their first meeting, they could not have imagined that they wouldn't be apart again until Leo died from lung cancer in 1998.

After this chance meeting, the couple got down to some serious dating. They married in 1957 and not long after their wedding, Eileen Ryan discovered that she was pregnant. She gave birth to a baby boy, whom they called Michael, on August 1, 1958. The couple, who had lived in Greenwich Village since their wedding, decided to make a big move after the birth of their first son. They packed their bags and moved to California, settling in the San Fernando Valley.

Once there, Leo achieved his first real success in the world of movies when he landed a part in a film called *The Story On Page One*. The film was directed by Clifford Odets and starred Rita Hayworth, Anthony Franciosa, Gig Young, Mildred Dunnock, Hugh Griffith and Robert Burton. However, Leo Penn's big break was laced with bittersweet irony. When Sean Penn was inducted into the prestigious Actors Studio as a lifetime member in late 1998, an accompanying interview with James Liston (the studio's director) was filmed for the Bravo series *Inside The Actors Studio*. At the beginning of the film, Liston pays tribute to Leo Penn, who had died ten weeks earlier. When Liston outlined Leo's accomplishments, he noted that Clifford Odets was the person who had named Leo Penn during the witch-hunts that had caused his blacklisting during the McCarthy era.

The Story On Page One was released in 1959, and the following year Leo made a brief appearance in the TV show *The Untouchables*. By this time, Eileen was pregnant again. Her condition could have stalled her own acting ambitions, she over-rode that consideration to take a small part in an episode of the TV show *The Twilight Zone* in the early half of 1960. By the summer Eileen was in the advanced stages of her pregnancy and unable to work. She gave birth at a hospital in Burbank on August 17, 1960; the couple called their second son Sean. Some 38 years later, in an online chat hosted by the internet service provider AOL, Sean Penn answered a question about whether he was from Irish descent or not, by saying that he was made up of a mix of Irish, Spanish, Russian and Italian blood.

11

Eileen was soon back on her feet and able to appear in an episode of *Bonanza* in 1961. The same year, Leo capitalised on the experience that he had gained directing episodes of *Gunsmoke* and *Bonanza* by nailing down some more work as a director, this time on the TV show *Ben Casey*. He had not yet established himself as a known director, but when the directing jobs dried up, Leo could always fall back on acting to make ends meet. He took a minor part in *The Gertrude Berg Show* in 1961, played an uncredited role in *The Birdman Of Alcatraz* in 1962 and made a small appearance in an episode of *Ben Casey* that aired in 1963. Although she now was pregnant for a third time, Eileen also picked up another small acting part in an episode of *Bonanza* in early 1962. The couple's third son, Christopher, was born on June 10, 1962. Like Sean, Christopher would follow in his parents' footsteps and become an actor. Michael would be the only child not to choose acting as a career, opting instead to become a musician and songwriter.

Leo's reputation as a solid, dependable TV director flowered during the early 1960s. Once it reached full bloom, he was able to work as a director for the rest of the decade without having to fall back once on acting work to keep the family afloat. After he directed an episode of the TV show *The Fugitive* in 1963, Leo worked on two other TV shows – *Voyage To The Bottom of The Sea* in 1964 and *Lost In Space* in 1965. He also worked on the TV show *I Spy* in 1965 and in 1966, he directed his first made-for-TV film, *A Man Called Adam*.

By now Leo was making a comfortable living, and no doubt pleased his young sons by directing episodes of *Star Trek* and *The Girl From U.N.C.L.E* in 1966. He followed those projects with work on the *Judd For The Defense* series in 1967 and the hit cop show *Hawaii Five-O* in 1968. By the time Michael was celebrating his 10th birthday, Leo had wrapped up a successful decade of work by directing several episodes of *Marcus Welby*.

In 1970, Leo and Eileen moved the boys to a new home in the chic resort of Malibu, taking a house in the exclusive neighbourhood of Point Dume. In his book *Like A Virgin, Madonna Revealed*, Douglas Thompson notes that the hillside house cost the Penn family three million dollars at the time.

Once they had moved, Sean was enrolled at Malibu Park Junior High School. Leo, whose career had now well and truly hit its stride, spent a chunk of 1970 directing his second made-for-TV film, a medical drama called *Quarantined*. He also busied himself with directing episodes of *Cannon, Cade's County* and *Ghost Story* for TV.

When they weren't at school, Michael, Sean and Chris spent their time in the ocean, which lay next to the family home. They all got into surfing and spent much of their free time learning to negotiate the famously stormy Malibu waves. By the time he was ten years of age, Sean was dreaming of becoming a geologist when he grew up, fantasising about a life that involved trawling and examining rugged terrains. But the dream gradually drifted away as he and his brothers became increasingly fascinated by surfing.

Won over by the lure of the waves, Sean abandoned all dreams of becoming a geologist and redirected his ambitions towards another goal: becoming a famous surfer. "There are waves I'll never forget," he told *Neon* magazine in 1998. "Surfing was purer then. People talk about how bad the '70s were musically and culturally but surfing was the one thing that was at its height. There was a spiritual aspect to surfing then. Now it's just a sport."

The Penn boys began to hang out with two local boys of a similar age, Emilio and Charlie, who lived nearby with their actor father Martin Sheen. The Sheens had also moved to California from New York. Their move occurred in 1969, just before the Penns made the same trek. Sean and Christopher hung out with Charlie and Emilio while Michael started to hang out with older friends. Michael was also obsessed with music and working towards forming his first rock'n'roll band. While his younger brothers surfed the waves, he spent a lot of time listening to Beatles albums in his bedroom.

Leo was constantly busy during 1972–73, directing episodes of *Barnaby Jones, The Girl With Something Extra, Columbo, Kojak* and *The Little House On The Prairie*. He was so in demand that he probably twisted a few arms to get his wife a small role in an episode of *The Little House On The Prairie* which aired in 1974. Leo directed a steady stream of episodes of contemporary TV shows in 1975, such as *Switch, Starsky And Hutch* and *Doctors' Hospital*.

The three Penn sons were growing up fast and Christopher, the youngest, bore the brunt of his brothers' rough-and-tumble teasing. "Until I became 14, it was older brother syndrome," he told *Empire* magazine some years later. "They beat you up every single day of your life and then the first time they get beat up, you never ever have to have a fight again."

Michael, who was a fairly proficient guitar player by the time he left Junior High school, put together his first band while he was at Santa Monica High School. The band covered songs by The Beatles, The Rolling Stones, David Bowie and Cream and Michael spent a lot of time in his bedroom writing what he would later describe as "earnest, downbeat" rock songs.

By 1975, Sean was a student at Santa Monica High School, known to locals and students as 'Samohi'. The school grounds were once used by director Nicholas Ray as a location for his seminal 1956 James Dean vehicle, *Rebel Without A Cause*. When I posted an email on the Samohi alumni online message-board asking former students to share their memories of Sean, I got two short emails back. Sean was apparently a member of the school tennis team as well as a keen surfer; one former student remembered Sean as not unlike the character he plays in *Fast Times At Ridgemont High*. It was at Santa Monica High School that Sean shared classes with Charlie Sheen, Emilio Sheen (later to act under the name Emilio Estevez) and another local boy called Rob Lowe. A decade later, all four would be successful actors and key players in a wave of young American actors and actresses tagged by one critic as 'The Brat Pack'.

Fate stepped in to steer Sean and Christopher towards the film industry when Leo and Eileen bought Christopher a Super-8 camera as a gift. The boys teamed up with the Sheen brothers and started to make their own short films. Sean later told *Film Comment* that they made a lot of "cops 'n' robbers stuff". He also joked that he always ended up "getting killed" rather than "doing the killing". Interestingly, Penn also later talked about one of these Super-8 films and how a brief moment gave him the desire to become an actor. He recalled that he and the other boys were busy filming one day when he caught himself momentarily looking down at the boots he was wearing. "I thought they looked like actor's shoes," Penn remembered. "And I know this sounds clichéd, but the idea of becoming an actor happened then."

The fifth member of the boys' group, school buddy Rob Lowe, was born in Charlottesville, Virginia in 1964. He met the Sheen and Penn brothers after his parents split up and he and his brother Chad were relocated to Malibu. As residents of Malibu and also students at Santa

Monica High School, it was inevitable that the three pairs of brothers would cross paths.

Sean wasn't particularly interested in high school and preferred reading books of his own choice and surfing to homework. Sometime circa this point he read *The Defense That Never Rests* by American lawyer F. Lee Bailey. The lawyer, best known for representing Patty Hearst, became an unlikely source of inspiration for the young Penn. When he finished reading the book, he set his heart on becoming a lawyer.

It was during this period that Sean, Chris and the Sheen brothers made a short film called *Looking For Someone*. Penn later explained during his interview for the *Inside The Actors Studio* profile that the inspiration for the film came from a prop of a severed hand. The Sheen brothers had just returned from the exotic shoot for Francis Ford Coppola's classic film *Apocalypse Now* that their father had starred in. They brought back the aforementioned prop, which mightily impressed the Penn brothers. Pretty soon, the severed hand had formed the basis of the film *Looking For Someone*, which Sean directed. He later commented that they'd had to draft in other surfers to act in it as they couldn't attract any 'real' actors. Sean himself remained a keen surfer. He told one interviewer that he surfed constantly for eight years straight, which goes some way to explaining how he was able to make Jeff Spicoli – the character he played in *Fast Times At Ridgemont High* – into such a cult icon.

Sean's new-found enthusiasm for law was abruptly curbed by his less-than-shining high school grades. He knew that his results would prevent him from getting accepted by any of the acclaimed law schools and promptly gave up on the idea. "I'd had it with school altogether," he later commented. "If I couldn't just go out and practise law, I would go out and be an actor." In 1993, Sean got the chance to practise law on screen at least, when he played an out-of-control, corrupt coke fiend lawyer in Brian De Palma's film, *Carlito's Way*.

Now that Sean had abandoned all ambitions of becoming a geologist or a lawyer, his sights were firmly set on acting. A key figure in the realisation of this dream was Peggy Feury, an acting teacher who died in a tragic head-on car collision in 1985. Feury, who had been a 'charter member' of the legendary Actors Studio in New York, founded the acting and theatre school the Loft Studio in Hollywood in 1973 with her husband, William Traylor. She had studied at the drama school at Yale for only one semester in 1945 before moving to New York. It was there that she became involved with the Group Theater before winning a two-year acting scholarship to attend the Neighbourhood Playhouse. When she graduated, she landed a part in a Broadway play called *Me and Molly* with Paula Strasberg (wife of Lee Strasberg).

Once Feury fell in with Lee Strasberg's circle, her career was made. After he became the Artistic Director at the Actors Studio in 1949, he hired Feury as a Teaching Assistant. She became a key proponent of the 'Method' school of acting and worked alongside future stars such as Marlon Brando, Montgomery Clift and Steve McQueen at the studio. Strasberg was so impressed with Feury that he later entrusted her to take any classes that he was unable to attend. Presumably it was around this time that Leo Penn was inducted into the Actors Studio as a life-time member.

Feury married Traylor in 1961. It soon became apparent that most of Traylor's work would be coming from Hollywood and the more he worked in California, the more the couple considered moving to Los Angeles. After talking this predicament over with Strasberg, Feury was hand-picked by the master to move out to California to set up the Lee Strasberg Theater Institute. Over time Feury and Paula Strasberg drifted apart, until finally Feury broke from Strasberg's influence and formed the Loft Studio in Los Angeles. The Loft Studio didn't set out to teach any new styles of acting, instead specialising in teaching Strasberg's sensory-based acting techniques as well as personal scene instruction.

Sean Penn gravitated to the Loft Studio while he was still a student at Santa Monica High School. The way in which he became aware of the studio remains unclear: his parents may well have told him about it or he may have learned about it from the Sheen family. Most likely, Leo – as a member of the Actors Studio – already knew Feury and Traylor.

Sean Penn was only 17 when he first dropped by at the Loft Studio. He was initially wary of studying acting because he believed that it was a natural, organic process that could not, ultimately, be taught. However, what Penn saw and learned inside Feury's studio would change the course of his life. "I was seventeen when I first went to the Loft," he told *Premiere* in 1990 as part of a celebration of Peggy Feury's life. "I hadn't had any experience and I think I was the youngest one there. I'd use my key to the Loft and sleep there. I'd be there 24 hours a day." Penn later said on *Inside The Actors Studio* that he spent four days a week at the Loft Studio and that each session lasted for roughly five hours. He then said that he would spend roughly the same time again rehearsing for roles and practising methods and exercises that he had learned from Feury at home.

The list of names who also went to the Loft Studio to learn and expand their acting technique with Feury and Traylor includes Eric Stoltz, Anjelica Huston, Lily Tomlin, Meg Ryan, Michelle Pfeiffer and Ellen Burstyn. Stoltz remembered the Loft Studio as "a sanctuary" and a place that was always a hive of activity. Penn, like the others, totally fell under Peggy Feury's charismatic spell. "Peggy had something that made her particularly suited for being an acting teacher, which is that she had lived a life that seemed so well observed," recalled Penn. "When you would do a scene in class, she'd get a look on her face, and she'd tell you a story about something. So immediately you were disarmed of whatever restrictions you had about how you were going to attack this problem, because you thought you were going off on a tangent with her."

Feury's personal approach to teaching and acting appealed to Penn and drew him in. "What was so special about Peggy wasn't about technique," he recalled later. "It was on a much more personal level. And it was always completely genuine." Jeff Goldblum saw the same quality: "She was interested in the deep psychology of the individual." Penn told *Premiere* that he felt blessed to have worked with such an inspiring teacher: "I think I got really lucky. I think I would have been very discouraged at other places and probably not done the work I did at the Loft." When he reflected back on her personality after her death, Penn had fond memories of her. "She was really such a strong positive presence," he remembered. "Without sounding poetic, that's what I remember, just always that warm smile, and the twinkling eyes and on to some story about this or that, and the revelation that comes from it." He also discussed Feury's influence when promoting his debut effort as a director *The Indian Runner* in 1991: "Peggy operated on the whatever works theory and she applied it to each person individually, focused on their strengths and weaknesses." Penn has also talked repeatedly about one of Feury's techniques which involved placing an 'uncommon thought' on a 'common matter'. This method taught Penn to see everyday things in an unusual, detached way and hence to bring a fresh, unclichéd approach to his performances.

Interestingly, Chris Penn also hung out a lot at the Loft Studio. Some biographies claim that he was spending time at the studio as early as 1974, when he was 12. It's difficult to ascertain whether this is true or not, though, like his older brother, Chris certainly studied under Feury.

As Sean and Chris worked hard at the Loft Studio, Leo continued to notch up the credits while Michael was playing local venues with his band. During 1976–77, Leo directed episodes of *The Bionic Woman* (1976) and parts one and three of a three-part TV mini series called *Testimony Of Two Men* (1977). Leo also briefly returned to acting in 1977, taking a part in a made-for-TV film called *Sixth And Main*. The film, which was directed by Christopher Cain, saw Leo act alongside future *Police Squad* and *Airplane* star Leslie Nielsen.

By the time Sean was getting ready to graduate from high school, he already had a fair bit of acting experience under his belt. "I was doing a lot of little plays but I wasn't getting the parts I wanted," he recalled in a late 1998 interview with *Newsweek*. "I'd open the show, then I'd be backstage for an hour, then I'd do a scene. Next thing I know, I'm at curtain call and I didn't feel like I did anything."

Sean Penn graduated from Santa Monica High School in summer 1978, but continued to attend the Loft Studio. The same year his father Leo was busy directing the films *Dark Secret Of Harvest Home* and *Columbo: The Conspirators* for TV and managed to set Sean up with a great break. Leo had a word with an old director friend of his, Kenneth C. Gilbert, who was at the time directing a string of episodes of the TV show *Barnaby Jones*. Gilbert was happy to help Leo's middle son out and Sean was cast in an episode called 'School Of Terror'. An article in *American Film* magazine in 1986 reported Penn's sole line as: "Looks like she shoots horse to me – mainlining." This solitary sentence got him his all-important SAG (Screen Actors Guild) membership card.

Sean, now out of high school, enrolled at Santa Monica Community College where he studied to be a mechanic. Quite why he was taking classes with a view to becoming a mechanic while hanging out at the Loft Studio remains unclear. "At least I can articulate the various aspects of an American-made motor," he told *Newsweek* wryly some 20 years later. However, Penn hated being a student and dropped out after just one quarter at the college to return to his real love: acting. He managed to get himself hired as a production assistant to actor/director

Pat Hingle at the Los Angeles Group Repertory Theater, a job that he held for the next two years. Again, the way in which Penn landed the job is unclear. It's probable that he was tipped off to it by Feury and Traylor, although Hingle's extensive work as an actor for TV shows and made-for-TV films may well have meant that the introduction came through Leo. Hingle, who was born in 1924, was commonly known as 'Pat', though his full name was Martin Patterson Hingle.

During 1979, Leo directed episodes of *Murder In Music City*, *Tales Of The Unexpected*, *Hart To Hart* and *Eishchied*. Sean learned the ropes while working for Hingle. He also won parts in two small productions at the theatre. The first was in a play called *Earthworms*; the second was in a play called *The Girl On The Via Flaminia* which was put on at the Gene Dynarksi Theater in Hollywood. Penn's enthusiasm and his good performances in both plays impressed Hingle, who accordingly gave Penn the chance to direct his first play, James Leo Herlihy's *Terrible Jim Fitch*. Around the same time he had another stab at directing, this time on a play that he wrote in a Los Angeles workshop.

Now that Penn was determined to make it as an actor, it was just a matter of nailing down a decent break and then using it to get a foot in the door of the film world. His views on acting were shaping up too: "I think Stella Adler is the one who said your talent is your choice", Sean observed to Bravo's *Inside The Actor's Studio* in 1998. Leo solved his son's how-do-I-get-a-foot-in-the-door headache when he found himself at the helm of a made-for-TV film called *Hellinger's Law*. The film was a pilot for a TV series starring Telly Savalas that never got off the ground. The director presumably leaned on the producers and casting agents to get Sean the part of 'Don', a small role but one that would give him another stepping stone to fame.

The film was first shown on TV in 1981 and Penn, wasting no time, was eager to use his appearance in this film to get further work. His plan worked and he found himself playing a bit part in Sam Wanamaker's *The Killing Of Randy Webster*, another made-for-TV film. Wanamaker would later act alongside Sean in Leo Penn's *Judgment In Berlin*. Then as now, the U.S. film industry was an incestuous circuit, and Leo's contacts must have been invaluable for his ambitious son.

The Killing Of Randy Webster also featured a young actress called Jennifer Jason Leigh, the daughter of actor Vic Morrow and actress/ screenwriter Barbara Turner, who would again work alongside Penn in

Fast Times At Ridgemont High. Jason Leigh, who was born in 1962, had attended acting classes given by Lee Strasberg, when she was only 14. Like Sean Penn, Jason Leigh would also find future acclaim for her committed attitude to 'method' acting. On one film shoot she became notorious for keeping a journal in her character's name.

In late 1980 Sean packed his bags and headed for New York City, with a view to making it on the theatre circuit. The move was also prompted by his inability to find an agent in Los Angeles who would take him on. Once settled, one of his first moves was to audition for a play, called *Heartland*. Penn landed the part and suddenly found himself treading the boards at the Century Theater in New York alongside Kevin Heelan, Larry Nicks, J.C. Quinn, Ben Slack and Martyn St David. The play, which only ran briefly, was directed by Art Wolff who later observed: "Maybe it is Sean's ability to become so many different characters – so totally different from one another – that is his attraction to young people who want to be somebody else." Clearly Sean Penn the method actor was already taking shape.

This theatre experience further encouraged Penn in his desire to become a serious actor – an enthusiasm that he hadn't got from his TV work. He later said that because he did a lot of theatre work at the start of his career, it gave him a respect for the profession that would later highlight any time that he was acting in a vehicle that didn't feel satisfying.

As it turned out, it wasn't a disaster for Sean that the play crashed and burned after a short run. After one night's performance, a New York-based agent came backstage to talk with him. She enthused over his performance and then offered to represent him. No sooner had Penn calmed down from this potentially exciting break than the agent told him that there was a film currently being cast that she thought he might be right for. He auditioned for the film – a drama set in a military academy – which was called *Taps*.

Harold Becker had at the time just directed the acclaimed film *The Onion Field*, which starred James Woods and John Savage. He had also directed *The Black Marble*, which featured a future close friend of Penn's, the actor Harry Dean Stanton.

Meanwhile, the rest of the Penn family were as busy as ever. Leo was directing episodes of *Mr Merlin*, *Bret Maverick* and *St Elsewhere*. Michael was fronting a new, far more serious band, called Doll Congress. They played live in the Los Angeles area as often as they could. He also turned to the family profession to keep himself afloat, taking bit parts in TV shows such as *St Elsewhere*, which Leo presumably helped him get.

Shortly after the audition, Sean – who had blown Harold Becker away with his reading – received the news that he had landed the part and found himself signed up for his biggest break yet . . .

TWO

Sean De Niro

Things were moving fast for Sean Penn. He had grown up making Super-8 films, learned his craft with Peggy Feury and bloomed under Pat Hingle's wing. He had also directed two plays, hit the boards in two plays in New York, notched up three counts of TV work, been wooed by an agent and landed a part in his first big screen feature film. Not bad for a 21-year-old.

Taps is a film about young men at a military academy. The screenplay was adapted by Robert Mark Kamen, James Lineberger and Darryl Ponicsan from a novel by Devery Freeman. When the General (played with typical muscular charm by George C. Scott) tells his youthful cadets that the academy is going to be closed down because the land has been sold to real estate developers, they fight the closure as if the developers are enemies in a wartime situation. The General falls sick with a heart attack and is rushed off to hospital, whereupon the Cadet Major, Brian Moreland (played by Timothy Hutton), finds himself in charge of the young men and boys. Spurred on by their wishes, Moreland instigates a siege. He and the other cadets decide to barricade themselves in the academy in protest against the planned closure.

Timothy Hutton was the familiar face in the chaos. He had already won the Best Supporting Actor at the 1980 Academy Awards® for his performance in Robert Redford's *Ordinary People*. Hutton, who like Penn was born in 1960, would also later act alongside Penn in *The Falcon And The Snowman*. He took acting as seriously as Penn and spent a lengthy period of time researching the life of a cadet major. As well as reading books about military figures such as General Patton and General MacArthur, Hutton also spent time at the Valley Forge

Military Academy, along with other actors from the film, shadowing a real-life cadet major. "I stayed in the barracks at the Academy," Hutton told *Films & Filming*. "Hung out with my counterpart, marched with them, went to officers training school and voice command and viewed films of similar subjects – *if . . .*, *The Bridge*, *All Quiet On The Western Front*, *Lord Of The Flies* and others." He also read Herman Melville's *Billy Budd*.

Taps broke Penn and a youthful Tom Cruise, playing a cadet who eventually cracks as the police and National Guard surround the academy. Cruise, who was born in 1962, had arrived on the set of *Taps* fresh from making his feature film debut in *Endless Love*. Penn plays Alex Dwyer, a peroxide mop-top who fervently believes in truth and honesty. When he realises that Cadet Major Moreland has taken things too far, he delivers a powerful monologue, urging Moreland and the cadets to give themselves up. Penn steals the film with this monologue, which is the highlight of the movie.

Even though Penn's part in the film was nowhere near as significant as the roles played by Hutton and Cruise, he nevertheless took the whole project very seriously. He insisted on staying in character throughout the shoot, even going so far as to ignore anyone who didn't address him by his character's name. If a fellow actor or crew member called him 'Sean' he would refuse to answer; he only responded when he was called 'Alex'.

This heavy-handed 'method' approach led to some cast and crew members teasing Penn and giving him the nickname 'Sean De Niro', according to Margy Rochlin in *American Film* magazine, but his performance – solid, occasionally incendiary – set Penn's career in motion. He and Cruise were singled out as actors to watch in a review of the film that appeared in *Variety* magazine at the time.

To prepare the young actors for their roles, Harold Becker subjected his cast to a compulsory 45-day induction course at the Valley Forge Military Academy in Pennsylvania. The exhausting training spell worked the actors into shape and educated them about the cadet's life. Becker put his cast through agonising rehearsals that mostly involved perfecting military drills. Becker knew that he had to get the cast to act as if they really were cadets, otherwise the inauthenticity would fail to draw audiences in. "It was necessary for that sort of thing," Hutton told *Films & Filming*. "All the marching and the drills were very hard work."

Hutton also praised veteran actor George C. Scott who makes a dramatic impact in the first 20 minutes of the film before being taken into hospital. For the rest of the film, he continues to exist as a powerful character and role model for the cadets even though he's not seen again after the heart attack. "He was only there for a few weeks, but all the kids really liked him," remembered Hutton. "It was amazing just to stand by him and see him at work – a real experience to see such discipline and concentration."

The studio – Fox – felt that the film was going to bomb at the box office. It was, after all, a film about the rigidity of military academy training. The subject matter (the impracticality of military training in a problematic, peacetime situation) was hardly the kind of thing that was going to draw in the crowds. Moreover, it was dismissed by critics and industry insiders as a dull, plodding drama about a bunch of robotic cadets immaturely wrestling with issues of honour and allegiance when their beloved training academy gets sold out for money. "The film never decides whether it has come to praise or bury the military tradition," wrote Richard Schickel for *Time* magazine. However, *Taps* surprised everyone by becoming a box-office hit when it was released at the very end of 1981. Apparently, a lot of teenage cinema audiences were queuing to see Hutton – who became an overnight heartthrob – in the film. Hutton wound up getting nominated for a Golden Globe (in the Best Motion Picture Actor category) in the 1982 awards. Penn's performance in the film – including a memorable tearful outburst directed at Hutton's character – attracted a lot of interest, if no award nominations.

Penn later told the *New York Times* that he celebrated the end of the *Taps* shoot by heading back to Los Angeles: "I had money in my pocket for the first time so I went back to California." When he got there, he discovered that his agent had been approached by a female director – Amy Heckerling – who was in the process of overseeing auditions for a high school teen comedy. The film, which had a $9-million budget, was called *Fast Times At Ridgemont High*. Via Penn's agent, Heckerling arranged for the young actor to drop by for an audition. She had a part in mind: that of a perpetually stoned surfer called Jeff Spicoli.

As soon as Penn completed his audition, Heckerling knew that he was the one to play Spicoli, a key role in the film because it provides a comic centre to the plot. "There were lots of people who read for the part of Jeff Spicoli," Heckerling recalled. "But there was something about Sean's presence that told us he was right, that the quality was there."

Penn later told Salon.com that he felt Spicoli was the kind of character that he had encountered frequently during his surfer days. He observed that no one had put that kind of personality into a film and commented on the fact that kids like Spicoli were getting high and surfing all along the California coast line. He was confident about the part, and felt secure about improvising with the role because he felt as though he "knew the character, the rhythm of the character".

The film was adapted from a lengthy journalistic commission. *Rolling Stone* magazine had sent a young journalist, Cameron Crowe (later the director of grunge film *Singles*), back to high school for a semester to find out what American youths were thinking and doing. His fly-on-the-wall findings became first a report for the magazine and then the screenplay, *Fast Times At Ridgemont High*.

The film is typical teen fare, the sort of thing that would later be endlessly recycled through TV series such as *Beverly Hills 90210*, *Dawson's Creek* and *My So Called Life*. The film's focus on sex, cars, rock shows, first dates, getting stoned, drinking, the tedium of school, teenage pregnancy, abortion, dumb pocket money jobs at the mall, annoying parents, old fart teachers and romance would also inspire a wave of hit teen films in the '80s including *The Breakfast Club*, *Pretty In Pink*, *Sixteen Candles*, *Ferris Bueller's Day Off* and *Some Kind Of Wonderful*.

One of the more hilarious scenes in the film has Phoebe Cates in the school canteen teaching Jennifer Jason Leigh how to give a blow job, using a carrot to explain her technique. This, like other scenes in the film, tapped into the teenage fascination with sex. For a lot of the film, Jennifer Jason Leigh's character is exploring her sexuality, as she moves from losing her virginity in a casual sexual encounter through a teenage pregnancy and abortion to a belief that sex works best in a romantic relationship. Some of the film's sexually related content caused problems with the censors. Amy Heckerling told *Films In Review* that she had been forced to cut scenes to get the film's rating down from an 'X' to an 'R'. "I didn't think it was very fair," she commented in retrospect. "I thought it was a much tamer movie than others I've seen."

Heckerling was also told to remove a scene in which a male character gets undressed during a casual sex scene. "I've seen a great deal of nudity," she told *Films In Review*. "Full frontal nudity. And here we have one shot where the boy is getting undressed and you don't really see anything but they (the MPAA) made us blow the shot up." She was also asked to make cuts to a scene in which Jennifer Jason Leigh's character is seduced in her parents' bath house by her boyfriend's older brother. "There's this scene while they're doing it in which her head is getting banged against the couch," she explained. "When we showed it to high school audiences at previews, they all laughed." Amazingly, Heckerling was told that unless she removed the shot of the head banging against the couch, then the film would have to have an 'X' certificate.

Of Penn's performance, Heckerling was highly complimentary: "You hear talk about people going out on a limb. He'll (Penn) go out on the tiniest twig." So much of the film's knockabout charm stems from Penn's performance as Jeff Spicoli; even today, Spicoli is a cult hero for prestigious dope smokers and sun-tanned surf dudes. Once again, Penn's intense acting methods made him stand out from the rest of the cast. For the entire two-month shoot, Penn stayed in character. "Sean never answered to any name except for 'Jeff', 'Spicoli' or 'dude'," recalled Cameron Crowe when he was asked about his memories of the shoot. This method was so comprehensive that Penn would also only answer to these names when he was at home as well. He apparently left answering machine messages using Spicoli's name and even went so far as to tell his friends and family that he would only answer to his character's name. This acting style led even more industry people to start talking him up as a new Brando or a new De Niro.

One day, Penn's commitment to the Spicoli character frightened everybody on the set. He was standing silently waiting to shoot a scene. To everyone around him, he was simply smoking a cigarette and thinking about what was coming next. Suddenly, he stubbed his cigarette out on the palm of one of his hands. When he was asked what he was doing by concerned onlookers, he dismissed their concern, telling them he had suddenly realised that he had slipped out of character for a moment and needed to shock himself straight back into Jeff Spicoli's mind and body. Penn clearly felt that if he wandered back to his own personality, then his performance would suffer, and abruptly punished himself for losing concentration during a tightrope walk of extraordinary seriousness. Such self-punishment certainly seems extreme, but at the same time it demonstrates a passionate and admirable commitment to his craft. Amy Heckerling watched all of this play out and was very impressed. "He's going to be an incredible artist," she told a reporter. Seconds later she added: "He already is." Few people involved with the film could believe how much energy Penn was investing in the role of a stoned surfer. Several years later, when Penn was being lambasted by the media as a bad boy with a penchant for violence, Heckerling defended him, describing him as "the sweetest, most co-operative, hardworking, creative guy I've ever worked with. I'd heard a lot of things about Sean but I worked with him every day for two months and he was very different from those things I hear."

Penn's performance in the film is hilarious. It is also – when seen within the context of all of his work – an uncharacteristically light-hearted part for such a heavyweight actor. There doesn't appear to be a single moment in the film when he isn't totally in sync with his character. Unlike so many actors who are just starting out, Penn never once seems to be trying too hard. His stoner vocabulary (a series of unintelligible ramblings around the word 'dude') undoubtedly inspired the Bill & Ted films that came out in the '90s. His sun bleached surfer mop (almost shoulder length), shorts and sneakers give him the look of the consummate surfer.

Some of the scenes that feature Penn are wonderfully funny. When a pizza delivery boy turns up in the middle of Mr Hand's class, it could only be Jeff Spicoli who ordered the take-out. Similarly, when Mr Hand calls by Spicoli's home and enters his bedroom, he finds Spicoli at war with a bong, surrounded by walls that are covered with *Playboy* centrefolds. Every aspect of Spicoli's character is spot-on and, as Penn suggests during the Actors Studio interview, this was because Penn had been a serious surfer himself and was therefore perfectly qualified to play the part.

The film's ending – which takes place in a general store – sees Judge Reinhold's character (Brad Hamilton) foil an attempted robbery by a stick-up artist (played by Penn's friend James Russo). Spicoli, who had been in the bathroom, comes out to see Reinhold pointing a gun at the would-be thief. Instead of appearing frightened, or doing something to help his friend, Spicoli simply chuckles at the severity of the situation. His totally unphased reaction – the same throughout the film – is an hysterical caricature of a stoner.

The film also featured a galaxy of future stars such as Phoebe Cates, Eric Stoltz and Nicolas Cage as well as the aforementioned Judge Reinhold, and earned good notices when it was released in 1982. "Believe it or not," wrote Marjorie Bilbow in *Screen International*, "behind the crass vulgarities of hard selling in the States lurks a pleasantly funny-touching portrayal of teenagers nowhere near as black as they're painted."

"The really good part of *Fast Times* is Sean Penn as a spaced out irresponsible surfer," raved *Variety*'s reviewer. "As previously proved in *Taps*, Penn is a joy to watch at work, even when his role has no particular plot importance." Paul Taylor, wrote in *Monthly Film Bulletin* that Penn's character was the film's "U.S. marketing hook" but didn't refer to Penn by name. For him the film fitted "remarkably snugly into the post-*American Graffiti* niche." The entry for Sean Penn in *The International Dictionary Of Films & Filmmakers: Actors And Actresses*, highlights his role in *Fast Times At Ridgemont High*, praising Penn's "considerable technical skill in a comic vein". The praise also extended to Cameron Crowe who notched up a nomination in the 1983 WGA Awards for Best Comedy Adapted From Another Medium.

On a more personal note, Penn was also to fall in love during the film shoot. One of the actresses in the film – Pamela Springsteen, sister of singer/songwriter Bruce Springsteen – caught Penn's attention. The two started dating and before long Penn had met Bruce himself, one of his favourite songwriters. Penn's interest in Springsteen's music – in particular a song on the *Nebraska* album called 'Highway Patrolman' – would end up forming the basis for his debut film as writer and director, *The Indian Runner*. The romance between the couple burned brightly and quickly and it was only a matter of time before they were living together in an apartment in New York City. Penn proposed, plans were made and a wedding date was allegedly set for February 20, 1983.

Meanwhile, Sean was taking his method acting to even greater extremes in preparation for a tough, violent gang film called *Bad Boys*. The major difference between this project and the other roles that Penn had tackled up to that point was that this time, Penn was the film's lead actor. For the first time, he was the star. *Bad Boys* was directed by Rick Rosenthal, who had previously directed a TV series called *Darkroom* as well as *Halloween II*. The screenplay was written by Richard Di Lellio.

Penn's mostly silent role meant that he had to act with his body and develop a physical acting language to convey the unspoken. This was where Feury's excellent 'uncommon thought' on a 'common matter' method proved to be vital. There are many charged scenes in the film in which Penn screens his character through an array of intense looks, moody stares and macho body language that inevitably reminds the viewer of early Brando performances in films such as *On The Waterfront*, *The Wild One* and *A Streetcar Named Desire*. This time, to get into the head of his character Mick O'Brien, a brutal gang-member-turned-locked-up-juvenile-convict, Penn had a wolf's head tattooed on his right forearm. He was planning to have his teeth filed and capped too before his mother stepped in and told him that maybe it wasn't such a great idea.

Penn has often spoken of the preparation for a part as journalism, a kind of quest for information and details. Like Harold Becker and Amy Heckerling before him, the director Rosenthal was impressed by Penn's ferocious commitment to the part and saw the same fiery passion in his young star. He told *Films & Filming* about one episode involving Penn that scared the hell out of him. One day, on location in Chicago, he had to personally stop Penn from snatching a woman's purse. When he asked Penn what the hell he thought he was doing, Penn told him that he was only doing what he felt was necessary to 'become' Mick O' Brien. He thought that the theft would turn him into O'Brien and erase any uncertainties that the actor might have about his character. The director, who was still puzzled by the episode, asked Penn what snatching the purse would illustrate. Penn, turning deadly serious, explained that he wanted to know what criminal activity felt like. He said he wanted to tap into the emotions that came from such an act.

The deeper Penn went into character, the more fascinated Rosenthal became. When he was later asked by a reporter if he thought Penn's method was coming straight out of the Robert De Niro school of acting, he dismissed the comparison. Instead, Rosenthal chose to paint Penn as a powerful actor in his own right whose lack of peers inevitably leads critics to make the comparison with De Niro. "The only reason that people compare Sean to Robert De Niro," he commented, "is that Sean is the only actor of his generation who can really become a different person for each acting job."

Another anecdote from Rosenthal illustrated this theory even more clearly. "We went out with some Chicago cops (on a raid) so Sean could get a 'feel' of it all," recalled the director. "During the raid, some more cops arrived and thought we were criminals and told us to raise our hands. I complied but for Sean it was a chance to see what it's like for a gang member to take on a cop. He turned to the cop who was the size of an apartment and said 'Fuck you'. The cop picked Sean up and threw him into a wall. His nose was almost broken but later he told me it was at that moment that he finally became his character in the film." Again, Penn was using pain to break the barrier between himself as an actor and the character he was trying to portray. This painful authenticity was once again the catalyst that helped Penn erase any distance between himself and his character.

The film was also notable for the introduction of a new young actress, Ally Sheedy, who played Mick's girlfriend, 'JC'. Sheedy, who was born in 1962, had first found success at the age of 12 with a children's book that she had written called *She Was Nice To Mice*. Her first acting part of any note was in a made-for-TV film, *The Best Little Girl In the World*, which followed small parts in two TV shows: *St Elsewhere* and *Hill Street Blues*. Sheedy arrived on the set of *Bad Boys* fresh from having acted in *War Games* opposite Matthew Broderick. Afterwards she went straight from the set of *Bad Boys* to shoot *Oxford Blues*, opposite Penn's high school buddy, Rob Lowe.

Sheedy's performance as JC is a powerful buffer against Penn's moody performance. When she is brutally raped by a rival gang member (whose brother O'Brien has gunned down), she calls O'Brien who is locked up in a juvenile correctional facility. After learning of the savage rape, he escapes from the facility so that he can see her. The scene in which the young lovers are reunited at JC's family home is one of the film's most powerful moments. O'Brien holds JC while the juvenile correctional facility's warden waits downstairs. At one point O'Brien cries and breaks down, in a charged and intense performance from Penn, exposing the emotions behind his hoodlum character's hard shell.

Ally Sheedy found working with her co-star to be something of a learning experience. "I was so fortunate to have worked with Sean Penn in my first movie," she told *American Film* magazine. "Even when I wasn't working, I watched him all the time. His script was always open, his pen always out. In every single job I've done since then, I've thought a lot about his approach, the way he takes his work so seriously."

When the film came out in 1983, it received mixed reviews from the critics. "Penn is nothing short of terrific in the key role which, given a minimal amount of dialogue, calls for him to rely primarily on his emotional and physical abilities," gushed the review in *Variety*, continuing, "It's a subtle, studied performance that others might likely have played more broadly to less effect." By contrast, the film was dismissed by *Monthly Film Bulletin*, whose reviewer summarised the terse drama as "an old-fashioned juvenile delinquent saga".

Bad Boys is an uncompromising film that stretches Penn to the limits of his budding talent. Much of the film is set in the juvenile correctional facility where O'Brien strives to survive in an environment that is ruled by violence and corruption. O'Brien finds himself having to fend off attacks from cliques of inmates while the facility staff try to 'save' him from a life behind bars. He ends up in ascendancy over the other inmates after he beats the jail bullies with a pillow case filled with cans of Coca Cola.

The final, brutal fight between O'Brien and a rival gang member, whom he knows is one of JC's rapists, is bloody and dramatic. Desperate to get out of the facility as a free man, O'Brien is forced to protect himself as the gang member, still determined to avenge his brother's death at O'Brien's hands, plots to murder him. Finally, when the inmates take bets on who will kill whom first, he has to defend his honour, even though he knows that it will probably cost him his freedom. The movie, which was filmed on location in Illinois, grossed a modest $9.2 million at the American box office when it was released in 1983.

A genuine Sean Penn oddity also came about during 1982. He had a small part in a period piece film called *Summerspell*. The storyline revolves around a Fourth of July family get-together at a ranch in Texas. The finished product was shown at a few American film festivals during 1983 but failed to attract a distributor. For reasons best known to a small Los Angeles-based distribution company called Margin Films, *Summerspell* was finally given a cinema release in 1999 when it was shown at a handful of screens in the San Francisco area. Reviewing the film for *Culture Vulture* at the time of its belated release, Arthur Lazere wrote: "There is some nice cinematography, shots of the dry Texas hills in a subdued palette, a few scenes thoughtfully lit or angled for dramatic effect. But even this minor accomplishment sinks beneath the writer/director Lina Shanklin, who can, with a straight face, start with a sunrise and end with a sunset even as mother puts her arm protectively around daughter's shoulder." He concluded: "directing is conspicuous by its absence".

Penn took a short break from the film circuit to return to the theatre. He auditioned for a part in a play called *Slab Boys* that was scheduled to make a run at a theatre in New York City. He landed the part and was subsequently busy with rehearsals in New York for a while. This also meant that when the play started, Penn could earn money while living with Pamela Springsteen in their New York City apartment.

The rest of the Penn family were also busy working at the time. Leo had returned to acting and taken a small part in a made-for-TV film called *The Horse Dealer's Daughter*, which aired on TV in 1983. Michael Penn was busy building up a local following with his band Doll Congress. Christopher Penn had also launched his career as an actor, landing a supporting role as a member of Matt Dillon's gang in Francis Ford Coppola's black-and-white masterpiece, *Rumblefish*. The film, which hit cinemas in 1983 boasted a very cool cast that included Dennis Hopper, singer/songwriter Tom Waits, Diane Lane and Mickey Rourke as 'The Motorcycle Boy'. After *Rumblefish*, Christopher Penn won himself a part in the football film, *All The Right Moves*, which catapulted his childhood friend, Rob Lowe, to stardom. It was becoming abundantly clear that there was yet another talented actor in the Penn family.

When *Slab Boys'* run came to an end, Sean Penn drove from Los Angeles to see his brother Chris on the set of *Rumblefish* in Tulsa, Oklahoma. It was here that he met actor/director Dennis Hopper (an encounter that Penn later said had "a big impact" on him) who would become a key friend and advisor to him. The young actor watched Hopper at work and saw that he had a lot to learn. In conversation with *Interview* magazine in 1994, Penn re-told a story about one particularly magical moment that happened while he was watching Hopper on the set. "In the script there's a scene where Dennis' character tells the Matt Dillon character about his mother. Matt says something like, 'Was our mother crazy?' And Dennis' character says, 'No, your mother wasn't crazy. She just saw things differently than other people.' And that was the essence of the scene. Well, all of a sudden Coppola says 'Action.'

'Dad, was our mother crazy?' 'No, your mother wasn't crazy. She wasn't crazy. She just saw things – she saw – she saw buffalo's feet on an elephant! Have you ever seen rainbows going up a duck's ass? No, your mother wasn't crazy.' Well, now I knew that everything I had learned about acting I could just throw out."

THREE

The Truth Machine

After acting in *Slab Boys* and befriending Dennis Hopper, Sean Penn signed up for his next film project – *Crackers* – which was directed by Louis Malle. The film, which cost $12 million to make, only happened after a project that Malle had been working on with Dan Ackroyd and John Belushi fell apart. Malle, who was riding high at the time after the success of *My Dinner With Andre* and *Atlantic City*, had become fascinated with a news story that was circulating at the time. In Malle's own words, it was a story about "an extraordinary character, a swindler who was offering people an offshore tax evasion scheme." The swindler fiddled people's money to great profit until he was caught, whereupon the FBI used him and an Arab sheikh as human bait to entrap a series of other fraudsters. This became known as the 'Ab Scam'. Malle found the story fascinating and figured that the topic could be fleshed out as a screenplay that would make "a political satire and comedy".

He took the idea to screenwriter John Guare, who knocked the story into a screenplay. Malle then shopped the screenplay around, managing to win Dan Ackroyd and John Belushi's interest. The screenplay's provisional title was *Moon Over Miami*, the setting for the action. The project was taking shape nicely but collapsed when two tragedies occurred. First, Malle had to fly back to France when he learned that his mother had died. Then, John Belushi, whose name had guaranteed Malle a green light for his project, was found dead at the Chateau Marmont Hotel. On hearing the news, Columbia – who were keen to get the project off the ground based on the potential box-office returns that would result from an Ackroyd-Belushi partnership – immediately went cold on the project.

When Malle returned to Los Angeles, he found out that Columbia had been more interested in the potential star power than they were in the screenplay itself. However, determined not to let the project wind up gathering dust on a shelf in his office, he began talks with Dustin Hoffman and British actor Bob Hoskins, while John Guare worked on a stronger draft of the screenplay. The re-writes dragged on and after a year of meetings and talks, Malle lost his patience with the ill-fated project and decided to work on something else.

A producer, who had been chasing Malle around with a view to having the Frenchman direct a re-make of the 1958 film *Big Deal On Madonna Street,* suddenly found that Malle was interested in the project. The Italian comedy, which milked a considerable amount of humour out of a bungled robbery, was now Malle's primary focus, even though he had turned the idea down on numerous occasions while trying to get *Moon Over Miami* made. Jeffrey Fiskin, who had written the screenplay for *Cutter's Way,* was brought in to write the screenplay.

Once Fiskin and Malle had spent time scouting potential locations, they decided to set the re-make in San Francisco's Mission district. The budget was soon eaten up by hiring a cast that included Donald Sutherland, Sean Penn, Jack Warden, Wallace Shawn, Trinidad Silva and Larry Riley. To cut corners, some unknowns were hired too, including Christine Baranski, who took the part that had been played in the original by Italian actress Claudia Cardinale. Malle later felt that the Italian cast – with stars such as Cardinale and Marcello Mastroianni – was far superior to his own cast which he cryptically described as "odd, bizarre and interesting". Malle became disillusioned during the shoot too. "I hated being on the set," he later confessed. "I kept asking myself, what am I doing here?"

The film, which flopped at the box office, didn't give Penn much space to show off the acting talents that made *Bad Boys* such a powerful film. Like most of the cast, he felt unsure as to what Malle expected of him. The director's disinterest in the project affected less experienced actors like Penn deeply. It was also difficult for him to go from being the star of *Bad Boys* to being a young actor working with veteran talents such as Donald Sutherland and Louis Malle.

After an arduous editing process – because it was a big studio picture there was a crowded editing suite at all times – the film was dismissed with indifference by the critics. *Variety* magazine described the movie as: "a mild little caper comedy". The review in *Monthly Film Bulletin* wasn't much more enthusiastic. The review slated the film as "yet another remake to add to the growing heap that seems to indicate either an imaginative bankruptcy in Hollywood or an unwillingness to subscribe to the Reaganite regressions that are the order of the day."

Even though the reviews were less than warm, Louis Malle was nominated for the Golden Berlin Bear Award at the 1984 Berlin International Film Festival. Even if that panel considered the film a successful one, Penn, like everyone else involved in the project, felt stung by the flop film. He dusted himself down and immediately went to work on a far superior film called *Racing With The Moon*. Penn didn't know it yet but the film would also bring about changes to his personal life. He hadn't married Pamela Springsteen – the relationship had fizzled out and the wedding had been called off. Penn's affections were soon elsewhere. He fell in love with his *Racing With The Moon* co-star, Elizabeth McGovern. The mutual attraction was instant. "I really tried for it not to happen," McGovern later said, "but I just couldn't fight those blue eyes."

Elizabeth McGovern was born in Evanston, Illinois in 1961. When her law professor father was transferred from Northwestern University to UCLA, the family moved out to Los Angeles. McGovern started acting in school plays when she was a student at North Hollywood High School. After graduating, she studied acting at the American Conservatory Theater in San Francisco and the Juilliard School Of Dramatic Arts in New York. With a devoted acting background like that behind her, it was no wonder that she and Penn hit it off.

McGovern first came to attention in Robert Redford's *Ordinary People*, acting alongside Timothy Hutton – another connection between her and Penn. The young actress was hand-picked for the film while she was still a student at Juilliard. After *Ordinary People*, her performance in Milos Forman's *Ragtime* earned her an Academy Award® nomination for the Best Supporting Actress award. She then worked with Dudley Moore in Marshall Brickman's *Lovesick* before really showing her talents in Sergio Leone's epic gangster tale, *Once Upon A Time In America*. This film brought her in touch with heavyweight actress Tuesday Weld, edgy actor James Woods and Sean Penn's hero, Robert De Niro.

By the time she met Penn on the set of *Racing With The Moon*, it would appear that the two were fated to fall in love. The quaint period love story gave Penn room to breathe and the necessary space for him to once again excel. As mentioned earlier, Penn was by this point prone to leave answering machine messages in his character's name and it's tempting to wonder if he was in or out of character when he fell for McGovern. Was their budding romance perhaps an extension of their acting methods? Were they falling in love as Sean and Elizabeth or Henry and Caddie?

The film was directed by Richard Benjamin and written by Steven Kloves and was shot on location at Fort Bragg and Mendocino. Benjamin's previous directing credits included *City Heat*, a 1930s crime thriller starring Clint Eastwood and Burt Reynolds, and the Peter O'Toole vehicle *My Favourite Year*. Set in California in 1942, *Racing With The Moon* is a coming-of-age tale. Penn plays Henry 'Hopper' Nash. He and his best friend Nicky (played by Nicolas Cage) are two young blue-collar men who try to maximise what little time they have left before they get drafted into the Second World War. Henry falls in love with Caddie Winger (McGovern), a rich girl from the other side of the tracks. Nicky falls in love with a more down-to-earth girl and has a less satisfactory experience. The bittersweet tone, which stems from Nicky and Henry's fear that they might not make it home from the war, is the only compensation for an otherwise slow-paced, if enjoyable film.

Richard Benjamin was the latest of Penn's directors to be blown away by the young actor's passion and commitment. "Sean is a truth machine," admitted Benjamin. "He can spot anything fake – scenes or in dialogue. Sometimes when I had a problem I would go to the screenwriter, but often I would go to Sean." When Penn was being hounded by the media a few years later, Benjamin – like Amy Heckerling – rallied to his defence. "I find him quite exceptional," gushed Benjamin. "And I'd much rather work with a talented actor than a bad one who likes to go on talk shows."

According to Christopher Andersen's Madonna biography *Madonna Unauthorized*, it was around this time that Penn began to show signs of a volatile temperament that would get him into so much trouble during his marriage to Madonna. Andersen claims that there was trouble on the *Racing With The Moon* set one day when Penn went berserk on learning that a male reporter was interviewing Elizabeth McGovern in her trailer. Andersen alleges that Penn became inflamed with jealousy and started rocking the trailer from side to side, throwing McGovern to the floor. (Andersen also alleges that prior to dating McGovern, Penn had also conducted a brief but 'highly publicised' affair with the actress Susan Sarandon after he had left Pamela Springsteen.)

The reviews for *Racing With The Moon* were much more positive than the ones for *Crackers* and Penn, let loose in the lead part, naturally became the centrepiece of the reviews. The *Monthly Film Bulletin* review, which appeared circa the film's release in early 1984, summed the piece up as a "sweet, likeable film". The main thrust of the review was devoted to Penn's performance. "Penn is an offbeat but plausible romantic figure," wrote the reviewer, "capable of giving an edge to this sort of conventional fellow." The review also noted that Penn "finds in Hopper a useful vehicle for his caustic charm". However, the performance of Penn's co-star was less warmly received: "Elizabeth McGovern can do nothing with the incoherent Caddie," bitched the reviewer, "except flash her sweet pudding face." The review in *Films & Filming* was equally Penn-centric, commenting that Penn "just gets better and better even as you watch him" and praising *Racing With The Moon* as "One of the best films to be released this year."

Penn's infamously wilful nature reared its head when he was requested to take part in publicity for the release of *Racing With The Moon*; he showed a total disinterest in promoting the film, much to the chagrin of the producers. Although he was by now starting to become a big name in the U.S. film industry, no one was amused when he agreed to only do one interview – with *Newsweek*. He later gave his own version of this curiously self-destructive decision in an interview with *American Film*. "I got the bum rap primarily for *Racing With The Moon*," he reflected. "There was a producer – a couple of producers – who needed to find a scapegoat because they couldn't figure out the best way to promote the movie. Private conversations between the producer and me were divulged to the press."

Penn felt that once the shoot was wrapped, his job was over. His argument was that he was an actor, not a member of the film's publicity team. He had invested a great deal of emotional energy into bringing Henry Nash to the screen as best as he could and wasn't interested in endlessly talking about his method or the film's plot or his co-stars (who also included Crispin Glover and Michael Madsen). He was also bummed at not being allowed into the editing suite so that he could veto takes that he didn't like. Sherry Lansing, who was one of the film's many producers, was not amused by Penn's attitude. "His career will be over if he doesn't change," she mused. "He's talented but he's also self-destructive."

When the film bombed in grand style, the producers pointed the finger at Penn's refusal to do press. "I'm not the first actor who didn't feel he had something to say to the press all the time," said Penn in 1991. "But I'm the first one they went after, as far as I know." Penn turned the tables in that interview though, blaming the film's producers. "They just dumped it," moaned Penn. "And I'm the one that fucked it up, right, 'cause I won't do interviews." He elaborated on this point in an interview with the *New York Times* the same year. "I wasn't even a famous actor at the time but it became this thing," he commented, ruefully. "Ah – now we've got a label for him. He's the guy who doesn't support his movies. And then I got married to her." The 'her' was, of course, Madonna.

Whatever the feelings about his post-production involvement with the feature, nobody could dispute Penn's commitment to his part. His dedication to establishing the character's authenticity even extended as far as stunts. When it was time to shoot a dangerous stunt involving a train, Penn tried to persuade Benjamin to let him do the stunt, rather than use a stunt man. He told Benjamin of his concern that if a stunt man did the scene then the audience would be viewing the scene through the eyes of a stunt man rather than through Henry's eyes. This kind of perfectionism was typical of Penn's dedication to 'the work'.

Things were looking considerably brighter for Sean's brother Christopher, who appeared in the hit film *All The Right Moves* and then followed this role with a part in *The Wild Life*, a made-for-TV film directed by his father. Leo supplemented work on the film by directing *Paper Dolls* for TV. In fact, the only Penn who wasn't finding it easy to get a break was Michael Penn who was still toiling away with Doll Congress.

The film that Penn chose to do next – *The Falcon And The Snowman* – heralded his arrival as a remarkable actor. His performance in the film may owe be heavily reminiscent of Robert De Niro's role as 'Rupert Pupkin' in *The King Of Comedy*, but it is still an astonishing piece of acting.

The Falcon And The Snowman was directed by British filmmaker John Schlesinger, whose impressive CV included *Billy Liar, Far From The Madding Crowd, Midnight Cowboy* and *Marathon Man*. The film, which had an $11.5-million budget, was adapted for the screen by Steven Zaillian from Robert Lindsay's book. When Schlesinger landed the director's job on the film, it was a return to form after a spell spent directing for TV. The film was based on a true story. Christopher Boyce and Andrew Daulton Lee, two middle-class Americans, caused a national scandal when they sold classified government information to the Soviet Union. Schlesinger cast Penn as Andrew Daulton Lee and Timothy Hutton as Christopher Boyce. Penn grew a moustache for his role as the sleazy drug dealer-turned-wired seller of government secrets – giving him a distinct resemblance to De Niro's 'Rupert Pupkin'.

At the time of the film's release in May 1985, Schlesinger told *Screen International* that "we've been pretty truthful to the facts of the case." The facts of the case were as follows. Boyce and Lee had grown up together in Los Angeles in comfortable, middle-class homes. Boyce was a falconer and political idealist, while Lee was a cocaine and heroin dealer who had been busted several times in his teenage years. When Boyce discovered that the CIA were interfering in foreign government policies, he worked with Lee to sell insider knowledge to Russia. After two successful years, they were caught. Boyce was sentenced to 40 years in jail and Lee was given a life sentence. Hutton researched the role endlessly, even before the project had found backing, and once the project was green-lighted, he established a relationship with Boyce via telephone calls. Boyce worked closely with Hutton, giving him plenty of character information (in particular outlining and describing his emotional state) at every step of the story. Hutton admits that the role "took over" his life for the best part of two years, and freely admitted at the time of the film's release, that he had become "obsessed" with the subject. Another interesting dimension to the film was the casting of Pat Hingle as Andrew Daulton Lee's father. Pat Hingle had, of course, taken Penn under his wing at the Los Angeles Group Repertory Theater. Now the roles were reversed: Hingle, who had once given Penn a break by hiring him, was now Penn's key supporting actor. It may well have been that Hingle's presence drove Penn to stretch his character to the max, to push the envelope as far as he could.

Influential film critic Pauline Kael attacked Penn's hysterical, edgy - performance when the film was released. "You get the impression that Penn thinks the only part of the character creation that's authentic is the groping," she wrote. "He abdicates half the actor's job – the projecting and the shaping. You feel as if the artist had disappeared and you were left watching a twerp playing a twerp." Penn exploded on reading the review, later telling *American Film* that he had Kael's piece pinned up on his "piss wall". He rebuked her attack, commenting, "Who is she to say what is or is not acting?"

Interestingly, Penn told *Film Comment* in late 1991 that he personally wouldn't have cast himself as Daulton Lee. He told the magazine that he would have liked to have seen the part played by a youthful Richard Dreyfuss. However, whatever his subsequent feelings about the film, the whole thing is held together by Penn's heavily De Niro-ized perform-ance that gains intensity throughout the film as his character spirals further and further out of control. Similarities are apparent between his role in this film and his role as a lawyer in *Carlito's Way* – in both he's twitchy, hyperactive, a bundle of electricity paralysed by drug abuse.

Once again, even though both Penn and Hutton gave outstanding performances and supporting actress Lori Singer was also very good, the film flopped and was condemned to only a short run at cinemas. When its run came to a close, *The Falcon And The Snowman* had only grossed $17.1 million, a very modest return on a film with an $11.5-million budget. On the plus side, the reviews were still Penn positive. *Variety's* reviewer commented, "Penn is left with the shallower part of the dete-riorating druggie, to which he nonetheless adds necessary dimensions," adding that both Penn and Hutton were superb. *Monthly Film Bulletin* argued that the interplay between the actors gave the film its power: "Sean Penn's hyperactivity as he veers between coked-up over-confidence and smack-induced snivelling, contrasts usefully with Hutton's uptight, inexpressive intensity." Vincent Canby of the *New York Times* described the film as "a very curious though effective entertainment, a scathing social satire". For *Newsweek's* David Ansen, the film was a "kind of darkly comic illustration of the banality of contemporary evil".

The film premiered at a theatre in Los Angeles in February 1985 and Penn did little to make up for the stink that had followed his refusal to promote *Racing With The Moon*. Instead of wisely getting stuck into a meet-and-greet with the celebrity and industry guests at the after-screening party, he hid behind a tree, according to an article in *People* magazine. The news report said that Penn spent almost the entire party behind a "potted tree". When Lori Singer wanted to congratulate her co-star on his performance, Penn requested that she do so behind the tree. *People* magazine also observed that this behaviour was positively normal compared to another night prior to the premiere party when Penn had run into his fellow actor friend Harry Dean Stanton after a party at Spago's on Sunset Boulevard. Penn had put his jacket over his head on seeing photographers trying to snap him with Stanton. He then zipped the jacket up and carried on a conversation with Stanton through the zipped-up jacket.

Penn's own father has described him as "moody and he likes mischief," and at this period in his career this was never more true than when the young actor was around photographers. Douglas Thompson, the author of *Like A Virgin: Madonna Revealed*, notes that a female photographer told him a story about a run-in with Penn at a publicity event. "He told me he had a water pistol, and if I didn't leave he was going to fill the pistol with urine and squirt me." Sean Penn, soon to be the tabloids' favourite actor, was beginning to earn himself a testy reputation.

FOUR

Big Deal On Madonna Street

It's a safe bet that when Penn took up an invitation to visit the set of a video shoot for the new single by Madonna, he had no idea what lay ahead of him. Romance, a wedding, continuous intrusive hounding by the world's media, arguments, a series of public punch-ups with the paparazzi, heavy drinking, court room appearances, a spell in jail, a disintegrating marriage and, finally, divorce.

When Sean Penn turned up on the set to watch Madonna live out her Marilyn Monroe fantasies in the video for the 'Material Girl' single, he was a rising star and was rumoured to be earning about $1,000,000 per film. He'd been on magazine covers and guested on TV shows. But although he was used to a degree of celebrity, he'd tasted nothing like the kind of fame that his bride-to-be was courting and getting.

By 1985 Madonna was already a global icon. The pressure that Penn suddenly found himself under when he pursued Madonna would later blow his career off course and lead to a lengthy sabbatical. The pop star, who was born on August 16, 1958, was enjoying sales figures of 3.5 million copies for her *Like A Virgin* album when she and Penn first crossed paths. The story of their meeting is told in a different way in each of the two primary Madonna biographies. Christopher Andersen, in his book *Madonna Unauthorized,* claims that Penn happened to be on the set because the video's director, Mary Lambert, was a friend of his and she invited Penn to tag along for a day. Madonna spotted Penn wearing a leather jacket and sunglasses and knew exactly who he was. This fleeting glimpse swiftly turned into something else. Madonna herself is quoted as saying that she was suddenly overcome with a "fantasy that we were going to meet and fall in love and get married".

That may be so, though Andersen notes that the fantasy must have soon dissolved because Madonna then threw Penn a cold stare and ignored him for the rest of the day's shoot. Douglas Thompson, in his book *Like A Virgin: Madonna Revealed* also states that Penn and Madonna met on the 'Material Girl' shoot but he paints a less romantic picture. According to Thompson, Madonna later commented, "I didn't feel swept off my feet but he is somebody whose work I had admired for a long time."

Thompson's slow-moving telling of the story contrasts with Andersen's fiery account of the rest of that fateful video shoot. According to *Madonna Unauthorized,* at one point during the day Madonna told Penn to get out, though quite what prompted this outburst is never fully explored. Andersen then reports that Madonna softened up and gave flowers to everyone who worked on the shoot. He claims that Madonna, realising that she hadn't had flowers sent over to Penn, abruptly ran off and returned minutes later with a single rose, which she gave to him.

When Madonna and Penn met on the 'Material Girl' shoot, they were both in theory already taken. Madonna was still seeing Jellybean Benitez and Penn was by this stage engaged to Elizabeth McGovern. The actor and the singer may have been involved with other lovers, but sparks were clearly flying between the two of them. And in truth, they seemed like a good match. After all, Madonna was born on August 16, 1958, and Penn was born on August 17, 1960. Madonna considered this to be a good omen. "We were born one day apart and he and I have similar temperaments," she later told a reporter. Perhaps rather spookily, Madonna also said that she saw similarities between Penn and her own father. "When I squint my eyes," she said, "he almost looks like my father," although this was probably just another classic Madonna quip designed to shock and thrill in equal measure. Penn wasted no time in asking Madonna out. He had taken notes at the video shoot and knew exactly how to woo her. Andersen says that when Madonna and Penn went on an early date in Los Angeles, Penn drove Madonna from his Malibu home to Westwood Cemetery. The reason for this brief drive was soon revealed. Madonna's idol, Marilyn Monroe, was buried in the cemetery.

According to *Like A Virgin: Madonna Revealed,* the relationship got off to a flying start. "I'd never known Sean happier," Chris Penn later recalled of the relationship's early days. Penn's childhood buddies were similarly positive about the two. "Sean's always been misunderstood," Charlie Sheen told Douglas Thompson. "And probably most about how much he adores Madonna." His brother Emilio Estevez was singing from the same song sheet: "I thought that was a lifetime partnership. I'd never write them off." Their dad, Martin Sheen, weighed in with some paternal perspective: "You just wanted it all to be perfect for them for they really were a well-suited couple."

In *Madonna Unauthorized*, Christopher Andersen's version of events has the romance getting off to a far slower start. He states that a friend of Madonna's – Erica Bell – received a phone call from the superstar shortly after her initial encounter with Penn on the video shoot. Andersen quotes Bell as saying that during the phone call Madonna raced down a list of celebrities that she had met since the two friends had last spoken. Bell is quoted in Andersen's book as saying that Madonna was as excited about having met Penn as she was about meeting Elizabeth Taylor. Andersen doesn't detail a speedy romance. He states that Madonna and Penn were busy having dinner at Café Central in New York when Elizabeth McGovern appeared out of nowhere to join the would-be couple. Andersen reckons that this incensed Madonna – stirring up a blizzard of jealous emotions – and says that she stormed off leaving Penn and McGovern to finish dinner without her. McGovern – who was expecting to marry Penn that April – must have wondered what was going on.

Andersen then claims that the tables were turned a week later. No longer in New York but instead back in Los Angeles, Madonna and Penn allegedly had a bust-up at her apartment after Penn flew into a jealous rage over rumours that Madonna was dating Prince. Andersen states that Penn stormed out of the apartment and Madonna slammed the door behind him, whereupon Penn turned around and punched a hole through the wall. Madonna later showed the damage to close associate Melinda Cooper. When Andersen interviewed Cooper, she told him that Madonna was intrigued by Penn's temper. "She thought it was great," Cooper revealed. "Sean's violent streak appealed to her back then and she likes pressing men's buttons."

After this initial explosion, Andersen notes that the couple gradually drew closer. Erica Bell told him that she saw Penn as a classic rebel figure film star, the kind of moody James Dean figure that would effortlessly attract a woman like Madonna. She was also drawn to Penn because he was well-read. Bell told Andersen that Madonna went from being moderately interested in writers to suddenly dropping names such as Charles Bukowski and J.D. Salinger into everyday conversation. It is only at this stage, after some intense early developments, that Andersen has Penn drive Madonna from Malibu to Westwood Cemetery to visit the grave of her idol. Thus, in Anderson's version of events, this quirky romantic date came hot on the heels of some mutual jealousy and some serious movement towards a one-on-one relationship.

Madonna's star – already shining pretty brightly – went into orbit when Susan Seidelman's film *Desperately Seeking Susan*, opened at over 1,000 screens across the U.S. in April 1985. The film attracted instant attention after Seidelman asked Madonna if she could deliver a dance track for a sequence in the film. Madonna, in collaboration with Steve Bray, wrote 'Into The Groove', which not only plugged the film via the continuous radio play that it received, but gave Madonna another giant smash hit single.

Madonna prepared for her forthcoming tour by jogging six miles a day and eating a strict vegetarian diet. She also spent some time hanging out with Penn and his fellow actor and actress friends. Most of them belonged to the group tagged by the media as the 'Brat Pack'. The term did not amuse Penn, who later threw a fit about it to a journalist. "All it is, is a condescending load of shit," he complained, "written by some person with a big vibrator up his ass."

As *Desperately Seeking Susan* cleaned up with young cinema-goers, Madonna began her much-anticipated Like A Virgin tour. Every time her show hit a new city, the coverage brought her an even greater level of fame. In *Madonna Unauthorized*, Andersen claims that at this point Madonna was simultaneously chasing Prince while being chased by Penn. He also says that Prince, although heavily into flirting with Madonna, never once allowed himself to seduce her or to be seduced by her.

Penn, meanwhile, was following Madonna from show to show – Andersen notes his appearances at concerts in Detroit, Miami and San Diego. He also contradicts the notion that Madonna was more interested in Prince at this time by relating that Madonna introduced Penn to her father after one show on her tour, which hardly sounds like the act of a woman who was only vaguely interested in her suitor.

When the tour reached the Universal Amphitheater in Los Angeles, Penn reciprocated the gesture and arranged for Madonna to meet his parents. Andersen quotes Erica Bell on her theories as to what Madonna was thinking at this point. Bell told him that although Madonna had called her from Cleveland early one morning to tell her how bored she was on the road and how much she was thinking of Penn, Bell still felt that Madonna wasn't as passionate about Penn as she had been about Jellybean Benitez. Even so, by now it was safe to assume that both Benitez and McGovern were out of the picture.

Shortly before Madonna's Like A Virgin tour began, Penn was busy preparing for his role in James Foley's *At Close Range*. The film was to be shot in America's Deep South. Foley, who had known Penn for years, was still dining out on good notices for *Reckless*, a broody, moody film that starred Aidan Quinn. *At Close Range* was based on a screenplay written by Elia Kazan's son Nicholas, and had a working budget of $6.5 million. The idea for the screenplay stretched back to the late '70s, when Foley was studying at USC (University of Southern California). It was during that time that he read a newspaper story about a crime family whose run of criminal activity came to an end when father and son were forced to turn against each other.

The story originally centred on the Johnston family murders in Pennsylvania's Brandywine River Valley in 1978. The son of a crime gang leader and his 14-year-old girlfriend were ambushed by two of the boy's uncles after his father had put a $15,000 contract out on him. The girlfriend died from one bullet but the son survived eight separate gunshot wounds. Foley had shown Penn the article and the latter expressed an interest in transferring the story to the big screen. However, even though the author of the article, Elliott Lewitt, had given them permission to transform his piece into a film, the pair had tried unsuccessfully to find an interested backer. The story, which was considered "too dark" by most of the producers who had expressed an early interest in the project, was finally given a green light by John Daly of Hemdale.

At the time of the film's release, in April 1986, Foley summed up the plot to *Film Comment* thus: "*At Close Range* is about a sleepy town and a kid who's been in hibernation until he comes alive with an enormous turbulence. I wanted the colours and look of the film to reflect that." However, even when the project was finally off the ground, all did not run smoothly. The small budget available meant that heavy-weight actor, Christopher Walken (as sleazy crime leader Brad Whitewood), had to work for deferred payment. The main expense for Foley to accommodate came from the large number of set-ups needed. Many scenes were shot in Tennessee, just outside Nashville and because there was no suitable source of electricity available, the crew had to bring a huge generator for lighting. This, along with the fact that the crew ended up moving to 68 different locations in 48 days, rapidly ate through the budget. The film was a family affair for the Penns, with Sean playing Brad Whitewood Jr, his brother Chris playing his half-brother Tommy and their mother, Eileen Ryan, played their grandmother.

As part of his characteristic dedication to the role, Penn put on 30 pounds and worked out ferociously in order to convey a more powerful physical presence. Comparing his appearance in *The Falcon And The Snowman* with that in *At Close Range* reveals a vast difference. In the former, he is skinny, sleazy and moustached; in the latter he has peroxided his hair bleach blond, eaten himself into a stocky shape and pumped iron to give himself a muscular frame. The new-look Penn was the result of arduous sessions with a personal trainer, Ray Kaybartaf. Penn had done his homework and had a very definite idea of how to play his part. From very early on in the film, his appearance and acting recall the Brando of *The Wild One* and *A Streetcar Named Desire*. This was probably intentional as Foley's favourite films are those made by directors such as Elia Kazan and Nicholas Ray, two key post-Second World War American directors. Foley admitted that, like Penn, he was mostly interested in the film because of the "father-son thing". The director liked the fact that Penn's character was not turning to crime (mostly stealing tractors) because he had an amoral streak, but because he wanted to get close to the father he had never known. For this reason, Foley needed an actor who could capture the understatement of the role. "An actor had to draw attention to himself without saying too much," Foley explained to *Film Comment*. "While everybody around him is screaming and yelling and shooting at each other. It flies in the face of many conventions. And that's why I felt it could work only when Sean became involved with the project."

Most importantly, Foley acknowledged that Penn's presence made the process of filmmaking much easier. "I was confident that I could tell a story, so I was more relaxed. And with Sean being my best friend – having had a relationship and a dialogue with him for years – the making of the film was just a follow-up to the months before that, when we spent every minute together." Foley elaborated on the special kind of relationship he had with Penn in an interview with *American Film*: "For each scene that any individual actor is involved in, I feel a collaboration with him in that area. With Sean it goes beyond that. Our partnership is the whole movie." To *Film Comment* he revealed, "Sean is a director's dream for knowing the medium he's working in . . . he knows how to make any act or gesture, however simple, like cigarette smoking, more expressive."

When *American Film's* Margy Rochlin visited the set to write a feature on the making of the film, Penn's ascending star – she reported that Penn was at that time getting between $1 million and $1.5 million a film at the time – was very much on display. His increasingly hostile attitude to the press resulted in Rochlin being issued with provisos for her presence on the set. She was told to stay out of Penn's "line of vision" and also not to bother him until the day's filming had been wrapped. Rochlin revealed that the unit publicist also spent the day hard-selling an image of Penn, revealing trivia about Penn's exercise regime (he ran six miles a day) and also the shoot (Penn and Christopher Walken drove out to Tennessee from Los Angeles in a pick-up truck for the filming).

When Penn did talk to Rochlin, he enthused about the freedom he was finding, working with a close friend. "I feel this is my first movie not for hire," he revealed, "my first movie that didn't have to do with this long chain of business people." Rochlin found that Penn, who had recently been arrested for throwing rocks at two English journalists, was a hot potato as far as the crew were concerned. One crew member told her: "Sean was very professional but people walk on cat's feet with him because they never know from one day to the next whether he'll be gracious and charming or act like a punk."

Rochlin also discovered that the film's producer Elliott Lewitt and Nicholas Kazan were less than happy with what Penn and Foley were doing with the screenplay. The main complaint was that they saw the work in progress as straying from the facts of the original story and that Foley and Penn were making it more of a rites-of-passage film. "I feel the film that has come out of seven years' work is a much diluted

version of the film that I hoped would result from that work," complained Kazan at the time.

In its finished form, Rochlin's article picked up the interview with
Penn some six months after he had married Madonna. That part of the
article caught Penn on the eve of flying out to Hong Kong to start
shooting *Shanghai Surprise* with his new wife. When asked about preparation for the role, Penn exhibited a notable reluctance to talk about
his technique. "Any discussion defeats the purpose of what is on
screen," said Penn. "Preparation is all hogwash. It takes the mystery out
of movies." The interview revealed a maturing Sean Penn, one who was
starting to ease up somewhat on his exhaustive preparation methods.
He had not bothered to go and visit Brad Whitewood Jr as part of his
research because he didn't feel it necessary. When asked if he was still
insisting on crew and cast members calling him by his character's name
for the duration of the shoot, he said that he had stopped doing that
during *Racing With The Moon* because it put him on edge whenever he
encountered someone who "felt resentment" and "didn't want to do
it". In other words, some co-workers found his approach unnecessarily
pretentious and whenever Penn sensed that, it affected his ability to
keep in character. Penn did make some interesting comments about his
technique though, explaining that he often found shoots exhausting
because he felt as though he was condensing an entire character's life
into a matter of months. To safeguard against the emotional overload
that this caused, he often imagined his character as being like the
process of building a cage, in order to maintain an aspect of personal
space. When the shoot was over, he mentally released the character from
the cage.

The shoot also had serious significance for Penn's personal life.
Madonna frequently flew down to Nashville, Tennessee to spend short
bursts of time with him. It was on one such visit that she and Penn
decided to marry. When Penn's friend and mentor Harry Dean Stanton
interviewed Madonna for London's *Time Out* magazine in 1986, he
asked her who had proposed to whom. Her reply was characteristically
unorthodox. "Sean asked me to marry him," the singer recalled. "But he
didn't say it out loud, I read his mind. So I read his mind back to him . . .
[I said] 'Whatever you're thinking, I'll say yes to.' That was his chance.
So he popped it." Dean Stanton asked for further details and Madonna
happily obliged. She explained that the proposal had been made "in

Tennessee, at the Something Inn. We were out in the middle of nowhere and 7-Eleven was the high point of interest there." The couple decided to get married on a Sunday morning. Madonna was in the middle of her daily exercise cycle. Some articles claim she was leaping up and down on the bed, improvising her usual workout to fit the circumstances. When asked by Dean Stanton, Madonna confirmed that she had accepted Penn's proposal on the spot. "Of course I did," she gushed. "I'm a woman of my word. Then we went to the 7-Eleven and bought a whole bunch of jawbreakers and celebrated. Sean is my hero and my best friend."

The couple's family and friends were surprised by the news of the engagement when it leaked out to the press. In *Madonna Unauthorized*, Christopher Andersen says that Madonna's friend Erica Bell expressed concern at the match, due to Penn's allegedly violent streak. Madonna laughed off Bell's fears, telling her that Penn reminded her of her brothers when she was growing up with them.

Andersen also claims that Penn, who had for some time carried a gun with him wherever he went, started to take Madonna to a shooting range for target practice and told her that he had once fired one of his guns at McGovern during an argument. The bullet allegedly blew McGovern's watch clean off her wrist. Andersen says that Madonna found this story "funny" and made a point of bragging about it to Erica Bell who told her that she was playing with fire. But whatever the couple's feelings about each other, the intrusive hounding that Penn and his fiancée were forced to put up with from photographers and journalists was starting to get to the young actor. Madonna was more used to the attention, but Penn found it hard to have his every move shadowed by money-crazed paparazzi.

A week after the proposal, news of the engagement reached the world's media. Madonna's publicist confirmed the story. When Andersen talked to Erica Bell about the engagement he was told that Bell was knocked out when she heard the news. "She told no one she was going to marry," Bell explained. "Even his family didn't know about it until they saw the news on TV."

Andersen states that Madonna's entourage, which included a high head count of gay men, were less than enthralled about her decision to marry Penn. One of Madonna's inner circle, Ed Steinberg, told Andersen: "It was sickening to hear him (Penn) call her friends queers and fags. Everybody hated him." Erica Bell contradicted this view, stating that Penn was actually jealous of Madonna's gay male friends because they were able to get closer to her than he could.

The couple, once again hiding away at a hotel in Tennessee, were pushed to breaking point by two freelance journalists, Laurence Cottrell and Ian Markham-Smith, who were chasing a juicy story on commission for the *Sun* newspaper. Penn had clocked the stalking pair when he had waved Madonna off on her daily jog. When she came back, Penn saw the journalists rush in for an exclusive series of photographs. Andersen alleges that Penn snapped when he saw them and picked up a rock. He warned off the journalists, telling them that they were not to take any photographs. When Cottrell asked Penn why he was getting so angry, the actor shouted: "You take my picture and I'll break your fucking back with this rock!" He then apparently ran towards the journalists and threw the rock, which struck Cottrell in the back, before starting to strike Cottrell with his camera. Andersen reports Cottrell as saying: "Penn was acting like a madman".

When Cottrell had hit the ground, Penn turned his anger towards Markham-Smith, whom he allegedly punched in the face. Cottrell wasted no time and snapped pictures of Penn attacking Markham-Smith. Penn then hurled a rock for a second time at Cottrell. When the fracas was over, the journalists went straight to the nearest police station and filed their version of what had just happened. Police officers arrived at the superstar couple's Nashville hotel later that day and arrested Penn on two misdemeanour counts of assault and battery. Once arrested, Penn was brought before the Night Court commissioner who presented him with the charges and set bail at $1,000. Madonna was utterly supportive of Penn, arguing that his outburst was the result of extreme provocation. She disliked the paparazzi as much as Penn and felt that her fiancé had simply been trying to protect her from an invasion of privacy. She was as annoyed as he was with rumours that were then circulating claiming that she was already pregnant.

The engagement was the hottest thing to hit the world's newspapers and gossip columns in years. If reporters weren't drooling over that or Penn's paparazzi punch-out, then they were feverish about yet another news item which would dominate July 1985. This time, the scoop concerned nude photographs of Madonna that dated back to her early days as a struggling young singer in New York.

Penthouse and *Playboy* both announced that they had bought nude photographs of the superstar and were intending to run them as scandalous spreads. The pictures, which dated back to the end of the '70s and the dawn of the '80s, were hardly flattering. Unfortunately for the Material Girl, sources of these photographs were endless. Madonna had posed for art classes, artists and photographers back then – all for typically minuscule posing fees. *Penthouse* stated that they were going to run a selection of pictures as a major, lengthy special feature. *Playboy*, on the other hand, had bought photographs from a shoot done by acclaimed photographer Lee Friedlander as well as from Martin Schreiber. Andersen alleges that each photographer was paid $100,000 for their pictures. The Freidlander photographs – like many of his nudes – reflected a raw, realistic style.

Lee Friedlander's monograph *Nudes*, which features photographs from the same shoot that the *Playboy* pictures originated from, offers a series of photographs of women with armpit hair, unshaven legs and often hairy arms – for a purpose. Friedlander's style is strictly natural, his photographs pursuing a real (heavily European) document of female beauty rather than the kind of airbrushed beauty to be found in fashion magazines.

When he shot Madonna, she sported armpit hair as well as body hair. The *Playboy* photographs show Madonna in this typically European look: a far cry from the Madonna that her fans and observers had become accustomed to. Once *Penthouse* knew that *Playboy* were racing to get their Madonna nudes to the news stands ahead of their rival, Andersen claims that their publisher – Bob Guccione – struck back by offering Madonna $1 million to pose nude for a new, contemporary shoot. His proposal offered her the photographer of her choice. Not surprisingly, she turned him down. Unfortunately for her, Madonna was unable to prevent either magazine from going to press because she had signed release forms at the time of the shoots, permitting the photographers to use the resulting pictures in whatever way they wished.

No sooner had Madonna weathered all this than she learned that Stephen Jon Lewicki, the director of a rough, cheaply shot soft porn film that she had appeared in called *A Certain Sacrifice*, was planning to release the film to the home video market. Madonna had her legal team attempt to stop the distribution of the video but the judge ruled against her as she had signed similar release papers to those for the photographic sessions and had therefore waived her rights. By the time Madonna was singing on stage in Philadelphia for the American half of the Live Aid concert, *A Certain Sacrifice* was available on video and both *Playboy* and *Penthouse* were racing to get their Madonna special issues on sale.

The clock was ticking and the wedding date was getting closer. Andersen claims that Erica Bell told him that she had asked Madonna if she was going to arrange a pre-nuptial agreement to protect her fortune if the marriage failed. Bell told Andersen that Madonna had indeed had her lawyers draw up such an agreement. Madonna and Penn were being hounded night and day by journalists desperate to find out when the big day would be. Some of the more persistent sleuths spotted the couple leaving the Los Angeles Court house on August 12, where they had picked up a marriage licence. The date itself – which only the couple and close family knew – was set for August 16, 1985.

The invitations – which were designed by Michael Penn – went out to select guests and stated that the wedding ceremony itself was going to begin at 6 pm. They also stated that although the wedding was going to take place in Los Angeles, the exact location would only be revealed shortly before the event itself. Therefore, the invites asked guests to RSVP with a telephone number through which the location could be circulated at a specified time. The reasons for this kind of secrecy were obvious: to keep the paparazzi away and to allow the bride and groom some privacy on their wedding day. Interestingly, the RSVPs were to be sent to 'Clyde Is Hungry Productions' which would later become better known as Penn's film production company.

Although the primary focus was the wedding, Madonna and Penn were also shopping around big-name Hollywood producers in search of a film to do together. One of the screenplays that went further than the 'no thanks' stage was *Blind Date*, a film that would later get made with Bruce Willis and Kim Basinger in the leading roles.

The hotter the couple became, the more producers were sweating it out trying to woo the dream team to a project that would automatically garner enormous exposure given their involvement. Producers could hear the sound of tickets being torn by the million at cinema foyers all over the world. The only headache was finding a screenplay that the couple were interested in committing to.

By the time Penn had finished the shoot for *At Close Range* and Madonna was done with her Like A Virgin tour, the two celebrated their decision to marry by moving in together. The home that they chose as their love nest was in the Hollywood Hills and the house itself, it transpired, had once been home to legendary actor John Barrymore. Douglas Thompson found out that the couple were paying $1,300 a month to rent the place.

Andersen's Madonna biography lays on details about the stag and hen nights with a broad brush. He reveals that Penn had a big boozy bash with close friends including his brother Chris, Tom Cruise, Robert Duvall and Harry Dean Stanton. The ensuing party is alleged to have featured a stripper. Andersen also relates that Madonna – out with a dozen close friends – held her hen night at a mud wrestling club in Hollywood called the Tropicana. Douglas Thompson's biography is more precise about the facts. He states that Madonna had a wedding shower that was presided over by Nile Rodgers' girlfriend, Nancy Huang. The shower took place at Huang's apartment on Manhattan's Upper East Side. Apparently, along with guests such as Mariel Hemingway and Alannah Currie from the Thompson Twins, Madonna had invited six of her male friends, who came in full drag. In the interim, Madonna organised a wedding list at Tiffany's. Meanwhile, a venue for the wedding was being sorted out. It was finally decided that it would be held at the cliff-top Malibu mansion owned by multi-millionaire Dan Unger, who was a close friend of Leo and Eileen.

The wedding finally took place on Wednesday August 16 at 6 pm. Penn apparently welcomed guests by saying: "Welcome to the remaking of *Apocalypse Now*". Even though the guests were tipped off as to the location only hours before, someone leaked the venue and place and by the time the couple were exchanging vows, Malibu was crawling with reporters and paparazzi desperate for an exclusive. Madonna wore a white wedding dress designed by Marlene Stewart and Penn wore a Versace suit. A massive catering tent was set up on Unger's estate and white lily pads were set afloat in the swimming pool. The guests included Christopher Walken, Andy Warhol, Cher, Patricia Arquette, Martin Sheen, Diane Keaton, Carrie Fisher and many other A-list Hollywood celebrities. Security guards patrolled the grounds while other security men frisked all guests on their way in to prevent paparazzi from sneaking in wearing disguises.

James Foley was Penn's best man and Madonna's sister Paula was her maid of honour. Penn and Madonna were furious when the whirr of helicopters overhead practically drowned out their ceremony and shortly thereafter the message FUCK OFF appeared in the sand on the beach beneath Unger's estate. It has never been established if this message to the press was written by Penn, a guest (or guests), or if the couple had an employee write it. Whoever was responsible, it was certainly a humorous way to deal with the intrusive airborne media.

It has been alleged that Penn fired off several rounds from a handgun into the air out of frustration at the intrusion, but Penn himself insisted that nothing could have spoiled his day. "I had a beautiful wedding," he told *American Film*. "There was that helicopter interruption but they could have gone ten times further and still couldn't have interrupted that great, beautiful wedding. They gave it their best shot though." In a comment that perhaps revealed more about the true strength of Penn's feelings on the paparazzi than he'd intended, he continued: "Those were non-people to me though. I consider myself very human and very moral and I would have been very excited to see one of those helicopters burn and the bodies inside melt."

Afterwards the couple checked into the Highlands Inn in Carmel (just up the Pacific Coast Highway from Malibu) under aliases. The $225-a-night room should have brought them privacy. However, when they sneaked down to Clint Eastwood's restaurant The Hog's Breath Inn, they were spotted and their honeymoon hideaway was leaked to the press.

The next step for the world's most famous twosome was to go house hunting. They settled on a $3.5-million mansion in the canyons of Malibu, which they promptly surrounded with an electrified fence and steel spikes on the tops of all walls. Things seem to have taken rather a strange turn after the wedding. Andersen and Thompson both claim that Madonna began to see a psychiatrist several weeks after the happy day. She apparently tried to get Penn to do the same but he refused. According to Andersen, another sign of early marital problems came when Madonna bought a $900,000 apartment in New York City and registered it – unlike the Malibu mansion – in only her name. Madonna was already flexing her gigantic buying power, and in retrospect this may have hurt her husband's pride.

In October 1985, Penn went back to Nashville to face the assault charges that had arisen from his attack on journalists Laurence Cottrell and Ian Markham-Smith. He was given a 90-day suspended sentence and fined a minuscule sum, perhaps in recognition of the provocation he had received. In 1991 Penn spoke to Bruce Weber of the *New York Times* about his past predilection for violent outbursts, commenting that he had a problem with "people who violated my liberties". He explained that throughout his relationship with Madonna he was constantly hounded. "There's the added thing of flashes in the eyes," he said. "The goading, the provoking." Clearly Sean Penn was not a man to tolerate infringement of his personal space. Unfortunately, he had just married one of the world's most famous women, and space infringement was one thing he would be getting plenty of from now on.

FIVE

A Tale Of Ordinary Madness

At the beginning of 1986, the newly-wed couple were set to start work on their first – and last – film together, *Shanghai Surprise*. The project was kicked into touch by former Beatle George Harrison, who approached Penn and Madonna with the screenplay. The film, which was to star Madonna as a missionary worker and Penn as an American drifter, was just one of a flood of film scripts that were sent to Madonna. Every major studio wanted her name on a film in progress. She and Penn boiled potential films down to two choices: the aforementioned *Blind Date*, a screwball comedy, and *Shanghai Surprise*, a homage of sorts to Hollywood movies from yesteryear, set in 1930s China.

The film was adapted from Tony Kendrick's novel *Faraday's Flowers* and Madonna envisioned the script turning into a film along the lines of *The African Queen*. George Harrison's Handmade Films had previously produced *The Life Of Brian* and *A Private Function* and this new $15-million project made the company the envy of producers all over the world, although such envy turned rapidly to relief when the finished product was released. The contracts gave Madonna and Penn salaries of roughly $1 million each as well as total script approval. Penn immediately threw himself into Mandarin classes.

Sean Penn and Madonna flew into Shanghai on January 8, 1986, direct from Los Angeles. Once they had acclimatised, the cast and crew moved on to Hong Kong. However, once on location the project rapidly ran into problems. Some areas of the shoot were beset with rats; to her horror, Madonna discovered that a swarm of them had set up home under her trailer. The shoot was often held up by Chinese gangsters. One day, a gang blocked off an entire street with a car – effectively trapping the celebrity couple – and only agreed to move the offending vehicle in return for $50,000. Another day, gangsters closed down a power generator, forcing the day's shoot to be abandoned. But legal organisations could be just as devious at causing headaches for the shoot. In *Madonna Unauthorized*, Christopher Andersen reports that the *Hong Kong Standard* put up a $500 reward for anyone who could point the newspaper's paparazzi to Madonna and Penn's hide-out or dropped off photographs of the couple at the paper's offices.

When the crew and cast arrived in Macao, Penn and Madonna checked into the Oriental Hotel. Douglas Thompson notes that the couple wore disguises when they went off to dinner and that security men sealed off the hotel swimming pool whenever Madonna wanted to take a swim. According to Christopher Andersen, it was at the Oriental Hotel that Leonel Borrahlo, owner of the *Hong Kong Standard*, tried to photograph the celebrity couple when they stepped out of a lift in the hotel. Penn allegedly went berserk and had to be held back by the bodyguards assigned to protect him and his wife. Sometime during the scuffle and exchange of words, Borrahlo – after getting caught up in the camera strap – traded the film in his camera in exchange for an exclusive interview with Penn. When it became apparent that the interview seemed less than likely to happen, Andersen claims that Borrahlo filed assault charges against Penn and sued for damages in the region of $1 million.

Madonna backed up her husband when he was taken to the Macao police headquarters for questioning over the incident. Handmade Films, dismayed to find that Penn was being billed as the "ugly American" in the native press, asked the film's publicist, Chris Nixon, to sort something out. Nixon came up with a plan. He suggested to Penn and Madonna that they stage a photo shoot for the local press. All Penn and his wife had to do was smile sweetly for a brief while and all the bad feeling – caused by the Borrahlo run-in and the fact that the couple hadn't given any press interviews since touching down in Shanghai – would dissipate.

Unfortunately, Andersen reveals that Penn wasn't interested in the plan. He states that Penn told Nixon that he should concentrate on plugging the film rather than appeasing the paparazzi. Andersen also alleges that Penn asked that Nixon be fired; his request was honoured by Handmade Films. Clearly there was little love lost between the two men. Thompson quotes Nixon as calling Penn an "aggressive, arrogant little shit". George Harrison flew out to visit Penn and Madonna because he was sick of hearing about all the problems that the film was encountering and tried to persuade them to do some publicity to help matters. After the visitation from the former Beatle, the couple finally knuckled down to the rest of the shoot in Macao, which proceeded relatively smoothly.

During the brief time out between Macao and England, Penn and Madonna made an appearance at the 1986 Berlin Film Festival to promote *At Close Range*. It was here that James Foley was nominated for the Berlin Bear Award. Afterwards, the couple arrived in England on February 24, to film exterior scenes in London and interior scenes at Shepperton Studios just outside London. The British media were out in force and during the couple's dash from the airport, Andersen reports that the Mercedes hired for the couple struck a photographer for the *Sun*, damaging his foot. He also mentions that Penn hardly helped matters by spitting at another photographer.

After that, the British media waged war on the couple, who they were now referring to as the 'Poison Penns'. (Back in the U.S. they were known as 'S&M' to the paparazzi.) Andersen says that when Polaroids taken for Jim Goddard, the film's director, went missing, the celebrity couple refused to shoot any more scenes until the thief was caught and the photographs destroyed. Penn didn't exactly calm down the storm when he told *Vanity Fair* what his favourite pastimes were. "I prefer the bar to the gym any day," the actor confided. "I like to drink and I like to brawl." It took a cleverly engineered press conference – organised by George Harrison – to cool the British media's dislike of Madonna and her husband.

When the shoot wrapped in late March 1986, Penn and Madonna returned to the U.S. ready to help plug the imminent release of *At Close Range*. Earlier, James Foley had asked Madonna to write a song for the film. He was hoping to repeat the successful formula that Susan Seidelman had struck gold with. The result, a hypnotic power-ballad called 'Live To Tell' was, just like 'Into The Groove', a serious marketing bonus for the film. Unsurprisingly, James Foley directed the promo video for the song (complete with footage from the film) which, like 'Into The Groove', became a massive hit, reaching number two in the UK and going all the way to the top Stateside.

Variety unflatteringly described *At Close Range* as a "downbeat tale of brutal family relations" on its release in April 1986. The magazine highlighted Penn as the film's key figure and saving grace: "violent without being vicarious, this true story runs the risk of being an audience turn off, though the presence of Sean Penn will give it a needed lift at the box office." Reviewing the film for *Monthly Film Bulletin* at the time of the British release in August 1986, Richard Combs commented on what he saw as the somewhat superficial way in which family relationships were examined in the film: "the father-son confrontation is followed by a coda in court, when Brad Jr breaks down at having to identify his father. But by this time, with the star's wife, Madonna, performing the theme song on the soundtrack, 'family' seems to have become a theme of no more than plangent show-business resonance." Combs attacked the film for refusing to engage with the worthwhile issues that it raised, describing it as a "flashdance of themes – about adolescent estrangement from and need for family, about violence in the family multiplied and complicated when violence becomes a family enterprise – that would have been more interestingly dealt with at close range. Into this heavily lyricised vagueness, the nouveau method playing of Sean Penn fits snugly." *Films & Filming*'s David McGillivray saw the film as another "male bond vehicle for another hot young star. The star in question is Sean Penn, unrecognisably transformed from the pot-bellied wimp of *The Falcon And The Snowman* into a swaggering muscleman." Whatever his image in the press, Penn was fast earning plaudits from those who had worked with him, especially his directors. Some years later, when Sean Penn had put his acting on the back burner to concentrate on directing, James Foley commented, "Sean is one of the greats. And it's a shame he's become a director, because there are already too many directors out there, but not enough actors of his calibre."

After the debacle surrounding the making of *Shanghai Surprise* had subsided, Madonna returned to her music career and spent most of April working on her third album, *True Blue*. "Now that I'm in love, all the songs I write I feel like I do it all for him," she revealed at the time, clearly still besotted with her new husband. If the *Shanghai Surprise* shoot had started to raise questions about Sean Penn's volatile attitude to the press and his ability to cope with the continuous surveillance that came with being Madonna's husband, then an incident that happened at Helena's on April 12 showed that he was close to breaking point.

Christopher Andersen relates that Penn and Madonna were spending a great deal of their nights hanging out at the bar with celebrity friends such as Jack Nicholson and Cher. On April 12, a songwriter from Madonna's pre-Penn New York past – David Wolinski – came up to say hello and, naturally enough, she embraced her old friend. According to Andersen, when Penn saw Madonna kissing the songwriter he went berserk and punched Wolinski, knocking him to the floor. Douglas Thompson quotes from the police report for his own account of the episode: "Suspect picked up a chair and started hitting victim with the chair and kicking victim while on the ground. Suspect then picked up a podium and was about to throw it on victim however was stopped by unknown citizen." Andersen says that onlookers such as Ryan O'Neal, Farrah Fawcett and Harry Dean Stanton were possibly involved in restraining Penn. Andersen found out from various Madonna sources that the events of that night scared the hell out of her. One of these sources, Melinda Cooper, told Andersen that Madonna was freaked out because "when he drank, Sean was too violent for her to control".

When *At Close Range*'s American screen run came to a close after a short time, it had only grossed just over $2 million – a poor return on a film that cost roughly $6.5 million to make. It was during the failure of the film's initial release that Penn began to unravel. Andersen relates that Penn and Madonna got into a massive shouting match in a club called the Pyramid in New York City and that Penn – apparently drunk – 'shoved' Madonna up against a wall during their argument. Andersen claims that the argument was over Penn's uncertainty as to whether Madonna was being faithful or not. One of Madonna's former intimates, Bobby Martinez, told Andersen that one night at a club in New York, he heard that Penn was looking for him. Martinez told Andersen that he saw Penn, spotted a gun tucked inside the actor's suit and fled the club because Penn looked "nuts" to him.

The summer of 1986 was all Madonna's. Her *True Blue* album topped album charts all around the world and she had a huge, controversial hit with the 'Papa Don't Preach' single, which dealt with the theme of teenage pregnancy. She also acted alongside her husband in a play by David Rabe called *Goose and Tom-Tom*. Penn, Madonna and others rehearsed the play in New York and put on a one-night-only performance in front of a celebrity-soaked audience at the Lincoln Center. Madonna and Penn were joined onstage on August 29, 1986, by

Harvey Keitel, who would later star opposite Madonna in Abel Ferrara's *Dangerous Game*.

After the show, Penn and Madonna stopped in at the Ginger Man restaurant for dinner. When they left the restaurant, a gaggle of photographers was waiting to ambush them. One of them – Anthony Savignano – followed the couple to their apartment building where, he later told Christopher Andersen, Penn suddenly turned around and swung a punch at him. Penn missed and then apparently spat at the photographer. Savignano, having got the scoop he was after, busily snapped away. According to Andersen, Savignano pushed Penn away and Penn then punched him. Another photographer who was present – Vinnie Zuffante – then became Penn's target. Andersen relates that Penn attacked Zuffante and then disappeared into the apartment building. More bad press for the trouble-prone Penns.

Meanwhile, *Shanghai Surprise* was released, to a dismal reception. The film, which had been talked up as a modern day *Casablanca*, *African Queen* or *His Girl Friday*, proved a complete dud at the box office. It went on to gross a mere $2.3 million – a dismal return against the $11 million that the film had cost to make. To be frank, the film is an embarrassment and Penn and Madonna both hated the finished product. Penn, in garish make-up, thick stubble and a horrific '80s hairstyle, is barely recognisable throughout. The dialogue is pathetic, the sets dreadful and the cinematography a farce. The attempts at intrigue, comedy and drama all fall flat. *Variety*'s review in September 1986 was harsh, but typical: "If *Shanghai Surprise* was the best project Sean Penn and Madonna could find to star in together, the screenplays floating around the industry these days must comprise a sorry lot indeed." For good measure, the reviewer added that Madonna's character "makes no sense at all."

Richard Combs, writing in *Monthly Film Bulletin*, didn't have anything positive to add either: "the film fails to cohere, since the husband and wife pairing can't disguise the fact that Madonna, a 'performer' in the wider sense, doesn't play well against Sean Penn, an actor in a more concentrated sense." Not content with that, he then laid into the director, Jim Goddard, complaining that: "Goddard shows no signs of having mastered the rhythms or idiom of screwball." *Films & Filming*'s Sally Rowland was even meaner: "Madonna in bright red lipstick looks throughout as though she is reading her lines off an autocue and Penn, while displaying a skill for comic timing, otherwise looks extremely disaffected by anything that happens. He manages to maintain the same morose expression whether he has a gun pointed at his head or Madonna between the sheets. The much touted sexual chemistry (the new Bogey and Bacall, Goddard would have us believe) is sorely absent."

By way of explaining at least partly why the film had been so bad, in October 1991 Sean told *Premiere's* Michael Tighe, "I fucked up the whole thing. I drank a fifth of Scotch until five in the morning, took a shower, and went to work." The film brought Sean Penn's so-far meteoric rise to fame to an abrupt end; he was suddenly at the centre of a stink. The film bombed, and he was rapidly gaining a reputation as a troublemaker. Penn's rapid slide from the quality of his performances in *The Falcon And The Snowman* and *At Close Range* to that in *Shanghai Surprise* raises obvious questions: was he under his wife's influence? Or was he deliberately trying to score a commercial box-office hit?

In *Madonna Unauthorized*, Andersen claims that Madonna and Penn were now arguing at home because of Penn's growing collection of handguns and rifles. She was apparently scared of his gun mania and persuaded him to put them away in a strongbox. Later, Andersen says that Penn bought even more guns and built a shooting range in the basement of their Malibu home. .

Even while the *Shanghai Surprise* disaster was in the making, Penn was spending time hanging out with the writer Charles Bukowski, who had become a friend. The grizzled poet, short story writer and novelist had made his name writing beautiful tales of his low-life existence on the poverty-stricken underbelly of Los Angeles. Penn loved Bukowski's way with words and would end up dedicating his second outing as writer/director, *The Crossing Guard*, to Bukowski, who died in 1994 when Penn was busy making the film.

Early in 1986, Penn saw a screenplay for a film about the life and writings of Bukowski. It had the working title of *Barfly*. From the moment he opened up the manuscript, Penn knew that he wanted to play the part of Henri Chinaski, Bukowski's fictional alter ego. In fact, Penn was so sold on the idea, that he told the project's proposed director, German Barbet Schroeder, that he was willing to play the part for one dollar. There was a condition to this, though: Penn wanted Schroeder to step down from the director's chair and make way for Penn's buddy, Dennis Hopper.

This seemed entirely unreasonable to Schroeder, who had paid Bukowski $10,000 in 1980 to write a screenplay based on his lifetime experiences. Bukowski had taken the money and then spent a considerable amount of time wondering exactly what to base the story on. Finally, he decided to shape the screenplay around two parts of his life: his time in Philadelphia and his life in Los Angeles with his first wife, Jane.

At this embryonic stage, Bukowski was referring to his work in progress as 'The Rat's Thirst'. By 1986, when Penn was pushing for Hopper to direct, the title had changed to 'Barfly'. Schroeder was trapped in a thorny situation. He had touted his idea around Hollywood to various producers to little or no interest. He was obviously excited that a major star like Sean Penn was saying that he would act in the film for one dollar but he hadn't banked on Penn wanting to hijack the project and wheel in Hopper. Not only had Schroeder and Bukowksi worked on the idea for almost six years but they had also assessed prospective actors for the role of Henri Chinaski. The pair of them had met singer-songwriter Tom Waits – an obvious candidate for the part – but couldn't decide if he would be a suitable actor.

After Waits, they had had similar meetings with James Woods and Kris Kristofferson. None of them had quite the qualities that Schroeder was looking for. So, having exhausted all logical avenues, Schroeder was stuck with Penn's demand. To make matters more complicated, Penn and Bukowksi had really hit it off and had now become close friends. In September 1987 Penn interviewed Bukowski for *Interview* magazine. The article featured a famous snap of Penn hanging out with his hero in the writer's back garden.

To try to come to an amicable compromise, Bukowski and Schroeder decided to ask Penn and Hopper over to Bukowski's home in San Pedro one night. However, when the meeting took place, Bukowski soon decided that he didn't like Dennis Hopper. This surprising clash of personalities wasn't helped by the fact that Hopper had quit taking drugs and drinking alcohol and was therefore a cleaned-up Antichrist to Bukowski, who embraced rather than struggled with his alcohol dependency. Bukowski was clearly suspicious of the reformed hell-raiser. As the legend has it, he later said of Hopper: "One time something was said, and it wasn't quite funny, and he just threw his head back and laughed. The laughter was pretty false I thought."

If Bukowski and Hopper had hit it off, then Schroeder might have been out of the picture. Instead, Bukowski took a dislike to Hopper that very evening and the tables turned. Penn and Hopper put forward an appealing cash offer to Schroeder that would get the film into production. The catch was that Hopper would direct, Penn would star and Schroeder would be relegated to the role of producer. Bukowski, a loyal man, wasn't having any of this and said that he was unhappy with Schroeder – who had brought the project to life – being pushed out. Once Bukowksi had made his feelings clear, Penn and Hopper both lost interest. It was an all or nothing situation and both duos subsequently took separate directions.

Hopper, however, told *Sky* magazine a slightly different story in 1988 that suggested that Schroeder was against him from the minute Penn mentioned his name. He explained that he and Penn had met on the set of *Rumblefish* and, during conversation, they had discovered that they shared a mutual admiration for Bukowski's writing. "When Sean was discussing doing the lead in *Barfly* with Bukowski, (he) wanted me to direct it. I said, 'Forget it, you'll never get it away from Barbet Schroeder because years earlier, when I was drinking, I'd caused a scene at Ma Maison by telling Schroeder he wasn't qualified to direct movies, that he'd made a couple of nice documentaries and he should stick with that. And it turned out they couldn't get *Barfly* away from Schroeder and Sean said, 'Well then I'm not going to do it'."

Penn continued to hang out with Bukowski, though. The writer's wife, Linda Lee, told Bukowski biographer Howard Sounes something about these meetings: "Sean wasn't such a huge star when we met him, although he was beginning to get there. He was just sort of a kid. He used to call us his surrogate parents. He would just come over here and tell us all his problems, sit and get drunk and chat and be away from that insane Hollywood." The admiration was mutual though as Linda readily admitted: "Sean liked Hank, and Hank liked Sean because Sean was willing to be with him in a natural way." The two of them often talked about poetry – Penn was writing his own poems by now and showing them to his mentor. At other times, Penn would turn up at Bukowski's house in a pick-up truck with actor buddies such as Harry Dean Stanton and Elliott Gould.

Once, Penn brought over a copy of his wife's new record though, according to Sounes' biography, Bukowski didn't much care for Madonna.

"Hank couldn't stand her," Linda Lee told Sounes. "He did not like her because he didn't believe in her." This fact didn't prevent Bukowski and his wife from being invited to a party at Madonna and Sean's home. It was at this party that Bukowski danced with Penn's mother, as Penn later recounted: "The pants are coming off. He is trying to take my mother's clothes off. My mother, at this point, is in her late sixties, and everybody is sitting back and saying, 'This is what he is supposed to do.' It was the first time that they had seen a legend actually behave like a legend."

Penn also found time to embrace a couple of rather offbeat projects. He was drafted in to lend his voice to a documentary called *Dear America: Letters Home From Vietnam*, about the experience of soldiers in the Vietnam war. The project saw him work alongside other star narrators including Willem Dafoe, old friend Charlie Sheen and early inspiration Robert De Niro. *Monthly Film Bulletin* dubbed it a "Who's Who Of the Hollywood Vietnam film" but felt that it was "a documentary with no argument to make, (it) often seems instead to be searching its compelling documentary material for correspondences to the war we've already seen recreated." The second oddity that Penn appeared in was a rarely seen film called *Cool Blue* that surfaced very briefly in 1988. Penn plays a tiny cameo as a character called 'Phil the Plumber'.

After his involvement with *Barfly* ended, Penn teamed up with Dennis Hopper to shoot a hard-hitting film about a pair of cops (played by Penn and old sidekick Robert Duvall) assigned to deal with street gangs in LA, called *Colors*. Barbet Schroeder did end up directing *Barfly* and cast Mickey Rourke in the part that Penn had so badly wanted. Faye Dunaway was cast opposite Rourke. "I went off and acted in a couple of movies and when I got back, Sean brought me *Colors*," Dennis Hopper told *Sky* magazine. "But it was a totally different script to that in the film we eventually made."

SIX

Here Comes Trouble

When Madonna and Penn returned to the U.S. after the *Shanghai Surprise* shoot, she was already thinking of another film to make with her husband. However, the plans were shelved while she focused on her new album and singles. Penn was busy working with Dennis Hopper in preparation for *Colors*. When the dust settled a little bit, Madonna narrowed all the possible film projects down to two films that she thought might be suitable. The first film project was called *Dead End Street* and was slated to be directed by Leo Penn. The second was a comedy called *Slammer*, to be directed by James Foley. In each case, Madonna envisaged herself starring opposite her husband but as events turned out, the plans were soon scrapped. By the time *Shanghai Surprise* had come out, and bombed, Madonna had completely gone off the idea of starring opposite Penn in another film.

In *Madonna Unauthorized*, Christopher Andersen says that while Penn was preparing for the *Colors* shoot, Madonna was busy masterminding a recording career for Levi's 501 model Nick Kamen. The speculation as to what her next film role might be ended when she signed up to do *Slammer* with Griffin Dunne starring in the role that director James Foley had originally wanted for his friend, Penn. The film was later released under the title *Who's That Girl?* Andersen claims that Penn — then on the other side of the country doing *Colors* while his wife was in New York doing *Slammer* — grew steadily more and more jealous about Madonna's close involvement with Griffin Dunne during the shoot. Although there is no evidence to suggest that Madonna had a fling with her co-star, Penn was apparently unable to get the notion that something was amiss out of his mind. Andersen relates that Penn was so plagued with jealousy that he moved out of the couple's home in Malibu and took refuge at his brother Chris's place instead.

The separation was tough. Penn appeared on *The Tonight Show* and said he was wearing a certain pair of shoes especially for his estranged wife's benefit. "For Madonna . . . wherever you are." By this stage it was clear that the marriage was running into serious problems, although days later the two were back together again in New York. Andersen says that they were continually arguing about two topics: Madonna's involvement with Nick Kamen and her devotion to a friend dying of AIDS, Martin Burgoyne. In both instances, Andersen alleges that Penn was jealous of the attention that his wife was lavishing on both friends.

Penn returned to the West Coast to work with his lawyers on the assault charges that he was facing after the Wolinski incident. When he heard that Madonna had hung out with Nick Kamen at the Live Aid show in London, he went berserk at Helena's, a Los Angeles club, in the company of his brother Chris. Andersen says he danced to 'Papa Don't Preach' and then got into a terse discussion with Chris who told his brother to either annul the marriage or file for a divorce. Apparently Penn, who carried a .22 pistol when he was out in Los Angeles, told Chris: "I'm going to annul her!"

In *Madonna Unauthorized*, Christopher Andersen claims that when Madonna returned to the couple's house in Malibu, she found the place littered with Penn's guns. On top of that, she had house staff throw out Penn's pornographic magazines and videos. Weeks later, she had checked into a nearby hotel. Andersen alleges that during this troubled period Penn drank heavily, stared at Polaroids that the couple had taken of themselves *in flagrante* and watched the home videos that they had reportedly shot of themselves when they were making love.

Madonna returned to the East Coast to finish shooting *Slammer* and to nurse Burgoyne. When 1986 came to an end, Madonna was still top of the singles charts with her latest release 'Open Your Heart'. However, things in her personal life were far from successful. She and Penn continued to argue until finally she split and the couple spent Christmas 1986 apart.

Sean Penn began 1987 before the Los Angeles Municipal Court charged with assaulting and battering David Wolinski. On his lawyers' advice, he pleaded no contest and was fined $1,000, sentenced to a year's probation and ordered to pay $700 court costs. This should have calmed Penn down. Instead, things got worse. Christopher Andersen alleges that Penn's rage at his supposed mistreatment by the press and authorities found a continued outlet in his arguments with Madonna. According to Andersen, Penn reportedly hurled a chair through a window and threw her into their swimming pool; she threw a vase at him and hit him. Worst of all, Andersen alleges that Penn stuck Madonna's head in their gas oven.

Colors turned out to be a highly controversial film. Penn and steely supporting actor Robert Duvall play two police officers whose turf is rife with gang-related crime and violence. The original script centred around two police officers: one white, his partner black. It was set in Chicago and revolved around the dealing of a narcotic available in a certain kind of cough syrup. Hopper thought this was a dumb plot hook: "I said, 'Give me a break, man. Make it cocaine, make it real, make it Los Angeles.'" He also suggested that the police officers should both be white and that one should be an older veteran of the force and the other a young passionate hothead. Indeed, although willing to have the film based around two police officers caught in the crossfire of gang violence, Hopper would have made the film "strictly about the gangs" if he hadn't been forced to toe the line by the producers.

Penn was taken by the script from the word go: "One of the things I really flipped about the script was that Michael Schiffer, who wrote it, wasn't trying to force likeability on anyone." This, for Penn, was particularly true of his part: "My character is not likeable at first but he grows as the movie goes along."

To get a realistic grip on the life of street gangs, Penn hooked himself and Hopper up with a photographer friend who covered the gang neighbourhoods. This enabled them to observe the way the gangs worked and the effects they had on their environment. Next, Hopper and Penn got in touch with an organisation called Operation Safe Street, which works from the Sheriff's department. Again, this helped them focus on the key issues at hand. Finally, they spent time with CRASH (Community Resources Against Street Hoodlums) which consists of LAPD police officers who work exclusively with gang-related crime. They took Hopper and Penn out with them which was the perfect way for Hopper to scout out locations. It also meant going into gang-controlled neighbourhoods such as Watts, Boyle Heights and

San Pedro. This was the most directly useful of their research pursuits because Penn and Duvall were to play two LAPD CRASH officers in Hopper's film.

Once filming began, Hopper's insistence on realism, soon led to problems. "We shot at a project in Watts that even the police won't go in unless there's a body lying there," Hopper explained. Some of the locations were touchy too. Although the crew was accompanied by heavy-duty security, gang members would stand around the set and then, hyped up by what they were seeing, would go off and start violent fights with rival gangs. Hopper later revealed that ten gang members were killed during the period of filming. One day the crew were filming a drive-by shooting and a real murder happened in the area just hours later. "It was a funeral scene for some members of the Bloods," Hopper recalled, "and two hours later, someone was killed a block away."

Hopper knew he was directing a dangerous film and had decided early on, when he and Penn were researching the gangs, that he would never mix the extras: "If I was shooting in a Crips area, I'd use Crips as extras. When shooting in a Bloods area, I'd use Bloods." Hopper also ignored the LAPD's request that he not use the real names of the gangs in case it incited violence or romanticised gang life. He used the real names because he felt that otherwise people would walk out of the cinema and feel as though they'd been spoon-fed a cheesy, unrealistic story.

Quizzed about Penn's poor box-office record on the eve of the release of *Colors*, Hopper commented: "I think Sean has a way of picking pretty hard pieces. Most of his movies are good, but he doesn't seem to make the most obvious commercial choices." When asked what it was like to work with Penn, Hopper was both generous and perceptive: "Sean's a very sweet, dedicated guy, but he's got a short fuse. I never punched out any photographers, but I got involved with some women who could pull my short fuse in other ways. I understand him."

Hopper's comment about Penn's 'short fuse' was a reference to an on-set fight that broke out in April 1987 between Penn and an extra, Jeffrie Klein, who one day had pulled a camera out of his pocket and started taking pictures of Penn during the shoot. The actor feared that he was being snapped by an undercover photographer. The story, as relayed in Andersen's Madonna biography, has Penn run over to the 5' 10", 210-lb. extra (who was paid the princely sum of $35 a day) and shout: "What are you doing taking pictures?" Klein who, Andersen discovered, was usually employed as a scrap metal dealer, replied that he was only taking photographs because he'd seen other extras doing the same.

According to Andersen, Penn then spat in Klein's face; Klein reacted by spitting straight back at Penn. All hell then broke out as Penn punched Klein in the face and continued to pound him until he was pulled off by some of those observing the fracas. Andersen reports that Penn and Klein were separated three times and that each time, Penn broke loose and attacked Klein again. When Penn was finally restrained, it dawned on him that he would now face charges of violating the conditions of his probation. Andersen then reports a key moment between the older, wiser Hopper and the young actor: "Hopper, who himself had conquered a long-time addiction to alcohol and drugs, urged his friend to check himself into a substance abuse clinic." Penn, although aware of the value of the advice he was being given, apparently told Hopper to mind his own business.

The immediate problem was that Penn now risked being jailed. In December 1998 he told *Newsweek*, somewhat cynically, that these clashes with paparazzi were down to a "lack of discretion relative to witnesses present". He also said that – in his mind – these clashes were "entirely justified behaviour". Penn was sick of being harassed, sick of being hounded and sick of being followed everywhere, and with hindsight, it's difficult to blame him. Who wouldn't have a short fuse after that kind of unwelcome attention?

Madonna biographer Douglas Thompson reports another bust-up between Penn and a photographer that happened around this time. Penn had apparently been spotted having dinner with an unknown blonde girl and on spying the two together a photographer named Cesare Bonazza, who was in the vicinity, saw a great opportunity for a potentially lucrative series of pictures. Bonazza snapped away until Penn spotted him and, according to the photographer, leaped into his truck and chased the lensman. Bonazza told Thompson: "He jumped from the truck and yelled, 'Come out of the car you motherfucker!' He reached under his T-shirt and pulled out a gun. He got in a shooting position with both hands grabbing the gun and pointed at me. He said,

'Give me the fucking camera, give me the fucking camera!' He was crazy, a lunatic." Andersen alleges that Madonna was seeing other men at this time, and even if the allegations were groundless, the rumours couldn't have helped Penn's state of mind.

On a more positive front, Penn learned a lot from working alongside the older, wiser Robert Duvall on *Colors*. It's clear that, like Bukowski and Hopper, Duvall became a paternal figure for Penn, who spoke fondly of working with him to *Sky* magazine: "Duvall is a constant reminder of what can be done. He never crosses the line of someone who is genuinely searching for the insides of a character. Day after day on the set of *Colors*, as we were playing these two characters, I would see him working things out, doing things, that were a lesson for me."

The film addresses the issue of street gangs through a filter of social commentary. It contrasts the hopelessness that breeds gangs (bad housing, poverty, unemployment) with the frustration that faces the CRASH and police teams that struggle to contain the appeal of crime (in particular the wealth that goes hand in hand with drug dealing) as well as the crimes themselves. Penn plays Danny McGavin, a hot-headed, idealistic younger officer who doesn't understand the tactics used by old-timer Bob Hodges, played by Duvall, to deal with the gangs. Penn wants to attack the gang problem by taking on every single criminal in Los Angeles; Duvall wants to maintain long-term relationships with gang members and leaders on the street in order to create a lasting peace. Penn is single and energetic; Duvall is married with children and anxious to make it to retirement without getting injured or killed.

Most of the film revolves around the tension between the tactics employed by Penn and Duvall. The more violent and aggressive Penn becomes, the more Duvall backs off. When Duvall requests a change of partner, Penn looks stunned. Duvall is a father figure for him and his youth and naivety prevent him from understanding Duvall's motivation. Once he becomes known on the streets as 'Pacman' (because he munches his way through the crime underworld), word goes out on the streets that he is bad news.

When Duvall is shot and killed towards the end of the film, Penn gives an astonishingly emotional performance as he kneels with his dying partner, dissolving into cries and screams. By the end of the film, he has a new partner, much like himself when he was first assigned to

Duvall. The new partner is full of Penn's old gung-ho attitude – the difficulties of the job haven't yet exhausted and jaded him, or wised him up. Penn has taken on Duvall's old role, warning his new partner of going at the gang problem too passionately.

Penn looks very comfortable throughout the film – which probably has something to do with one long-term friend (Duvall) being his co-star and another (Hopper) being in the director's chair. The characters' father-son relationship mirrors Penn's work with Christopher Walken in *At Close Range*. Penn adds some distinctive character traits, such as constantly combing and preening his hair, making his cop a picture of vanity. When he courts his Latina girlfriend, his bull-headed arrogance comes across in his strutting walk, displaying the kind of cockiness that Duvall's character has long since lost.

Not to be outdone by his wife's breakneck work pace, Penn agreed to host an episode of *Saturday Night Live*. His brother Michael, who had been forced to take bit parts in TV shows like *St Elsewhere* to support his career as a musician, which was at that point going nowhere, suddenly found his brother pulling strings to get him on the show as the live guest. Encouraged by his performance, he subsequently went off to write the songs that would become a successful album in 1989.

Madonna was training hard for her forthcoming tour, which would further support the sales of her *True Blue* album – at 17 million and counting at this stage. Her marketing whiz-kids decided to name the tour the Who's That Girl? Tour, which tied in nicely with the imminent release of James Foley's film of the same name. Madonna and Penn were not on speaking terms at the time and rumours spread that the couple were set to divorce. Madonna later complained: "I felt no one wanted us to be together. They celebrated our union and then they wanted us to be apart. There were rumours about us getting a divorce a week after the wedding. We fought that. You have to be really, really strong and immune." Her songwriting partner Steve Bray later added: "I think it was just two people who were basically incompatible at the end. They tried very, very hard to make their relationship work but in the end there was something inherently incompatible in their natures."

On Memorial Day 1987, Penn – who was now becoming increasingly desperate as his marriage slowly fell to pieces – was pulled over by police officers. He was speeding and had failed to stop his vehicle at a red light. When the officers talked to Penn, they also decided to conduct a drink-driving test; Penn failed the test and was arrested. A later blood test showed that he had a 0.11 alcohol content in his bloodstream, a fraction more than the legal limit of 0.1 per cent. The episode would later surface in Penn's screenplay for *The Crossing Guard* when Freddy Gale (Jack Nicholson) gets busted for drunk-driving. Penn later commented: "I can only think of one crime that I would turn somebody in for; if I saw them in the act, I would flag a cop. And I committed that crime. That was drunk-driving. All the other stuff, no regrets."

The crime, coupled with the probation violation that resulted from the very public bust-up with Jeffrie Klein, put Penn in a sticky position. He had now violated the conditions of his probation twice. Madonna – who was out of touch with her husband at this point – read about the incident in a newspaper. When hounded by the media with questions about whether Madonna and Penn were getting divorced, her publicist replied with a simple statement: there was not going to be any divorce. Madonna then took off for Japan where she was set to perform the Japanese leg of her Who's That Girl? Tour. She had just completed the tour and was back in the U.S. when Penn appeared before a judge for the two counts of probation violation.

On June 24, 1987, Penn was sentenced to a 60-day jail term to be served in Los Angeles County jail, by Municipal Court commissioner Juelann Cathey. There was a get-out clause though, which stated that the sentence would be reduced to 30 days if Penn behaved himself. Regardless of which sentence he ended up serving, Penn was to be put on probation for two years upon leaving custody. He was also advised to seek "psychological counselling".

Penn's sentence was due to begin on July 7, and in the meantime he went to Miami, where Madonna was scheduled to play a concert. The terminally on/off relationship was back on again. Penn and Madonna checked into a penthouse suite at a very exclusive country club and stayed there for four days straight. After their bed-in, Madonna played her Miami date with her husband in the audience, dedicating 'Live To Tell' to him. When it was time for Penn to go into jail, Madonna was playing a show in Chicago.

Amazingly, after a mere five days in jail, Penn was let out. The release was only temporary, but it was the kind of preferential scenario that only a star like Penn could hope to get. The reason for his release was work related. His father, Leo, had been given the green light to direct a made-for-TV film that would eventually be released under the title *Judgment in Berlin*. Sean was only too happy to lend kudos to his dad's project because it enabled him to repay the favour that his father had granted him by getting him cast in *Hellinger's Law*. The connection didn't end there, because Leo Penn also cast Sam Wanamaker – the director of *The Killing Of Randy Webster* – as an actor in the film. The arrangement with the courts and the jail was that Penn was allowed to fly to Berlin to shoot his scenes but as soon as he had finished his part, he had to fly straight back to the U.S. and return to jail. His sentence would also pick up exactly where it left off.

Judgment in Berlin is based on a true story, adapted by Leo Penn and Joshua Sinclair (who also co-produced the feature) from Herbert J. Stern's book of the same name. A man from East Berlin hijacks a flight by holding up a stewardess with a toy gun; he has two children in the West and is desperate to be reunited with them. The crew, believing the gun to be real, divert the flight. However, the plane runs into problems and the pilot has to make an emergency landing on an airstrip at an American army base in West Berlin. Once the plane lands, everyone aboard elects to defect from the East to the West. A federal judge, played by Martin Sheen, is flown in from the U.S. to preside over the complicated case.

Sean Penn plays Guenther X, an East Berliner who witnesses the hijacking and sees the stewardess being taken hostage. Later, in the lengthy trial, he proves to be a key witness and his testimony overturns evidence falsified by the authorities from East Berlin. When the plane lands, he and his wife and child defect. Penn's character becomes a taxi driver in the West. In one very short scene, Penn is seen driving a cab, recalling Robert De Niro's epic portrayal of an urban loner on the edge in Martin Scorsese's *Taxi Driver*.

Much of the film centres on an individual's justification in hijacking a plane in order to experience freedom. There are many jail scenes featuring Heinz Hoenig in the part of Helmut Thiele, one of the characters who help the hijacker make his escape. Penn, himself on temporary release from jail, must have brought something of that harrowing experience to his role. His key scene comes in the court rooms, a somewhat surreal situation for Penn, with his father directing the scene and his childhood friends' father standing in front of him playing the judge.

To play the part of Guenther X, Penn had to perfect a German accent. When he offers to testify, he is called up on the stand as a witness. During his seven-minute monologue, Penn stumbles uncertainly between words, a beautifully observed characterisation of an East Berliner to whom English is a new language and who is frustrated by his inability to express himself. When Penn's monologue becomes emotionally charged his voice waivers and tears fill his eyes. It's an astonishing piece of acting, a touching representation of a man who cannot believe he is finally free. The moment is made more poignant by the fact that Guenther's brother was gunned down by East Berlin authorities for attempting to escape to the West.

Once again, we're back to a familiar theme in Sean Penn's work: male relationships, be they between brothers, fathers or male friends. His monologue – which features certain facial quirks that recall Robert De Niro's acting style – again reveals his ability to seamlessly assume the personality of the character he is playing.

Empire reviewed the film in April 1990, when it came out on home video, and billed it simply as a "literate courtroom drama". Their praise was distinctly lukewarm. "Most people will be content to catch it on television," wrote the reviewer, "the medium in which (Leo) Penn is most effectively at home." Most of the plaudits went to Penn junior: "Sean Penn, son of director/co-writer Leo, grows his own accent for a good, tearful turn on the stand as a frightened East German witness."

Once Penn's scenes in *Judgment in Berlin* had been shot, he had to fly back from Germany and return to jail. Thompson claims that Penn received plenty of calls from Madonna while he was stuck in there and busied himself by writing a one-act play called *The Kindness Of Women*. Thompson says the play – about a rocky marriage plagued with sexual infidelities and heavy drinking – was later directed in Los Angeles by Penn, though this author has found no other reference to this play – either as a script or as a staged production – throughout the research for this book.

As soon as he was back under lock and key, a prankster sent Penn a highly tasteless package. When Penn opened it up, a copy of *Penthouse* magazine fell into his lap, containing eight pages of nude photographs of his wife. The story, which Andersen relays in his biography, is typical of the kind of intrusive button pressing that Penn had to endure throughout his marriage to Madonna. The parcel might have been sent by a sleazy journalist looking for an impulsive, angry reaction from Penn or by some psycho who simply wanted to torment him. But the identity of the sender was hardly likely to hold Penn's interest; he had bigger problems than a prank package. His jail cell was directly opposite the cell occupied by Richard Ramirez, the famous 'Night Stalker' who had terrorised the residents of Los Angeles. Although Ramirez was a danger, Penn was safe. "I was in the protective custody unit," he later told *Interview*. "All the inmates were separated on this particular floor of the Los Angeles county jail."

Apparently, a guard acted as a go-between when Ramirez requested Penn's autograph. When the guard relayed Ramirez' request to Penn, Penn jokingly told him that he might consider giving him his autograph but only if Ramirez gave him his. So, the guard returned with a note from Ramirez that read: "Hey Sean. Stay tough and hit 'em again." He then apparently signed his name, wrote 666, and sketched a picture of the devil and a pentagram for good measure. Penn wrote a letter back that touched on inmate kinship but stressed that, as far as he was concerned, he and Ramirez were from different planets. Penn paraphrased his note to *Neon* magazine in 1998 thus: "Dear Richard, it's impossible to be incarcerated and not feel a certain kinship with your fellow inmates . . . Well, Richard, I've done the impossible. I feel absolutely no kinship with you." When Penn later told *Interview* that in his opinion Ramirez was a "total fucking nutcase", he probably knew better than most what he was talking about.

Penn, who was bored out of his skull during his spell behind bars, spent his time reading. He dug into some essays by the French philosopher Montaigne and devoured some fiction by James Thurber. To his relief, he was freed for good behaviour after 33 days of his 60-day sentence. Madonna was waiting for him when he got out and they returned to their Malibu home.

However, all was not well between the couple. If, as Anderson writes, Madonna expected Penn to come out of jail a changed man, she was sorely disappointed, as he soon started drinking. To make matters worse, Madonna was in talks with producers about performing the lead role in a film version of *Evita*. Penn, who wanted a co-starring role along the lines of the *Shanghai Surprise* deal, was not on the producers' shopping list. Andersen claims that Madonna agreed with the producers that Penn would only be suitable for a supporting actor role, on a salary that amounted to about a quarter of Madonna's $1.6-million dollar fee.

Christopher Andersen relates that Penn, already jealous that his wife was now effectively worth $70 million, flipped when he heard about the *Evita* dealings and moved out of their Malibu home. He showed up at their New York apartment after a four-day silence, expecting to sit down to a Thanksgiving dinner with his wife. However, Madonna was still angry with Penn and told him to get out. To make matters worse, she also told him that she had instructed her lawyers to file for divorce. And with that, she went to spend Thanksgiving in Brooklyn with her sister, Melanie.

According to Andersen, Penn reacted by returning to Los Angeles and going on a drinking binge. When he saw paparazzi photographer Vinnie Zuffante in a bar, he insisted that Zuffante be thrown out. After this happened a drunken Penn couldn't be bothered to queue for the toilet so he went outside and took a piss on the outside of the building – in full view of passers-by. Madonna, who was meanwhile back out dating, was alleged to be involved with firstly *Bad Boys'* actor Esai Morales, and then John F. Kennedy Jr.

For days after the Thanksgiving bust-up, Penn kept trying to call Madonna so he could clear the air and patch things up. She refused to accept a single call. Ironically, when he stopped bothering to call she immediately started trying to call him. It was a basic lovers' psychology, but was clearly leading nowhere. On December 4, 1987, Madonna's lawyer filed divorce papers; the singer apparently felt that Penn had given up on their marriage. Christopher Andersen claims that Penn was by now also back out on the singles scene and partying hard with fellow actors including Michael J. Fox, Timothy Hutton and Judd Nelson.

Andersen claims that Dennis Hopper and Timothy Hutton both tried to get Penn to call Madonna. James Foley also stepped in, to tell Madonna that from his viewpoint they were both too in love to let their marriage drift away. Swayed by their encouragement, she decided to give Penn another chance. He was so happy at the news that he sent bouquets of flowers, silver balloons and love letters to his estranged wife and when he topped it all off with a singing telegram, she was suitably charmed back into his arms. Madonna laid down conditions though, insisting that Penn cut down on the amount he had been drinking, that he tried to control his anger and that he looked into seeing a counsellor. In return, Penn asked that they consider starting a family in 1989.

Despite the marital problems, Madonna pressed on with her heavy workload. Shortly after her reconciliation with Penn, she was back in New York to act in a TV adaptation of a play called *Bloodhounds Over Broadway*, written by Damon Runyon. The director was Martin Burgoyne, Madonna's old friend who had contracted AIDS. The shoot began around Christmas 1987 but the troubled project bounced from one obstacle to another and was only released in November 1989, some considerable time after Burgoyne's death.

Although she was now established as the world's top female pop star, Madonna remained determined to establish herself as an actress. To her great excitement, she now finally won a part in a David Mamet play called *Speed The Plow* that she had been aggressively pursuing for over a year. The part – that of an office temp called Karen – had originally gone to Elizabeth Perkins. When she left *Bloodhounds Over Broadway* in January 1988, Madonna put herself forward for the role. Her audition for Mamet and the play's director, Gregory Mosher, blew them both away and they promptly offered her the part. But according to Andersen's biography, the project was to prove an unpleasant one for Madonna. She later commented that she'd felt that other members of the production saw her as something of a vixen. Moreover, she felt that playing Karen's part night after night – the character is open to interpretation as a manipulative schemer – made her feel very unhappy. Like her husband she involved herself totally with the parts she played, and in this case that clearly resulted in unfortunate repercussions.

Colors opened in spring 1988, and became enmeshed in controversy from the start. On April 12, 1988, Curtis Sliwa, the notorious founder of the American Guardian Angels vigilante group, was arrested for trespassing on the Orion Pictures office premises as a protest against the film. As far as the Angels were concerned, the film would act as a catalyst for gang-related violence. On April 14, the Guardian Angels held a 12-hour long protest outside the Coronet Theater in Westwood, Los Angeles where the film was about to open. Six members of the Guardian Angels, including Sliwa again, were picked up by police officers for attempting to force their way into the Chairman of Orion's New York office. When the film opened at over 400 screens across the U.S. on Friday 15th April, all key urban cinemas were marked by a heavy-duty police presence. Three of the biggest cinemas in Los Angeles refused to screen the film for fear of violence. Five LA-based gang members were arrested during the night, most at a cinema in Huntington Park and two Hispanic gang members got into a brawl outside a cinema in Culver City. Due to these scares, the Chief of Police banned the United Artists Cinema in Colma, just South of San Francisco, from screening the film the following night.

Also on the Saturday night, a 19-year-old black youth was gunned down as he queued to see the film at the Regency cinema in North Stockton. The gang members who shot the youth were Bloods. To make matters worse, a bullet fired straight at the victim's head came through the other side and struck a 17-year-old girl, seriously injuring her. By Tuesday 3rd May, the Chief of Police for the Burbank district in Los Angeles – where Penn was born – issued orders preventing the area's multiplex cinema from screening *Colors* because, in his opinion, the film would draw a "gang type crowd".

On Thursday 7th July, three men were arrested for the Stockton shooting incident. A police statement at the time of their arrest explained that the gang members had apparently just come out from seeing the film and felt unhappy at the way their gang had been portrayed in the film. They took out their frustration on the black youth, whom they believed to be a member of a rival gang. This was the final straw for many self-appointed moral guardians who were convinced that the film was an evil and provocative incitement to even more gang-related violence than there already was.

The critics received the film casually. Robert Kimball, reviewing the film for *Films & Filming*, wrote: "What Hopper seems to be promising is a true to life, semi-documentary excursion through (LA's) war torn streets. What he delivers however is something quite different – a story too frequently indistinguishable from any weekly episode of *Miami Vice*." For good measure, Kimball paid the two leads a backhanded compliment: "Penn and Duvall both do commendable jobs with their less than brilliant roles."

Speed The Plow opened on May 3, 1988, at the Royal Theater in New York but Sean Penn was not there to help steady his wife's nerves – he was in Thailand shooting *Casualties of War* with Brian De Palma. De Palma's film is one of the toughest Vietnam films, easily standing alongside Oliver Stone's *Platoon*, Michael Cimino's *The Deer Hunter* and

Stanley Kubrick's *Full Metal Jacket*, as a corrosive document of a point-less war.

Right from the start, Penn was totally committed to what De Palma was trying to capture on film. "He knew his shit so well that no matter what anybody thought, there was going to be a very strong point of view on the screen," Penn told *Premiere*'s David Tighe in 1991. There were two weeks of rehearsals and one of Penn's first acts was to have a Chinese character that means 'Inner Strength' tattooed on his hand. He was also told by De Palma to go as far as he could with the role – that no 'limit' would be enough for the director. Thus encouraged, Penn – tormented by his ever-worsening marriage and shaken by his period in jail – threw himself into his part with a savage vengeance.

Penn's role was that of Sergeant Meserve, a man who orders his platoon to follow him into an amoral nightmare, the very name Meserve (as in 'me serve' my country) suggesting blind obedience and patriotism above all else. The snarling Sergeant orders his platoon to go along with his plan to kidnap a young Vietnamese woman from her village. The point of the kidnapping is made clear later in the film: Meserve wants to use the woman for a little "R & R" as he calls it. In other words, he wants to use the captive woman as a slab of meat for him and his men to gang-bang. When he orders every member of his platoon to rape the woman, he steers his platoon into a vile war crime. Penn gives a chilling performance as the wild-eyed and unpredict-able Meserve.

De Palma, the esteemed director of films such as *Body Double* and *Carrie*, became involved in the project as early as 1969 when he read an article by a Vietnam veteran called Daniel Lang then being serialised in *The New Yorker*. De Palma had himself managed to escape the draft. He explained to *Premiere*'s Steve Pond in autumn 1989 that he managed this because he "sniffed and ate everything I was allergic to and wheezed my way in to the draft board". Although, he had been moved by Lang's confessional piece about his harrowing experiences in Vietnam, De Palma left it there.

The story returned to De Palma some while later when a screenplay landed on his desk. The author of the screenplay, David Rabe, was himself a Vietnam veteran and after seeing *The New Yorker* piece too, he had begun to turn Lang's story into a screenplay. Rabe was in a strong position because he had written a successful play about the Vietnam

War called *Streamers*. De Palma loved Rabe's screenplay but didn't think it was going to be an easy project to get off the ground. After all, it was a touchy subject. Not only did most Americans want to sweep the Vietnam War under the carpet, but a film about a platoon that sexually enslaves a Vietnamese woman was hardly going to go down well with Vietnam vets and their families.

At this time, De Palma was riding high on the success of *The Untouchables*. "It's a difficult movie to get made at any point in your career," De Palma told *Premiere*. "But after *The Untouchables*, I was at a very good place to try. Even when we got the script written and we cast Michael J. Fox and Sean Penn, we still got put into turnaround by Paramount." The cold feet that most major backers were getting only ended after fate stepped in. Dawn Steel, who had been the Head of Production during the era when *The Untouchables* was made, suddenly made a career move. She got a new job "running Columbia Pictures" and stepped into David Puttnam's shoes. Almost immediately, she got in touch with De Palma and picked up *Casualties of War*.

Once that was taken care of, De Palma worked with a computer graphics program called Storyboarder to sketch out every scene in Rabe's screenplay so that the entire film, scene by scene, was mapped out to exact times and specifics. The cast and crew then took off for Thailand to start shooting. The heat of the jungle was an intense experience for all involved. "There was always something sort of crawling along or tripping up the wheels, or bugs flying into the lights kablooey," De Palma told *Premiere*. "I mean, imagine what it's like to turn on a bright light in a jungle. You've never seen so many flying things."

The film was released with poster copy that read 'Even in war – murder is murder'. Reviews for the film were for the most part positive. "*Casualties of War* is the strongest, the simplest and the most painful of the Vietnam movies," wrote Terrence Rafferty in *Sight And Sound*, around the time of the film's British release in late 1989, "because it isn't about how terrible it is not to understand what's going on around us – it's about the agony of seeing terrible things too clearly."

The review that ran in *Empire* in February 1990 was equally enthusiastic: "Both leading players (Fox and Penn) are exceptional and De Palma's flair for tension, at its best in the claustrophobic jungle and sharp battle scenes, is – like in *The Untouchables* – greatly heightened by Ennio Morricone's score." For John Pym, writing for *Monthly Film Bulletin*, the film had a clear message: "De Palma tells the story straight and old fashioned: everyone is a casualty of war."

Film Comment, the most prestigious of the American film magazines, singled out Penn's contribution for praise. "Penn exudes the physical and sexual confidence the part demands," wrote Gavin Smith. "Without Penn's performance, *Casualties* would merely be enthralling widescreen rhetoric." On a more general note he concluded that the film "is about the indiscriminate release of sexuality and aggression engendered by the removal of all civilised controls in war. What separates the boys from the men is the boys' penchant for going with the prevailing impulse of the moment – which in the war zone cannot be ignored. It is the supremacy of these impulses, that in a memorable performance, Sean Penn as Meserve, the Squad's Sergeant, understands and works from." Sean Penn had proved his worth as an actor once again; unfortunately, his turbulent private life was soon to undo much of the good that his acting talent had achieved for him.

Sean Penn's parents – TV producer/ actor Leo Penn and actress Eileen Ryan.

Sean Penn, as pictured in his high school year book.

Sean Penn and his younger brother, character actor Chris Penn.

Sean Penn and his older brother, singer-songwriter Michael Penn.

Sean Penn with his parents.

Sean Penn and Timothy Hutton in Penn's 1981 feature film debut, *Taps*.

Sean Penn as Jeff Spiccoli in the 1982 teen comedy *Fast Times At Ridgemont High.*

Sean Penn became close friends with Dennis Hopper (right) after the veteran actor/director worked with Chris Penn on Francis Ford Coppola's 1983 film *Rumble Fish.*

Veteran film director Hal Ashby whose films (which included *The Last Detail, Shampoo* and *Coming Home*) had a substantial impact on Sean Penn.

Sean Penn with his actor-buddy Harry Dean Stanton, best known as the star of Wim Wenders' classic 1984 road movie, *Paris, Texas.*

Sean Penn with fiancee #1, actress Pamela Springsteen (sister of singer-songwriter Bruce).

Sean Penn with fiancee #2, actress Elizabeth McGovern.

Sean Penn with the first woman to get him down the aisle, Madonna.

The infamous message to the paparazzi that was written on the beach on the celebrity couple's wedding day.

Hollywood rebel-actor-screenwriter-independent filmmaker John Cassavetes and his actress wife, Gena Rowlands, both of whom had an enormous influence on Sean Penn.

In 1985, two freelance journalists, Ian Markham-Smith and Laurence Cottrell (pictured here), working for the British newspaper the *Sun*, incurred Sean Penn's wrath when they door-stepped the actor and his wife to be, Madonna, in Tennessee. According to Madonna biographer Christopher Andersen, Penn yelled at Cottrell: "You take my picture and I'll break your fucking back with a rock!"

Husband and wife in the massive flop film *Shanghai Surprise*, 1986.

Sean Penn in Dennis Hopper's controversial 1988 film about Los Angeles gang life, *Colors*.

Sean Penn and his hero Robert De Niro in *We're No Angels*, 1989.

Sean Penn in *State Of Grace*, 1990, the film on which he fell in love with his co-star Robin Wright.

He went back on his vow to star opposite Al Pacino in *Carlito's Way*, 1993.

Sean Penn with Susan Sarandon in Tim Robbins' powerful 1995 film, *Dead Man Walking*.

Sean Penn and Robin Wright-Penn in Nick Cassavetes'
She's So Lovely, 1997, based on a screenplay written by
Nick's late father, John Cassavetes.

Sean Penn with co-star Jennifer Lopez in Oliver Stone's
1997 low budget film, *U Turn*.

Sean Penn with Robin Wright-Penn in *Hurlyburly*, 1998.

SEVEN

Downhill Slide

Penn was in Thailand for the summer of 1988. Meanwhile, Madonna was causing a box-office pile-up with *Speed The Plow*, for which ticket demand was unbelievably strong. She was also hanging out on the town with a new friend – comedienne/actress Sandra Bernhard. Madonna had met Bernhard during an early date with Penn but had never developed a friendship. Apparently, as relayed by Andersen, Madonna told her friend Erica Bell that she had had a dream in which she and Bernhard survived a major disaster and were the only two human beings left alive on the planet. Fate conspired to bring the two women together when Madonna went to see Bernhard's one-woman stand-up show, *Without You I'm Nothing*. Bizarrely, Bernhard told a story based on a fantasy of hers. In it, World War III breaks out and after the mass destruction . . . she and Madonna are the only survivors. Fired up by the coincidence, Madonna went backstage after the show and a friendship instantly developed.

For most of the summer, Madonna, Bernhard and *Dirty Dancing* star Jennifer Grey, hung out together, going from club to bar to club. The more Madonna and Bernhard were seen out together, the more the gossip spread. Bernhard's openly bisexual status gave rumour-mongers plenty of ammunition to start some 'Are they an item?' gossip. The rumours went national when Bernhard dragged Madonna onto *Late Night With David Letterman*. On the show, Letterman asked Bernhard what she and Madonna did on their nights out. He was alluding to the fact that they had been seen at a famous lesbian bar called the Cubby Hole. Bernhard, happy to play with the innuendoes, replied: "What do you think you do with a girlfriend? What do

89

you do when you go out with your girlfriend?" Letterman kept pressing the buttons, especially when Madonna appeared and joined Bernhard for the interview. Madonna joked that Bernhard was using her to get to her husband, a fact that prompted Bernhard to teasingly state that she had slept with both Madonna *and* her husband. It was all one big joke and a great ratings booster for Letterman. Much later, Madonna would reflect back on this period and tell an interviewer: "My friendship with Sandra was just beginning as my relationship with Sean was dying."

In August 1988, Penn flew home from Thailand, after finishing his part in *Casualties of War*. On his return he discovered himself a third cog in the Bernhard–Madonna friendship. Days after his return, Madonna celebrated her 30th birthday and a mere scattering of days after that, they celebrated Sean's 28th birthday. Then, to complete the trilogy of emotional events, the couple celebrated their third wedding anniversary.

The following month, Madonna pulled out of *Speed The Plow*, to concentrate on the writing and recording of a new album. As she worked on the record, Penn became involved in a production of a play called *Hurlyburly*, which had been written by David Rabe, the author of the *Casualties of War* screenplay. Penn agreed to act in the play only if it was staged in Los Angeles, so that he and Madonna could spend as much time together as possible. Once Los Angeles became the location for the production, Penn was in and participated in lengthy rehearsals, his wife often calling from a recording studio for some mutually inspiring chatter.

Penn had first been turned on to the play when he saw a production of it in New York and he subsequently came to feel that the play was the first redeeming acting part he'd had in a long time. Three years later he told *Film Comment*: "I realised I was just miserable acting. I felt emotionally on a downhill slide until *Hurlyburly*, where I had a part I liked in a play I thought was great, and a great writer, great director, hell of a cast (for the Los Angeles production, Penn acted alongside Mary Winningham, Belinda Bauer, Michael Lerner, Suzy Amis and Jill Schoelen). Perfect circumstances to do work in – and I was miserable. I realise now it was just like getting paid money to tear yourself apart." He was also aware that this personal conflict at the time was part of a larger context. "I don't know how much of that is coloured by all the baggage that came with my particular career, the marriage, all that stuff," he admitted.

When *Hurlyburly* opened, Madonna was not in the audience as the curtain went up. She arrived late with Bernhard. According to Andersen, there was a major argument between Penn and Madonna at a private after-show party at Twenty-20, a club in Century City, Penn allegedly screaming: "You cunt. How could you do this to me?" at his wife. An anonymous source that Andersen interviewed, commented: "Sean's fragile male ego was badly bruised. She was more famous than he was, made tons more money, and now she was rubbing her nose in the whole lesbian controversy. It's bad enough when a man thinks his wife is leaving him for another man – but for another woman? Sean just couldn't handle it."

On top of that, she had pursued and won the part of Breathless Mahoney in Warren Beatty's *Dick Tracy*. Her involvement in the film meant that her make-up pledge to Penn – to start a family – would be on ice for at least a year. Consequently, Madonna had apparently been less than open with Penn about her intentions to go for the part. Andersen claims that Penn, none too amused by her going behind his back to get the part, quietly fumed. When he learned she had signed all the contracts for the role, they had another bust-up. On Christmas Eve, Andersen alleges that Madonna hung out with Bernhard and Penn sought comfort with a stripper. Supposedly, Bernhard campaigned hard that night for Madonna to leave her marriage because of the unhappiness it was causing both her and Penn. Madonna apparently wanted to walk away but still loved Penn too much to do so.

The rest of the Christmas was no happier. After another argument, Penn moved out of their Malibu home and stayed with his parents. A matter of days – and various aborted phone calls – later, Penn gave up on trying to reach his wife and went over to their house, jumping the fence and breaking in. There followed one of the darkest incidents in the history of the couple's relationship. According to Andersen: "After slapping her around, he bound and gagged her, then strapped her to a chair with twine. He berated and beat her for two hours, then stormed out of the house." Penn went away and returned a few hours later. "Penn returned, swigging tequila from a bottle," continues Andersen's report. "And began tormenting her all over again." He then states that Penn untied Madonna, who made a run for it. She allegedly managed to get into one of their cars and, once she had locked the doors, called the police.

After that, Madonna drove to the nearest police station, arriving "bruised and bleeding" according to Andersen, and relayed the events of the past hours to police officers. Police then surrounded the couple's Malibu mansion and ordered Penn – via a bullhorn – to surrender. When he did, he was handcuffed and arrested. In his statement to the police, Penn alleged that Madonna had made up the whole story because she was angry with him for dating a stripper.

Douglas Thompson recounts this episode in greater detail. He says that at 4 pm on December 28, 1988, Penn jumped the fence and broke into the home he shared with Madonna. Thompson alleges that Penn then "put Madonna through hours of terror. He hit her. He tied her up and he humiliated her. He also sexually assaulted her." Thompson says that he asked police officers about the exact nature of the sexual offence but was given no details other than that the violence was "unique".

Andersen and Thompson report the same ending to this sad story. Madonna met with the Deputy District Attorney of Los Angeles County to state that she wanted to drop all charges, despite opposition from the police. Both biographers believe that the ensuing scandal that a court case would have raised was not something Madonna could face going through.

However, the singer did have her revenge: she filed for divorce on January 5, 1989, citing 'irreconcilable differences'. The pre-nuptial agreements were dragged onto lawyers' desks and the messy split began with the dawn of the new year. The pre-nuptial contracts meant that each half of the marriage got what they had brought into the marriage as well as what money they had earned during the marriage. Madonna was rumoured to be worth $70 million at the time of the split while Penn was worth something in the region of $5 million. During the settlement, Penn got the Malibu house and Madonna kept the New York apartment.

Madonna struck back fast. She bought a house in the Hollywood Hills for approximately $3 million, signed a sponsorship deal with Pepsi Cola for $5 million and caused a global sensation throughout March 1989 with the supposedly blasphemous video for her new single, 'Like A Prayer'.

The hits kept coming as 'Express Yourself' and 'Cherish' followed 'Like A Prayer' up the world's pop charts. To top off her latest run of success, she then started work on the *Dick Tracy* shoot with Warren Beatty. For Sean Penn it was time to lick his wounds and try to work out just what was happening to his life.

EIGHT

State Of Grace

Once Penn was cut loose by Madonna, he took on what should have been a dream project – a remake of the old 1955 movie *We're No Angels*. The somewhat lacklustre original, which was adapted from a French play, starred Humphrey Bogart, Peter Ustinov and Aldo Ray as three convicts who break out of a jail on Devil's Island and take refuge in a French shopkeeper's home. This new version was slated to be directed by Irish filmmaker Neil Jordan and was to star Sean Penn as the convict Jim opposite one of his early inspirations, Robert De Niro, playing another convict, Ned. The jail break in the film is instigated by the third member of their party, Bobby, played by James Russo, whom Penn described on an AOL LIVE internet chat almost ten years later as the funniest person in Hollywood to hang out with. After they escape the three characters become separated in a snow-covered landscape and take refuge in a small timber town where they are believed to be priests.

A multi-talented artist, Jordan had thus far in his career written a collection of short stories and two novels. His reputation as a director was based on three films: *Angel* (1982), *Mona Lisa* (1986) and *High Spirits* (1988); *We're No Angels* marked his Hollywood debut. The screenplay worked its way into Jordan's hands via producer Art Linson, who had worked on *The Untouchables* and was written by award-winning playwright David Mamet. It bore scant resemblance to that of the 1955 original, a fact that Jordan discussed with *Film Comment* in early 1990. "David's written a comedy about mistaken identities," explained Jordan. "It's a little fairytale with a very ironic twist to it. You know, everybody hopes that miracles can happen. And to these two strange, unfortunate guys, they do."

95

In 1991 Penn revealed to *Film Comment* that the experience of working on the film had not been entirely rewarding. "Art Linson, De Niro and I developed *We're No Angels* in a sense, so it was sink or swim together," he told Gavin Smith. "It was brutally hard. I guess that the cleanest way to say this is, I never understood – and I tried – what (director Neil Jordan's) point of view was. So I felt lost at sea." In short, Penn felt that he wasn't directed tightly enough and that consequently he worked within a personal stylistic framework that "wasn't in sync with everything else".

Penn also talked about the way in which he and De Niro worked on ways to synchronise delivery, both in terms of speed and tone, to debatable effect. "I don't think that the harmony was there enough," he reflected. "When it was there it worked, you know, sometimes you stumble on something everyone has the same idea about. But I think that a lot of stuff just got blurred."

Jordan had worked on revisions and different drafts of the screenplay with Mamet, helping to shape the narrative but never tampering with the latter's particular ear for dialogue. In Jordan's eyes, Mamet's dialogue was "hard Thirties, tough guy speech".

Interestingly, the director himself saw no problems with the way De Niro and Penn performed during the shoot. "I was very pleased with the way Bob and Sean approached that aspect of things," he told *Film Comment*. "What I associate with Bob is this kind of magnificent realism, but in this film, both he and Sean really stretched themselves to that level of farce." He explained how he, Penn and De Niro would have little meetings and exchange ideas about scenes and how the characters should behave. He also got De Niro and Penn to rehearse "on camera" so that they could get the right kind of performance for certain scenes.

Jordan also made a comment about working with the two actors that suggests that he might have felt slightly intimidated by actors of their calibre: "With actors like Sean and Bob, you start with that level of emotional integrity. However else you build on that, you'll never have less which is a great foundation for a character or performance." What he was perhaps saying was that he felt as though De Niro and Penn were, for him, capable of creating great work no matter what he did. Maybe he felt that they were the kinds of actors that didn't need intensive instruction.

If so, then Jordan made a fatal mistake; De Niro and Penn have always been vocal about their need for a director to work very closely with them on set. They need to be pushed, encouraged. For *Casualties of War*, De Palma told Penn that he could go as far as he liked with his role as Meserve, for there were no boundaries for him. De Palma threw down the director's gauntlet, challenging Penn to push his character to break-ing point and then some. If Jordan got only a half-hearted performance out of Penn, it may be because the actor felt that he was only given half-hearted direction.

The film was shot over a four-month period in Vancouver. The shoot started at the beginning of 1989 and wrapped in May 1989. The produc-tion racked up considerable expenses: it cost $2.5 million to build a dupli-cate 21-building period town in Mission, British Colorado and for the film's climax – the celebrations in a town on the U.S./Canada border – 700 extras were hired. For scenes in which there was meant to have been a snowfall during the night, real snow was trucked in for an authentic look. Jordan was very keen to have the landscape reflect a series of cine-matic references from old movies. He also wanted individual buildings to be constructed in such a way that for him, they suggested immediately powerful "emotional associations".

The Director of Photography, Phillipe Rousselot, talking with *Ameri-can Cinematographer*, cleared up yet another of the insane rumours that seemed to gravitate towards the actor. "Sean Penn given permission to okay scenes? That's ridiculous! He's really the nicest guy to work with. He couldn't have been more professional." Rousselot also talked about some of the more technical, and unusual, aspects of the shoot. "I was surprised by the fluctuating weather," he told the magazine. "And sometimes De Niro and Penn would decide to do certain lines with their backs to the camera."

The finished film did have the fairytale quality that director Neil Jordan had been striving for. Although the rapport between De Niro and Penn is strained to say the least, the film is held together by a series of amusing scenes that do provide some comic relief. The continuous mugging, face-pulling and chin-jutting on De Niro's part gets tedious very quickly but Penn, who seems constantly tense around the older actor, manages to pull off one of the film's genuinely funny scenes. It occurs late in the film, just as the Weeping Virgin procession is prepar-ing to cross the bridge into Canada. A priest announces the winner of a

lottery draw and it turns out to be Father Brown, aka Jim. The twist to
this scene is that the Prison Warden is standing in the crowd. Ned
sneaks off to free Bobby, who has turned up in the town's jail, and Jim
is forced to give an impromptu sermon. He opens his Bible and after a
lengthy excruciating silence, finds a little ticket for a handgun tucked in
the Bible. He starts to read the copy on the card, which states how dangerous the world is and how necessary a handgun is for self-protection,
and hilariously has to improvise when the copy extols the handgun's
virtues. The lengthy silences and delivery by Penn make for a highly
comic scene.

The problem is that this is a one-off scene in a film that is meant to be
a light-hearted comedy. The interplay between De Niro and Penn fails
to spark and often it's a case of the mentor intimidating the younger
actor. Penn was clearly in awe of the older actor and when he slips into
tough-guy mugging and accent, he often seems like De Niro lite. In the
context of the film, this isn't necessarily a bad thing, as De Niro's own -
performance is often cringe-worthy and absurdly laboured.

The film itself is a cute little conversion story as the two convicts
journey from a life behind bars for crimes they have committed to
redemption on the banks of the river separating the U.S. from Canada.
Ned unexpectedly leaps off the bridge to save Molly's (Demi Moore)
deaf and mute daughter and winds up not only saving the child's life but
also instigating her sudden ability to hear and speak. This is taken by the
priests and locals as a miracle. When the priests misunderstand Ned's
pleading with them (he thinks they know the truth about himself and
Jim and will turn them over) they believe that he is saying that his faith
had crumbled and that after the miracle he is a convert once again. The
priests bless Ned and Jim and indirectly instigate their conversion. By
the end of the film, Jim doesn't cross the bridge into Canada but instead
stays on at the mission. He is sheepish and confused about his motives
for doing so, but Jordan clearly intends us to see his story as one of conversion and redemption. Ned (De Niro) ends the film by crossing into
Canada (or so it would appear, he may turn back for all we know) with
Molly and her daughter. He insinuates that there is a story to tell and
Molly is happy to take his arm and start a new life.

The film's strongest scenes all feature Demi Moore who seems – like
every cast member except Penn and De Niro – confident and relaxed
with her character. Every time she appears, her tough single mother

character (who prostitutes herself to any man with $5 to fund her and her daughter) is beautifully played. It is perhaps her performance that saves the film from complete disaster.

In one key scene, Molly's daughter falls off a bridge and is in danger of drowning in a waterfall; Ned leaps off to save her and the statue of the Weeping Virgin follows them over the waterfall. By grasping hold of the statue, Ned is able to keep himself and Molly's daughter afloat. This, coupled with the fact that Molly discovers her daughter can speak and hear after the accident, inspires the assembled crowd to believe that a miracle has taken place. The connections are delicately handled here. Molly – a 'whore' – is redeemed by a weeping 'virgin'.

By the end of the film, as she crosses the bridge with Ned, Molly talks of taking holy orders. Her belief that God has dealt her a terrible life is picked up during Jim's impromptu speech about people being hurt and subjected to pain. As he improvises with a poetic ineloquence about the pain people suffer, we see Molly cry. The tear that rolls down her cheek mirrors the tears or raindrops that trickle down the cheek of the statue of the Weeping Virgin. Jordan is clearly having fun with symbolism here, creating a means by which Molly can be opened to a miracle and, consequently, redemption and conversion.

Overall, however, the film does not work as the light-hearted comedy it was intended to be. There are only so many times that Jordan can milk humour out of mistaken identity. There are plenty of vaguely amusing scenes that threaten major laughs but never deliver them. During the last fifteen minutes of the film, you can't help but wonder whether the whole thing would have worked ten times better if it had been played straight as a touching drama. The romantic interest that sparks between Molly and Ned is never developed and even at the end when they appear to be crossing the bridge into Canada and towards a new life, Jordan still refuses to commit the film to such a finale, leaving ambiguity to usher the credits in.

The attempt to create physical comedy (for instance, Ned trapped in the confession booth where he is trying to get his leg irons off while hearing a sheriff's confession) always falls flat. Even when Jordan is playing for laughs from the mistaken identity scenarios, the moment all too often degenerates into the flogging of a one-joke idea. There are only so many times that De Niro and Penn can pull forced faces and stare at each other as though they're Laurel and Hardy.

The film was savaged by most critics when it came out in 1990. *Empire* was kinder than most: "Both De Niro and Penn are obviously a long way away from their more traditional internalised roles here," the reviewer moaned. "But after the initial shock of seeing them capering around both manage to convince, with Penn particularly impressive, shedding the dumb cluck routine layer by layer with a skill and care reminiscent of Cagney." Pam Cook, reviewing the film for *Monthly Film Bulletin* wrote: "As if to compensate for the overall formlessness, De Niro and Penn deliver mannered performances overburdened with references to cinema's mad and madcap heroes, from The Three Stooges and James Cagney to John Goodman and William Forsythe in *Raising Arizona*." She felt that De Niro looked "particularly ill at ease, resorting to violent grimaces which seem to indicate that he received minimal direction (also implied by his credit as Executive Producer)". She wasn't as hard on Penn commenting: "Penn, belying his role as the novice of the acting partnership, acquits himself better and is reasonably convincing as his dim-witted, slack-jawed companion."

Penn's next project was another troubled one. This time, he played an undercover alcoholic cop who gets in over his head, in a New York-based film called *State of Grace*. The film was directed by Phil Joanou, who had also served as director for the U2 tour film, *Rattle and Hum*. *State of Grace* cast Penn opposite Gary Oldman, a British actor who shares Penn's admiration for actor/director John Cassavetes. Sometime later Oldman, like Penn, would write and direct his own Cassavetes-influenced film, *Nil By Mouth*, to critical acclaim.

When Penn and Oldman first met up, the introduction could have been potentially explosive. "Oldman sang 'Like A Virgin' at the top of his voice imitating Penn's ex-wife with exaggerated dance movements," explained Joanou to *Interview* magazine in 1990. "Penn laughed, however, succumbing to Oldman's decidedly devilish charm." Penn and Oldman seem to spark off each other throughout the film. Penn has said that he was drawn to the film because it again dealt with the theme of male relationships. This time, it concerned not only a boyhood friendship but also the troubled relationship between two brothers. The catch was that the boyhood friends re-met after a long spell during which they had lost touch. The reason for this soon becomes clear. Oldman's character is a gangster, Penn's character a cop who left Hell's Kitchen for a cop's life in Boston.

Gary Oldman steals much of the film's glory with his crackling performance. By comparison, Penn seems slightly straitjacketed by his role, which requires him to constantly maintain an expression of tormented guilt as he infiltrates his boyhood friend's crime network. Joanou spoke equally warmly of both his leads, however, particularly regarding the intensity that he was seeking from his cast and how they exceeded his expectations. "All that matters to me is emotion in a film," confessed Joanou. "I mean, when Sean Penn did his monologue, I choked up on the set."

Perhaps the most interesting aspect of the film is that it shows the beginnings of Sean Penn's relationship with his on-screen love interest, Robin Wright. If you watch the interplay between the two actors closely in the scenes that they share, you can sense the mutual attraction, the crackle of budding romance. At certain points in the film the line between art and reality becomes rather blurred. Witness the scene in which Penn and Wright walk along the street after she gets off her shift at the hotel early. Penn says that he was divorced six months earlier, eerily replicating the details of his off-screen life. This could just as easily have been Penn and Wright talking rather than their characters.

The finished film tries too hard to ape Martin Scorsese's *Mean Streets*. Gary Oldman plays a variation on Robert De Niro's classic Johnny Boy character and Penn is left to play the thoughtful, contemplative role that Harvey Keitel had in the Scorsese classic. The camerawork often tends to contradict the film's quest for realism by drifting into grand, sweeping statements that are neither naturalistic nor fitting. On the plus side, David Rabe, who re-wrote Dennis McIntyre's original screenplay, gives the actors plenty of authentic gangster dialogue, even though it sometimes lacks depth. Moreover, Penn, Oldman and Ed Harris make a great trio, and when the three are all sparkling, the results are powerful.

Penn, talking to *Film Comment* in 1991 (after he had vowed to never act again) spoke of similar problems during the shooting of the film to those he experienced with Neil Jordan on *We're No Angels*. Again, he was hinting that Joanou had not offered him the support and experience that he needed from a director. However, he also acknowledged that he had gained a lot from the shoot. "I liked Phil Joanou," Penn commented. "We didn't completely agree, but I still liked him and respected what he was doing. And technically, I learned things – which was part of the attraction. I knew Joanou was very knowledgeable about the camera and I also knew that where he wasn't knowledgeable he made up for (it) with aggressiveness."

He also talked about the role itself. "I wanted to work hard and focus my energies and really do the job even if I didn't feel like doing it," remembered Penn. "Because I'd had such a bad experience with *We're No Angels,* I wanted to get that taste out of my mouth." Looking back, he felt that he was exhausted on the shoot and the more he put into the part, the more it drained him. The result was that he felt he was unable to give his best performance no matter how hard he worked. "I think I was in need of a vacation," he said later. "I put myself under a lot of pressure and a lot of juices just weren't flowing."

Penn, probably depressed after *We're No Angels* and the bitter feelings left over from his divorce, found some comfort in his burgeoning relationship with Robin Wright. Fresh from a burst of the limelight with *The Princess Bride,* Wright was cast as the sister of Gary Oldman's gangster character. She and Penn had met for the first time back in 1986. "We were both in a coffee shop," she told *Neon* in 1998. "We looked at each other for about ten minutes. He bummed a cigarette." At that time, though, Penn was married to Madonna and Wright, who had made her name by acting in the TV soap opera *Santa Barbara* for four years, was married to fellow *Santa Barbara* actor Dane Witherspoon. However, her marriage was already on the skids and it was destined to last no more than six months after this first meeting with Penn.

Robin Virginia Wright was born in Texas on April 8, 1966. Her parents had separated by the time her brother was born. When she was four, her mother packed Wright, her brother and their belongings into a car and drove all the way from Texas to California, where they started a new life. "She became very successful selling Mary Kay cosmetics," Wright revealed to *Interview* in 1992.

When Wright was 14, she started working as a model. Her mother was very supportive when her daughter said she wanted to accept a modelling contract and gave her permission to go to Japan for modelling shoots when she was 15. After her stint abroad, Wright spent time modelling in Paris. She then returned to Los Angeles and abandoned modelling for acting.

Her big break came when she landed a part in *Santa Barbara.* "It was great," she later said of her time on the U.S. soap opera. "Having had no training and no confidence and being very young, it taught you to be on your toes and (taught you) a lot of technical tools to use." When she was 20, Wright married Witherspoon. It was during her long spell on *Santa Barbara* that Wright went to audition for a part on Rob Reiner's *The Princess Bride*, winning out over 500 actresses to take the part.

Wright and Penn developed a close friendship during the *State of Grace* shoot and when they weren't working, they were hanging out together. Wright talked about how she and Penn got together when she was profiled for *Interview* in April 1992. "When we read for *State of Grace* it was like meeting an old friend," she told Michael Kaplan. "We got to know each other during the filming but the relationship began after it had wrapped."

The film, which premiered at the Montreal Film Festival, met with mixed reviews when it went on general release. *Variety's* verdict in September 1990 read: "Penn is excellent as Terry, who drinks too much and who ultimately gets too personally involved with his mission." However, the overall conclusion was that the film contained a "grimly downbeat plot and languorous pacing". Tom Charity, reviewing the film for *Sight And Sound* in June 1991, felt that the director was somewhat out of his depth: "Spielberg protégé Phil Joanou, best known for U2's *Rattle and Hum*, strains to accommodate the rigorous moral interrogation of a Sidney Lumet precinct drama within the extravagant rhetoric of the gangster film."

The reviews reflected the audience's view as well. According to the Imdb web-site, the film only grossed $1.3 million at American cinemas. Penn, who had thrown himself wholeheartedly into the part as usual, was bitterly disappointed by the film's reception.

By the time *State of Grace* was in the can, Penn and Wright were dating. "We were both going through our own things with other people at the time," Wright recalled to *Interview's* Michael Kaplan. "But when we got back to LA and after the stress of filming ended, we started spending time together." Wright made it clear that she and Penn had been aware of a mutual spark between them for some while: "We always had a kind of familiarity with each other. Unlike the dating syndrome − now we can consummate, now we can't, now we can − it was always like, 'Oh God there you are. I feel like I've known you forever.'" Penn's sole comment on the new love in his life came a little later during a discussion of what he looked for in a woman. "It's about communication," he told *Interview*'s Graham Fuller in 1995. "If I click with somebody, my eyes stay straight ahead."

Other members of the Penn family were also going through some changes. Michael Penn had a hit solo album, *March*, on his hands. The album sold well after the first single 'No Myth' became an unexpected hit, although a second single, 'This And That', didn't fare quite as well. After this breakthrough, he didn't surface again until 1992 with the *Free For All* album which, unfortunately, failed to match the success of his debut album.

While Michael Penn was writing songs, Sean Penn was having them written about him. His high profile during the late '80s had led to two bands producing songs that name-checked him in song titles. The first was 'Madonna, Sean and Me', a song by New York band Sonic Youth. The second was 'Sean Penn Blues', by British band Lloyd Cole And The Commotions.

Meantime, Leo Penn had acted in some made-for-TV films as well as some episodes of the TV show *Matlock* during 1986. He had also directed episodes of TV shows including *Remington Steele*, *Paper Dolls*, *Columbo* and the aforementioned *Matlock*. Eileen Ryan, after acting in *At Close Range*, also appeared in *Matlock* as well as making appearances in *Parenthood* and *Winter People*.

Chris Penn wasn't doing so well. He was in the process of dealing with a serious drug problem. According to an article in *Uncut* magazine, Chris suffered a "five-year cocaine addiction in the mid-'80s which pushed the star to the edge of sanity and earned him an enduring reputation in Hollywood as a hair-trigger hell-raiser." Chris Penn described himself during this period of bingeing as "that guy who doesn't give a shit". The same article in *Uncut* claimed that during this lost weekend Chris Penn: "found himself in the Philippines smoking 'shaboo', a highly dangerous substance used in black magic ceremonies and said to be the speed-based equivalent of crack. The actor hallucinated for days as his heart rate rocketed to kamikaze levels." During the worst of this period – 1988–1991 – Penn hardly landed a single acting part.

Chris referred back briefly to this scary period of life when he talked to *Premiere* in October 1993. "I did drugs," he commented. "It was a bad fucking thing." In an effort to kick his crippling drug habit, he sought inspiration through prayer and started to attend church. In 1996 he also talked about the part that his brother Sean played in helping him clean up. "He was my main supporter when I went through my drug problems five years ago," confessed the younger Penn to *Empire*. "He was largely responsible for helping me get my life back together." Chris also talked to *Premiere* about the pressures of trying to emulate his brother's success. "He's my best friend. It's very difficult to establish yourself when you have a brother who's a great actor. But I'm my own artist – always have been and always will be."

NINE

A Man Under The Influence

"I don't get anything but grief out of acting now," Sean Penn told - *Premiere* in October 1990, at a time when he was still widely considered to be the finest young actor of his generation. Nobody could understand why such a talented artist – the only young actor capable of competing with the likes of Robert De Niro from the previous generation – would hang up his acting boots. Sure, it made sense that he would want to move over into directing but to many, it was not only a peculiar career move but a decision that robbed the acting profession of one of its most committed, passionate and inspiring talents.

Penn was disillusioned, tired and keen to find a new path. He felt that he was over with acting, that it had become a soulless purpose, a job that wasn't making him happy anymore and he was sick of investing enormous amounts of energy in parts that ended up gutted and neutered in the editing suite. He wanted to stop draining himself, stop giving his all to projects that were misunderstood or mismanaged. When he let this bomb drop, Penn was temporarily based out in Omaha, on the dusty plains of Nebraska, the primary location for his debut effort as writer/ director – *The Indian Runner*. Nebraska's grim, deserted landscape had been romanticised in one of Penn's favourite films of all time, Terrence Malick's *Badlands*. The film starred Penn's childhood next-door neighbour Martin Sheen opposite Sissy Spacek. A gritty throwback to late Sixties American cinema, *The Indian Runner* revolved around the troubled relationship between two brothers – one a moralistic small-town cop, the other a damaged Vietnam veteran. The finished film made it clear where Penn was coming from. Penn's Cassavetes-like vision was dialogue intensive, mood sensitive and anti-narrative, and was devoted to realism, anti-clarity, pro-emotions, pro-mystery. In short, it was anti-'Hollywood'. The look and feel of the film made Penn's influences clear: Hal Ashby's *The Last Detail*, Bob Rafelson's *Five Easy Pieces*, all of John Cassavetes' work, *Badlands*, Peter Bogdanovich's *The Last Picture Show* and Robert Altman's *Nashville*. Penn's aesthetic ideals were rooted in an American cinema that had long since been pushed out by a studio system obsessed with repetitive, sequel-driven blockbusters.

Just as Penn had sought out friendships with Dennis Hopper, Harry Dean Stanton and Charles Bukowski, he had formed a bond with John Cassavetes during 1987. The actor/writer/director/producer soon became another mentor to Penn. Cassavetes embodied everything that was romantic about filmmaking. He juggled highly paid acting jobs (in films such as *The Dirty Dozen*) with his own independently made films – ragged, raw, realistic pieces that are generally regarded as the first truly independent American movies. Cassavetes mostly funded these projects out of his own pocket and turned his home into a free-style set, film lab and editing suite. Everything was done his way. The films he directed – *Shadows, A Child Is Waiting, Too Late Blues, Faces, Husbands, Minnie And Moskowitz, A Woman Under The Influence, The Killing Of A Chinese Bookie, Opening Night, Gloria, Love Streams* – were anti-narrative efforts, committed to realism and the truth at all costs. Many find the films unendurably long, but Cassavetes' work is not concerned with plots or action, only the mysteries of human interaction. His unrelenting focus on the actors tends to make these films talk-intensive. Of his eleven films, three were co-produced with studios *(A Child Is Waiting, Too Late Blues* and *Gloria)*. The other eight were entirely made by Cassavetes outside the studio system – they were 100 per cent independent. The golden eight that he made himself had, and continue to have, an enormous influence on Sean Penn's work as a writer, actor and director.

John Cassavetes assembled a film family around himself, employing the same faces again and again: his wife Gena Rowlands, Ben Gazarra, Seymour Cassel, Peter Falk, his mother Katherine Cassavetes, Gena's mother Lady Rowlands, his own children Nick and Zoe. It was a case of all hands to the pump. In this way, Cassavetes' purest work was never tampered with or affected by external forces, because he laboured alone. He was often driven to desperate measures to get his films developed – even going to the extreme of re-mortgaging his house to pay for the making of *A Woman Under The Influence* – and fought the independent fight at all costs. Sean Penn learned a great deal from Cassavetes' working methods and would subsequently also make his own films family affairs. His mother acts in *The Indian Runner* and the lead female part went to close friend Patricia Arquette. Penn's father acts in *The Crossing Guard*, as does his wife Robin Wright. Penn was aware that the simplest way to accomplish a pure vision is to do it with those you love and trust. However, Penn didn't fund *The Indian Runner* or *The Crossing Guard* out of his own pocket – he had to look externally for financing. Cassavetes made each stage of each of his eight autonomously produced films as and when he had the time and the money to press on. Penn committed to a regular production schedule for *The Indian Runner* and shot the film in seven weeks. He was – to an extent – at the mercy of the producers and the cast. Names like Dennis Hopper didn't have the time to work slowly, so Penn had to work fast.

Penn has never explained how he got to meet John Cassavetes nor how they came to be friends. Long before Penn was out on location in Nebraska, most people who knew him thought that his debut effort as director was going to be *She's De Lovely*, a screenplay written by John Cassavetes back in 1980. In the words of Cassavetes expert Ray Carney, *She's De Lovely* is "in the vein of *A Woman Under The Influence*, it's another entry in the cycle of films of love and hate, of fear and adoration that Cassavetes has created." During 1987 John Cassavetes dusted off his screenplay *She's De Lovely* because he wanted to make the film with Penn in the lead role as the tortured Eddie and Penn started hanging out at the home that John Cassavetes shared with his actress wife Gena Rowlands.

Penn and Cassavetes worked together on the script, acting out various scenarios and testing the authenticity of dialogue; these acting sessions led John Cassavetes to sit down and rewrite the script. But just when their schedules were finally in sync and the project looked like it might happen, Cassavetes fell sick. He was diagnosed as suffering from cirrhosis of the liver and it rapidly became clear that it would be impossible to get the film made because he was unwell. When Cassavetes died in 1989, Penn optioned the screenplay for a reported $30,000. Earlier – when Cassavetes became ill – Penn had taken the screenplay to another left-of-centre director, Hal Ashby. The veteran filmmaker had directed another of Penn's favourite films – *The Last Detail* – which starred

Penn's friend Jack Nicholson, and expressed an interest in directing the script. Penn committed to working with Ashby but just as they started to firm up the project, Ashby too fell sick, with pancreatic cancer. Again, this made the possibility of getting financing impossible. In late 1988 Ashby died from what newspapers reported as liver and colon cancer. According to an anecdote in Peter Biskind's book *Easy Riders, Raging Bulls,* Penn made a touching gesture at the funeral. After seeing a street sign that read 'Ashby' in Los Angeles, Penn had helped himself to it. Biskind relates that the sign "leaned against the base of the podium" on full view throughout the funeral.

Once Ashby and Cassavetes were dead and Penn had optioned the screenplay with Gena Rowlands' blessing, he decided to try to get the film made himself. He made some calls and in each case, proposed that he direct it himself. There was plenty of interest until possible investors found out that Penn wanted to make the film in black and white. The interested parties immediately got cold feet and told Penn that they were enthusiastic about him directing the film but not if it was in such a box-office-unfriendly medium. Penn, always a fighter for what he believes in, refused to compromise, and the investors walked. There and then, the project bottomed out. Penn became distracted by *We're No Angels* and then *State of Grace*. Inevitably, the screenplay went up on Penn's office shelf and gathered dust. In April 1990, a news piece appeared in *Screen International* revealing that "Sean Penn has decided to postpone directing *She's De Lovely* based on a screenplay by John Cassavetes. Instead, he'll make his screen directing debut this summer with *The Indian Runner*, an original script by . . . Sean Penn. The family drama is being produced by the (Thom) Mount Company."

The original idea for *The Indian Runner* stretched back almost a decade to when Penn was just into his twenties and engaged to Pamela Springsteen. One night, in the New York apartment that he shared with Pamela, he was listening to Bruce Springsteen's dark, all-acoustic album, *Nebraska*. He felt himself becoming increasingly drawn to the song 'Highway Patrolman'. The song was about two brothers and their damaged relationship. Penn sat and listened, images flooding his mind, a screenplay about a troubled relationship between two brothers flowering inside him. When he told Pamela about his sudden connection with the song, she grabbed the phone and called her brother. Once she'd explained why she'd called, she put Penn on the line. Penn revealed to

Premiere that he'd told Springsteen: "I'd like to make a movie out of that song some day. And he said something like, 'Oh, okay'."

At the same time, Penn stumbled across a book called *Indian Running* by an anthropologist called Peter Nabokov. The book – based on an ancient Pueblo Indian ritual – "Re-examines the history of Indian Running as a spiritual, as well as practical tool", in Penn's own words. The book fascinated Penn and he filed it away for future reference.

Like all dreams, Penn's didn't come true overnight. Everyday life got in the way as much as earning a living did. Later, as he began to see acting as a torturous process rather than his raison d'être, he began thinking about the project again. When he was on the shoot for *We're No Angels*, he bounced the idea off his co-star Robert De Niro, who was also working towards directing his own film – which turned out to be the formidable *A Bronx Tale*. However, De Niro, who was certainly interested in doing something with Penn, didn't take the idea any further at the time. Penn had been thinking about making the film for years. He told interviewers that he'd had a lot of "different pictures" whirling around in his head and gradually, some of them settled long enough for him to sit down and flesh them out into a story."

Penn came to make *The Indian Runner* fresh off two acting jobs that had left him exhausted. True to form, he was investing so much of himself in his roles that he wound up absolutely drained. "I feel like I tear myself up emotionally for money," he told *Premiere* out in desolate Nebraska. "I started thinking more and more about doing something else, and that's what this is." In 1991 Penn told the *Los Angeles Times'* Kristine McKenna that his commitment to acting had started souring around the time of the *Hurlyburly* play, reiterating that it wasn't a question of acting no longer challenging him, but of acting challenging him too much. He also said that he was aware that all "psychological growth" was painful but that normally this process is not about getting up "at six in the morning for money". Penn wanted *The Indian Runner* to work out right, for it to perform at the box office and be taken seriously by the film critics. He wanted a break from acting and directing seemed the natural way to go. Like his idol John Cassavetes, he was also chewing over the idea of acting only for the money and then investing the money into his personal adventures as a director.

Penn was also busy cleaning his act up, eager to shake off the 'bad boy' tag that had been dogging him since his marriage to Madonna. He also talked to *Premiere* about how he had cooled his reputation as a drinker: "I think I've had about six beers and two Scotches the whole time I've been here. It used to be all day, every day – and I never did any rehab thing or anything like that – but I just drink on the weekend, that's about it." Penn had been doing some serious growing up and stepping out of the limelight to direct a personal, poetic film was as good a way to underline those changes as any. He was suddenly the boss, giving orders rather than receiving them and making others perform for him, rather than being the one under pressure to perform.

Next, Penn mentioned the project to playwright David Rabe, who had become one of his close friends. He too was interested, but said he'd chew it over for a while. Edgy and keen to not waste any more time, Penn sat down and started writing the screenplay himself. He had seen enough screenplays in his decade of serious acting, and figured he might as well have a go at writing one himself.

The words came thick and fast. He suddenly found himself dusting off Peter Nabokov's *Indian Running* and giving it another read. "During the writing process," Penn told *Film Comment*, "I started thinking about how it represented certain themes I was interested in." Penn decided to take his interest one step further, so he tracked Nabokov down to his teaching post at the University Of Berkeley. Penn spoke to him, explained his interest and asked if Nabokov and he could meet to talk more about his book.

Nabokov was only too happy to help the actor out and he suggested that Penn come and see him. Penn flew up to Berkeley and spent a day with Nabokov. "He gave me a one-day crash course – slide show, lecture, the whole bit," Penn later recalled to *Film Comment*. Penn left Nabokov's office wired on ideas, his brain working overtime. When he got back to his home, he returned to his typewriter and worked a mystical, spiritual angle about *Indian Running* into the screenplay. It was hardly a commercial idea to weld this particular ancient ritual into the film but it added a unique ingredient, an element that was pure Penn: idiosyncratic and perhaps overly ambitious, but undeniably written from the heart.

"The film wrote itself very, very quickly, in about a month," Penn told *Interview* magazine. Set in Nebraska in 1968, *The Indian Runner* concerns the relationship between two brothers – one (Joe Roberts) is a gentle, mild-mannered cop with a family; the other (Frank Roberts) a hell-raising alcoholic Vietnam veteran with a violent temper. Penn told

Film Comment in late 1991 why he had returned to the idea: "The thing that touches me most in terms of relationships is brothers. More than a man and a woman or father or son or any of those – brothers. Something just rings in me, I can't explain it."

By this stage in the development of the project, Penn's engagement to Pamela Springsteen had long since been filed away as history. Still, he figured that he would need Bruce Springsteen's approval if he was going to get backing and make the film. More distractions surfaced and Penn put his screenplay away in a drawer; at the time he was more interested in developing *She's De Lovely*. After Cassavetes and Ashby both died and Penn had realised that he wouldn't get backing for the script, he found himself left staring at two screenplays: the Cassavetes one and his own. Fate stepped in to make Penn's decision for him.

Producer Don Phillips, a throwback to the shoot for *Fast Times At Ridgemont High*, bumped into Penn. The two got along well, as they had on their previous film together. Penn gave Phillips a copy of his screenplay. He wanted an honest opinion on it, so he told Phillips that it was a screenplay that had been sent to him and that it had been written by a prisoner called J. Club McPhee. To juice the story up, Penn also told Phillips that McPhee was on death row at San Quentin. Phillips took the manuscript with him to read and was blown away; the quality of writing immediately connected with him.

What happened next kick-started Penn's dream. Phillips showed the screenplay to Thom Mount, a friend of his who was busy starting up his own production company. Phillips persuaded Mount that the screenplay was a great project with which to break in his new company. Presumably – although this bit of the story has never been revealed by Penn in any interview – Penn then came clean about J. Club McPhee's true identity. At this stage though, Penn must have been delirious with excitement because there was suddenly a real chance of his screenplay getting produced.

Phillips clued Penn up on what was going on with Mount. He then sent Penn back to his typewriter to work on tightening up some weak spots in the screenplay. In the meantime Mount, who had bought into Phillips' recommendation, went looking for the cash. He eventually got $10 million out of MICO/NHK Enterprises.

During this nail-biting time, Penn got restless. He'd finished the rewrites on his screenplay and wanted to get to work on bringing his vision to life. He sat twiddling his thumbs while the long-winded contractual aspects of the project dragged on. When Mount finally had the deal sewn up, Penn was thrilled, as he told *Premiere*: "I don't think anybody else in town in his position would have funded this. I have no track record and what track record there was, was not necessarily favourable."

The casting was slow too, as Penn struggled to get some serious players on board. Charles Bronson only agreed to play the brothers' subdued, melancholic father when the backing was secured and the contracts signed. Dennis Hopper, who plays the bartender in the film, had the same reservations. Like Bronson, he only became fully involved in the film when all the fine print had been tied up.

There was a degree of risk for all involved. Penn had never directed a film before. His reputation was as a great young actor; no one knew if he could carry his talent onto the other side of the camera. Plus, his bad boy tag probably put the frighteners on some potential backers. The project finally got a green light and regardless of what anyone thought, Penn still carried weight. He certainly wasn't going to sit back and play puppet for the investors. Penn fought to get one-time *St Elsewhere* TV star David Morse signed up to play the sober-toned older brother, Joe Roberts. Morse wasn't an obvious choice but Penn, having seen him in a film called *Inside Moves*, was sold on the idea. *Inside Moves*, which was directed by Richard Donner and released in 1980, pitched Morse against the immensely talented actor, John Savage, whom Penn cast in *The Crossing Guard*.

Penn, knowing that the rage-consumed younger brother had to be played by an actor who possessed polar opposite qualities to Morse, settled on Viggo Mortensen, the ex-husband of Exene Cervenka, a one-time member of LA new wave band, X. Mortensen – like Morse – was an unlikely choice but Penn knew that he was his man. Again, like Morse, Penn made his decision based on Mortensen's work in the David Anspaugh-directed film, *Fresh Horses*, which was released in 1988. To get Mortensen in the right frame of mind for the shoot, Penn arranged for him to spend time with a friend of his who was a member of a Hell's Angels chapter. This seemed like the perfect preparation in Penn's mind because he'd envisaged Frank Roberts to be like a "barking dog that bites" from the moment that the character took shape in his typewriter.

The key role of Frank's girlfriend, who becomes pregnant and gives birth in the film, went to the relatively unknown Patricia Arquette, later to marry Penn's acting buddy Nicolas Cage. Arquette was yet to make her name at this point and Penn was once again fighting for the right acting talent rather than hiring from the Hollywood star system. He wanted it to be as 'independent' a picture as possible. This ambition was partially realised in the unusual casting. To heighten the realism of this 'family drama', Penn cast his mother in the role of Mrs Baker; he roped in a writer friend of his, Harry Crews, to play the part of Mr Baker.

Once everything was sewn up, Penn and his crew headed for Nebraska where the seven-week shoot began. On set, Penn pushed his cast to the limits. He apparently bit Mortensen's right hand one day, in a bid to get the actor into the necessary mind-state to shoot a scene as he intended it to be shot. Mortensen later commented: "He tries to help us in different ways. It's just one he picked that day . . . He clamped down and it was too late to do anything. So I tried to stay really still like you would with a rabid dog."

That these kinds of performance-pushing techniques were forever looming in the background during the shoot is hardly surprising. Penn, himself known for pushing roles to the limits, was never likely to be an easygoing director. His enormous devotion to acting was bound to influence the way he directed; indeed, he's often said since that the best directors to work for are always the ones who've acted themselves. Again, this kind of belief system harks back to John Cassavetes' infamous duel life as commercial actor and independent director.

Penn's commitment to the actors' performances – at all costs – is most evident in a scene in the film that is unexpectedly violent, perhaps the most violent part of the whole work. Frank Roberts sits down to a dinner cooked for him by his girlfriend, Dorothy (Patricia Arquette). There are peas on the dinner plate. Out of nowhere, Frank suddenly spits a mouthful of peas at Dorothy. Apparently, Arquette had no idea that Mortensen was going to do this, as she told *Interview* magazine in February 1992: "We didn't really prepare for it. We just figured it out something like two hours before we filmed it. And there was this scene after that scene that got cut out where Frank went out and fucked someone else. Originally, when we were blocking it, we thought of having him throw the peas and then rape her. That really would have been a topper!" Prepared or not, the look of shock and surprise on Arquette's face is genuinely disturbing.

The film is a sprawling epic. The opening shots of a snow-covered landscape set the cold, moody tone for what's to follow. It's tempting to speculate that the Joe/Frank fraternal relationship was based on Sean's relationship with his brother Chris, but neither of the Penn brothers have ever made any comment that might back that speculation up. The acting is uniformly superb. Charles Bronson delivers a solid, touching cameo as the boys' father who kills himself after his wife dies and Dennis Hopper is excellent as the bartender with a neat line in alcohol-soaked philosophising.

The Roberts family slowly disintegrates throughout the film. By the time the credits roll, Joe Roberts has lost his father, mother and brother. The scene in which Joe slices his hand with broken glass to show his alcoholic, troubled good-for-nothing brother just how important family is makes for a dark, intense moment. The final scene in which Frank snaps and repeatedly bashes Hopper's bartender over the head with a chair (while his girlfriend is busy giving birth to their baby) is violently disturbing. It's a scene that is recalled in *The Crossing Guard* when Freddy Gale (Jack Nicholson) raises a chair, ready to strike a man in a restaurant. The film climaxes with Dorothy giving birth to Frank's baby while Joe chases Frank along dark, ominous stretches of highway. Penn ends the film with an ambivalent quotation from Tagore: "Every new child born brings the message that God is not yet discouraged of man." The words either place (perhaps futile) hope in Frank and Dorothy's child as the carrier of Frank's redemption or ironically mock the damaged legacy of violence that inevitably gets passed from generation to generation.

Frank's uncontrollable rage and anger leads the viewer naturally to wonder if the character is Sean's alter ego. In 1991, Penn told Bruce Weber of the *New York Times* that he could understand why audiences might think that the character Frank was based on him but commented that ultimately, it was too easy a reference to make. "I don't feel like I have a closer relationship with any one character more than another," he concluded.

Penn told *Film Comment* that he often created moments such as the pea-spitting to fire up performances, to get to the core of the delivery: "You do anything you can to make it feel real. And yet I think it's important to always go in with a lot of trust and then, even if you feel it's gone, you say, it might be worth trying something else." Penn's mission was to connect with the truth. He would generally let a scene play out once, just to see how the cast interpreted the scene. Sometimes they'd nail it in one, other times they'd come at it in a diametrically opposed manner to the way in which Penn had imagined it. Penn would sometimes go with the actors and actresses; other times he'd pool opinions and ideas and come up with a fresh perspective or create a situation that might get a better take. One example, which was reported in *Premiere*, had Penn call a take so that the cast relaxed. He had privately arranged with the Director Of Photography, Anthony B. Richmond (who had previously shot Abel Ferrara's *Cat Chaser* and Nic Roeg's chilling psychodrama *Bad Timing*) to keep the camera running and as it captured the cast off guard, Penn whispered instructions to Richmond as to who and what he wanted filmed.

"He basically has a very forceful style on the set," revealed Viggo Mortensen to the *Los Angeles Times* in 1991. "He really put his guts into this picture". The producer Thom Mount felt the same: "Watching Sean work I was reminded of John Huston. Like John, Sean is terrific with actors". "Sean's incredibly inventive with his camera," Dennis Hopper acknowledged. "He cares about his actors. He's got all the things a great director should have."

When the shoot had wrapped, Penn went in with the editor to start work on the editing. It was during this period that his quest for realism and truth came to life. "We just cut everything I didn't believe – every frame – without questioning whether or not it was important to the story telling," said Penn. After learning from John Cassavetes about the need for takes to be 'real', Penn was keen to eliminate anything that would make his film seem fake or constructed. "We'd look at it," Penn told *Interview*, "and say, 'Now it's up to the movie to tell us what it's about, because it rejected those scenes.' It's a living, breathing thing in a way and if you ask it, it will tell you. That's kind of how I look at or tried to look at the editing process." Penn completed his film by having veteran soundtrack composer Jack Nitzsche write the moody score.

Penn also made sure that he got Springsteen's approval during the final stages of editing. He was uncomfortable with giving himself the writing credit because he knew some people who saw the film would be aware of the Springsteen song. The last thing he wanted with his debut as writer/director was for people to think he had stolen Springsteen's taut narrative without crediting him. So, to clear the decks, Penn showed Springsteen a rough cut of the film and asked him if he was comfortable with his name being associated with the project. Springsteen – who had already talked at length with Penn about the project (and presumably what his song had originally meant to him and how he envisaged the characters) – was happy enough with 'the work' to give his consent to Penn's film. Sean Penn's directorial debut was now complete.

TEN

Badlands

By the time Penn had wrapped up work on *The Indian Runner*, he and Robin Wright had their hands full because Wright was pregnant. The pregnancy soon started to get in the way of Wright's career. She had landed the part of Maid Marion opposite Kevin Costner in *Robin Hood: Prince Of Thieves* but was replaced by Mary Elizabeth Mastrantonio a mere four days before shooting was meant to begin. Wright, who had put on weight because she was pregnant, was furious. "I was very upset at the time and feel annoyed even now," she recalled in 1992. "I could not understand why Meryl Streep, for example, is allowed to work while pregnant and I'm not."

On April 13, 1991, Wright gave birth to a baby girl whom the pair named Frances Dylan Penn. ("She is the greatest kid that ever was," Sean Penn told *Interview* magazine several months after he became a proud dad.) One-time 'bad boy' Penn was suddenly a happy father and there is little doubt that the birth of his daughter and the liberating experience of making *The Indian Runner* helped the actor move on to a new chapter in his life, taking him away from the self-destructive excesses of the late '80s and giving him a new purpose.

How and why the couple called their daughter Dylan depends on which of the various rumours you subscribe to. Most sources seem to believe the name is a tribute to Frances Farmer, Dylan Thomas and Bob Dylan. One person I spoke with had a less well-publicised version of the story. She claimed that they chose the name Dylan because of family friends who had a daughter called Dylan. Apparently, Robin Wright had a friend in California long before she was involved with Penn whose father was a gynaecologist. Wright's friend's sister gave birth to a daughter in the mid-1980s whom she called Dylan and Wright had always liked the name. When she was pregnant, her friend's father delivered the baby. According to this version of events, the family connection coupled with the gynaecologist's granddaughter being called Dylan too encouraged Penn and Wright to give their child the same name.

Once she was back on her feet, Wright was offered a part in a film called *The Playboys*, which was to be filmed in Ireland over the summer of 1991. Penn, unsure whether he wanted to act again, decided to accompany Wright and their baby on the shoot. "We all went over there," Penn told *Interview* magazine in 1995, "and I spent that time just being with my daughter and writing a script when she was in bed." The script was adapted from an unspecified 800-page novel, a challenge that Penn was happy to undertake himself. He was working on this adaptation day and night, certain that he wanted to continue writing and directing rather than return to acting.

When Penn spoke with Kristin McKenna of the *Los Angeles Times*, in August 1991, he seemed to be coming to terms with his past and preparing to get on with his new life. "I've always been fuelled to some degree by anger," the actor admitted. "And I think I've always channelled my anger constructively. I never hit anybody who didn't damn well deserve to get smacked and I don't have a single regret." He also told McKenna that the media hounding that he suffered during his marriage to Madonna meant that it was doomed because he was "in the eye of a media hurricane", adding that he now viewed felt the whole thing as a fiasco on every level. When McKenna asked him if he felt that the press had wrecked his marriage, he replied coyly: "The answer to that is no big secret to me." Asked how he felt about Madonna talking about him still, Penn responded: "I take what she says with a grain of salt." He also revealed that he hadn't seen her tour documentary *Truth Or Dare*. Work-wise, Penn announced that he was working on a new original screenplay called *A More Perfect Heaven For The Heart Of The Big Dog* as well as gearing up to produce *She's De Lovely*.

The Indian Runner opened in the U.S. in October 1991. Reviews were generally positive, with most critics noting Penn's promising potential. The review in *Variety* concluded: "Pic doesn't feel particularly improvised but it shares in common with the work of John Cassavetes, for example, a sense of commitment to the actor's process above all else, a belief that truth will best emerge from the combustibility of emotions between performers." Mark Kermode, reviewing the film for *Sight And Sound*, wrote: "*The Indian Runner* has all the hallmarks of an authentic early '70s period piece: lengthy, improvised, soul-searching conversations, punctuated with atmospheric footage of the grimy towns and barren fields of Nebraska, and accompanied throughout by the plaintive twanging of acoustic guitars." Kermode singled out Charles Bronson's cameo performance for praise, concluding that "occasional moments of haunting intimacy suggest that, if reined in by a firm producer or editor, Penn might develop into a director to watch". Reviewing the film for the *New York Times*, Janet Maslin paid tribute to the way that Penn "has framed even his film's most unruly episodes with unexpected delicacy". Maslin also noted the "ragged emotional reality" that recalled John Cassavetes. The comparison with Cassavetes' work was fitting. The film ends with the following dedication: 'In Loving Memory: Hal Ashby, Frank Bianco, John Cassavetes'.

Even though the reviews in the serious film press were enthusiastic, the film didn't fare well at the box office. The Imdb web-site cites the American box office takings as a mere $191,125. This low a return on what *Premiere* reported as being a $10-million budget was disastrous and Penn's hopes for future projects were dashed overnight. It might have been a moving, passionately crafted film, but it lacked mainstream appeal and most producers are only interested in seeing their investment pay off. Most viewers missed the point, the depth, the searing despair that Penn had tried so hard to capture, and stayed away in their droves.

The beauty and honesty of Penn's film was widely ignored. However, Penn was nominated for the Golden Leopard Award at the Locarno International Film Festival, an accolade that surely reminded him that a film's true success is measured by film-lovers and not box-office takings. Like his idol John Cassavetes, Penn quickly learned that eclectic, personal films often have limited commercial scope. When Penn was asked by *GQ* magazine in September 1998 if *The Indian Runner* broke even he commented, somewhat bitterly, "MGM would know about *The Indian Runner* but they'd misreport it, I'm sure. Nobody was looking out for it. It was pretty well dumped."

Once Robin Wright had finished shooting *The Playboys*, she, daughter Dylan and Penn flew back to the Malibu home that Penn had once shared with Madonna. What happened next remains unclear, though the end result was a split between Penn and Wright. At the time Penn was still working hard on his adaptation of the lengthy novel. It would appear that he hit a stalemate and began to sense that what he was writing wasn't hanging together as well as it had when he was in Ireland. "When I came back, I kept hammering away on that script," Penn told *Interview* magazine's Graham Fuller. "I also started to split with my daughter's mother. I was then living in this little apartment, babysitting a lot by day and drinking and writing at night. I couldn't crack the ending of the script. At that point I didn't know what I wanted to write about that I could direct." Neither Penn nor Wright has ever explained what their bust-up was about or why they couldn't overcome it. Whatever the reason, Penn split and moved out of the family home and into an apartment on his own. It seems as though he was drinking heavily again, possibly because he felt uninspired with the way that the script was going; he had hit a creative dead end. The failure of *The Indian Runner* had hit him hard and now to compound his problems, he was out on his own, estranged from the mother of his child.

His creative deadlock came to an end when Penn heard the news about Eric Clapton's young son Connor, who had fallen to his death from a window. The tragic accident affected Penn deeply and he couldn't get the story out of his mind. "It was such a wake-up call," reflected Penn in late 1995. "I started writing *The Crossing Guard* the next day and that just flowed." When Penn sat down to write about the accident, he wrote from the perspective of a father wracked with grief. Penn's screenplay grew around the idea of a loss that he felt would be impossible to cope with. The emotional screenplay was undoubtedly infused by his own sense of loss: he had 'lost' *The Indian Runner* to widespread indifference, and had now 'lost' Robin Wright and his daughter.

Penn was in the middle of writing this harrowing screenplay when Brian De Palma got in touch with him. "I got a late night call from Brian De Palma whom I'd worked with before," Penn later recalled. "I needed a chunk of change, because I had a kid now and bills to pay, and the part Brian was offering me in *Carlito's Way* was a good one plus it was with Al (Pacino) who I love, so I did that." It was the first time that Penn had felt the need to return to acting. He had turned down countless film offers over the previous few years, including a project that Mickey Rourke had tried to get him involved with. Penn would probably have done the nameless project out of his considerable respect for Rourke, but he was too busy writing his new screenplay to oblige.

Penn committed to *Carlito's Way* and was busy preparing for his role as David Kleinfeld, a cocaine-crazed lawyer, but he also continued to work hard on *The Crossing Guard*. When he finished a rough draft, he made some calls to see if anyone would back the project. After *The Indian Runner's* flop performance at the box office, Penn had a hard time fixing a deal that gave him full artistic control over the project. "I don't think the studios wanted to give two dimes to make another movie like *The Indian Runner,*" he acknowledged at the time of *The Crossing Guard's* American release. "And I needed to know that I could do it my way." At least he knew that his salary would help recover some of the debts that he had incurred making *The Indian Runner.*

Sean Penn arrived in New York, where *Carlito's Way* was to be shot, ready to throw all of his recent despair into the project. De Palma – who had taken on the project after first choice Abel Ferrara had turned it down – was a director that Penn knew and liked. He had spurred Penn on when they were shooting *Casualties of War* and Penn trusted the director's working methods. The $40-million film was about a gangster (played with typical energy by Al Pacino) who gets out of jail only to become drawn by forces beyond his control back into a life of crime. He tries to stay straight but finds it impossible. His lawyer David Kleinfeld is meant to be his buffer against a return to criminal activity but, instead, he turns out to be part of Carlito's undoing.

When the screenplay had first toured agents in 1989, it was rumoured that the film was to star Al Pacino and Marlon Brando, although it is unclear whether Brando was going to play David Kleinfeld. As things turned out, the role gave Penn the space to deliver a phenomenal acting performance. At times, it's difficult to recognise the man on screen as Sean Penn, because he is so physically and psychologically rooted in the Kleinfeld character. For the part, he wore John Lennon granny glasses and, it would appear, had his hair permed into an incredible bouffant, complete with a receding hairline. Ironically, the role also gave Penn a chance to act out his childhood ambition to become a lawyer.

Although many people believed that Penn only took the role to raise cash for the making of *The Crossing Guard*, his performance is so committed and passionate that it seems impossible he was seeing this as a cash-only job. Once again, his heartfelt respect for 'the work' won through. Even if he tried, it would appear that Sean Penn is incapable of delivering a bad performance.

Once he had finished work on De Palma's sprawling masterpiece, Penn returned to Los Angeles. He busied himself by working on further drafts of *The Crossing Guard* and making calls to friends and business contacts about getting the project off the ground. It seems that although Penn and Wright were in daily contact, the couple were still separated, although it remains unclear as to why.

During late 1992 and early 1993, the two were evidently back together long enough to conceive a second child. Bruce Kirkland, writing about Penn and Wright in an article for the *Toronto Sun* in August 1997 noted, "Penn once told me that Hopper was conceived on a surprise conjugal visit he paid to Wright when the two were severely separated, so much so Penn feared he might never even see her again." This 'surprise' led to Wright becoming pregnant for a second time and she gave birth to a baby boy on August 6, 1993. The baby's full name was to be Hopper Jack Penn. This time, the choice of names required no explanation: the 'Hopper' was for Dennis Hopper and the 'Jack' was for Jack Nicholson. In retrospect, it seems possible that the pregnancy and Hopper's birth prevented the couple splitting up for good.

In the winter of 1993, freak fires raged along the California coastline. The fire was first reported by California newspapers, radio stations and TV networks at the end of October 1993. However, the fires were difficult to control because strong winds were encouraging the spread of the flames. Thousands of fire-fighters battled with the blaze but were unable to put the fires out, and the devastation continued for some time.

By early November, the fires – which some newspapers reported as being caused by possible arson attacks – were spreading towards the Malibu area, sweeping down from the hillside forests. Penn was in Malibu driving in his car when he realized that the fire was heading for his house and raced home. He had so little time that he was only able to rescue his dogs and some framed photographs of his two children before getting out. He drove away in the certain knowledge that the house was going to be completely destroyed. When he talked about this incident to *Neon* magazine much later, Penn referred to the loss of the house as marking the end of a chapter in his life. "It was a weird house," he reflected. "Full of the sentinels of my regrettable past. The ghosts are all dead now." He was clearly talking about his marriage to Madonna and the way in which the fire had ended up neatly exorcising some of his personal demons.

Meanwhile, Chris Penn was enjoying a career renaissance after his part in Quentin Tarantino's *Reservoir Dogs.* Now clear of drug problems, the actor was anxious to make up for lost time and subsequently appeared in *True Romance* and *Short Cuts* – both well-received films. However, Madonna was clearly still a touchy subject for the Penn family. Chris told *Empire* that he was very uncomfortable when the opening *Reservoir Dogs* scene (in which the gang sit around a table in a diner and discuss Madonna) was being shot. "Originally Nice Guy Eddie had a couple of lines about Madonna which I cut because I didn't feel comfortable," explained Penn. "I stayed out of that conversation."

Penn's response to the fire was to buy a 30-foot silver Airstream trailer which he parked in a mountain canyon – part of the 50-acre estate that belonged to the destroyed house. By this time it would appear that Penn and Wright had once again separated. Most articles suggest that Penn's time in the trailer was a solitary one, a time during which he faced his demons and did a lot of growing up. He would drink whisky, smoke cigarettes and sit at his typewriter, pounding *The Crossing Guard* into shape. He also kept various weapons to protect himself. These arms included a series of handguns and a machine gun; Penn liked to call these his "home defence mechanisms".

Penn lamented this state of affairs – living in a trailer, separated from Robin Wright, separated from his children – in an interview with *Rolling Stone* magazine in 1996. "I don't consider that I have a home," he commented, in an interview during which he pissed into a wine bottle in a fancy restaurant while dining with Ashley Judd and Mira Sorvino. "I've got two kids and if I don't have them with me, it doesn't feel like I have a home. At one time I lived with a woman and two children in a house and that was my home. When my kids are with me I rent a house. That was part of the deal for me getting as many days with them. They love the trailer but she (Robin Wright) says it's better. She might be right, but the minute they walk out the door, I fall on my knees."

During the interview Penn also revealed to reporter Chris Mundy that he had a new tattoo, which reads NOLA DELIVER ME, the result of a hard night's partying out on the tiles in New Orleans. Penn also talked freely about the "wackos" who made a habit of trespassing on his 50-acre estate. He told Mundy that he had made seven citizen's arrests since he moved his trailer on to the plot. "I near cut the ear off one guy," confessed Penn. "I had excessive force charges against me. I cut his ear with a broken salad dressing bottle. He was one of five guys who broke in that I arrested one night when I had a house up there." Penn also made no bones about his gun collection. "I'm not going to be up there with my kids without a gun," he stated, assertively. "I've gone through the Los Angeles police academy weapons training (for the film *Colors*). I don't have one gun that I'm not an expert in." He admitted, though, that he has a "caution-hate relationship" with his gun collection.

Mundy found Penn in a surprisingly candid, reflective mood, probably because the star was drinking so heavily during the interview. "Nothing will rejuvenate you like vodka," Penn commented at one point. "My early twenties were engaged in the ambers." Penn also observed: "I'll tell ya the most naked thing I could say in an interview. I'm damaged. And I recognise that. But I have great faith in the resurrection of all beautiful things except innocence. Innocence is a constant and damage, to me, is gauged by how far you've gotten away from innocence."

Carlito's Way opened on November 10, 1993, and grossed $9 million in a matter of days; the overall American box-office takings peaked at $36.5 million. After a rash of flop films, Penn's name was finally associated with a commercially successful project. The film earned the cast two Golden Globe nominations: Penn and Penelope Ann Miller were nominated for best supporting actor and actress respectively. The film met with a lukewarm review from *Sight And Sound* at the time of its release in Britain in February 1994. "*Carlito's Way* stands to De Palma's career as *Cape Fear* stands to Scorsese's – it is the work of a man who needs a hit to prove that he can turn in a solid job of work that will make money," wrote John Harkness. "Worst of all, it feels like the work of a filmmaker marking time until something comes along that he can feel passion for." However, *Empire* praised Penn's performance as career-redeeming. Reviewing the film for the *Chicago Sun-Times* in December 1993, Roger Ebert followed suit, commenting "The acting here by Sean Penn is a virtuoso tour de force, one of those performances that takes on a life of its own. Penn is hardly recognisable beneath a head of balding, curly hair. He gives the lawyer a spoiled narcissism, a sneakiness and smarminess as we watch him steadily losing control to cocaine and greed."

On March 9, 1994, Penn's close friend Charles Bukowski lost his lengthy battle with leukaemia. Penn was torn up by his friend's death. On March 14, 1994, he solemnly attended Bukowski's funeral at the Green Hills Memorial Park in Los Angeles. Bukowski's widow, Linda Lee, asked Sean to deliver a personal eulogy at the ceremony, which was run by Buddhist monks.

This personal loss had at least one positive creative side-effect: *The Crossing Guard* was taking shape. Now it was infused with the grief that Penn felt over Bukowski's death and he eventually dedicated the film to the late writer. Penn had been talking with Jack Nicholson for some time about the project and Nicholson eventually agreed to star in the film as the father whose life is ripped apart when his young daughter is killed by a drunk driver. Once Jack Nicholson was on board, Penn found it a lot easier to get backing and his second directorial effort was soon off the ground.

ELEVEN

Emotions And A Message

Sean Penn presented *The Crossing Guard* at the Toronto International Film Festival in September 1995. In an interview with the *Toronto Sun* at the time, he described the film as being about: "the ways in which we paralyse ourselves and prevent ourselves from moving into the unknown territory where change is, where growth is, where hope is, to find the things we can pick and choose and control".

In the film, Jack Nicholson plays Freddy Gale, a man whose life is destroyed when a drunk driver hits and kills his seven-year-old daughter, Emily. The film concerns the emotional journey that Freddy Gale undergoes when the drunk driver, John Booth (played by David Morse, who had also acted in *The Indian Runner*) is released from the California Institute For Men State Prison after serving five years for manslaughter. Freddy Gale has been divorced by his wife, Mary (played, in an inspired bit of casting, by Anjelica Huston) because she found him to be too "weak" in the aftermath of their daughter's death. She is now with a new partner (played by Penn's friend, musician Robbie Robertson, ex of The Band).

Although little evidence is available to establish whether or not Penn and Wright were separated at the time, Wright appears in the film. She plays Jojo, a painter who becomes the love interest for John Booth. Wright has said that when she first read Penn's screenplay, she was deeply moved. "When I read the screenplay of *The Crossing Guard* for the first time, I started crying," she said. "That's what I want in a movie. Emotions. Emotions and a message." Penn, repaying the compliment, said that he cast Wright in the Jojo part because: "She's the only young actress with weight." Whenever Wright is on camera, she is filmed lovingly. There is one great moment where she stares straight into the camera. The audience is clearly meant to think that she is staring at John Booth here; I like to think that she's staring straight into the heart of Penn's film. She is confronting his message, questioning it, searching for answers.

Wright isn't the only person in the film who is close to Penn. His mother Eileen Ryan plays a customer who calls by Freddy Gale's jewellery store to complain about a ring. In one of the film's most memorable scenes, Gale sucks her finger and then rams a ring that she claims doesn't fit her onto the lubricated finger. Leo Penn also makes an appearance, playing a character called Hank, who can be seen in the film driving a tugboat; he only appears during one scene, in which we see John Booth at work. It's a blue-collar job and elements of the way in which Penn has these scenes filmed, subtly evokes comparisons with similar blue-collar work scenes in John Cassavetes' *A Woman Under The Influence*.

The casting of Anjelica Huston opposite her former long-term lover Jack Nicholson makes for some incendiary scenes. The most vital and charged scene involving the two of them happens when their characters meet at a diner in the middle of the night. During a soul-searching conversation, Freddy reflects back on how wonderful the marriage was prior to their daughter's death; Mary reflects on how much he has changed since the tragedy. He wants things to go back to how they were; she has accepted that their daughter's death drove them apart. When Freddy tells his ex-wife that he hopes she dies, the sheer nastiness in his eyes is hard to describe; it's a moment of supreme violence. He literally tears her apart with one remark and one flash of his eyes. When Penn was asked if he knew just how explosive this casting was going to be, he side-stepped the question: "To what degree their history played into their playing, I wouldn't be in a position to presume."

When Sofia Coppola interviewed to Anjelica Huston for *Interview* in 1994, she asked the actress if it had been hard to act opposite Nicholson as his character's estranged wife. "When you have a lot of history with somebody and there's a lot of emotion and a lot of pain," replied Huston, "it's good to be able to channel it into something. You can solve a lot of things through work." When Sofia Coppola asked her if she was afraid that the key scene in the diner was going to be a nightmare, Huston replied that she was aware of the dangers and risks of doing that scene but wasn't afraid. "Forgiveness is the only thing that really matters," she argued. This is a key theme in the film. How can Freddy and Mary Gale forgive the man who killed their daughter?

The film opens with a support group meeting. John Savage has a tiny cameo role as someone talking at the meeting whose monologue makes Mary Gale cry. It's a perfect way to set the mood for the film. During these brief scenes at the meeting, Penn intercuts scenes from a strip club. We see go-go dancers and strippers at the club. Freddy Gale is in the audience, smoking, drinking, sitting with a bunch of male friends. By juxtaposing the two scenes, Penn contrasts two ways of dealing with grief. We see Mary tackle her grief head on, which enables her to move on with her life. By contrast, Freddy is wallowing in his grief and trying to numb the painful feelings with drink, strip clubs and one-night stands with go-go dancers. When John Booth gets out of jail, we are presented with the other side of the situation. Penn explores the drunk driver's emotions, giving the viewer the chance to appreciate the guilt that John Booth feels. Our first sight of him is accompanied by a flash-back in which we see Booth smashing his head against the bars of his jail cell. (Penn introduces these characters by flashing their titles on screen: The Father. The Mother. John Booth.) It's reminiscent of De Niro striking his head against his jail cell wall in *Raging Bull*.

The strip club scenes are presented in a haze of grainy camerawork and mostly orange-red lighting and it's hard not to see the way that they're filmed and presented as a kind of quotation from very similar scenes in John Cassavetes' *The Killing Of A Chinese Bookie*. The Cassavetes influence is very definitely present in *The Indian Runner* and *The Crossing Guard*, something Penn freely admits. "I only want to make dramas that say something," Penn told *Neon* in 1998. "I don't want to do any bullshit Hollywood material which is just there to keep people munching on their popcorn. I think I know something about the human spirit and the kind of pain and joy we experience and so if there's any kind of theme that I want to address in my films it would have to be along those lines. Something real and serious, something that John Cassavetes would be proud of."

Penn uses a lot of slow motion and close-ups to add depth to the film and set the mood. The sequence that accompanies the opening titles – Nicholson walking to work along a crowded street while smoking a cigarette – goes a long way towards creating what Penn is looking for: a sort of masculine cool. Gale is seen throughout the film as a desperate man who has nothing left but his jewellery store. He is consumed with anger and the desire for revenge. Simply put, Gale wants to kill Booth, believing that this will solve his problems, almost as if by doing so he will undo the past and be able to start again.

Freddy Gale's life has fallen apart. When we see him in his office at work, countless bottles of alcohol stand on a cabinet; he seems lost in drink and the ghosts of the past. We repeatedly see him boozing in strip clubs and spending time with a steady string of anonymous dancing girls. As the film unfolds, striking parallels between the plot and events in Penn's own life emerge. Gale attacks a man in a restaurant, and when he raises a chair it's hard not to think of Penn's real-life run-in with David Wolinski at Helena's. When he is busted for drink-driving, Penn's own charge for the same offence comes to mind. Penn told *Interview* in 1995 that the film was all about "questions of guilt". He also touched on another theme: "Where do you put rage? And what is rage if not a buffer for facing loss?" Clearly his own experiences had forced Penn to do some serious soul-searching of his own.

It must have been hard to shoot the love scene between John Booth and Jojo. Penn told one reporter that the scene was "tense". This pre-supposes that he and Wright were separated at the time, and that the sight of his ex-partner in an intimate situation with another man bothered him. Wright must have felt comfortable though, or the scene wouldn't work as well as it does; for the viewer, there's no sense of tension or unease. Wright later paid tribute to Penn's directorial skills: "As a director, Sean is great, since he's an actor. He knows what an actor needs."

In another of the film's scenes, Jojo dances to a Salt-n-Pepa song that she's got blasting on a boom box. One critic hated this scene, but I feel that it's an interesting and successful scene. It seems full of love and doesn't strictly fit the character of Jojo, which is what makes it inter-esting. Penn has Wright filmed with immense affection and it's tempt-ing to wonder if he was telling her how much he loved her via this little scene.

The ending does, unfortunately, spoil the film. Gale chases Booth to a cemetery. It transpires that Booth has led Gale to his daughter's grave. Ironically, Mary had earlier berated Freddy for never having visited their daughter's grave; she pities Freddy because he cannot accept what happened and consequently cannot get on with his life. Moreover, she resents him for being weak at a time when she needed him to be strong. The showdown by the grave is accompanied by some insipid, schmaltzy music. Gale cries when he sees the grave – he can't believe that Booth knows where it is when he doesn't. Eventually, Gale and Booth link hands. Penn seems to be suggesting that the characters are united by their sense of loss. Although their lives have been destroyed by the same death, Penn is asking his audience to consider the two men as ultimately trapped in the same space.

It's an oddly tidy ending to a film that seems preoccupied with the complexities of human feelings, the lack of simple answers to questions this complicated. Quite how Booth and Gale can find peace is hard to imagine, though clearly Penn is asking the viewer to see the ending as a moment of pure forgiveness. Admittedly, when Gale gets busted for drink-driving he symbolically trades places with Booth and, we presume, learns something about the man he hates. However, such an isolated incident in the face of the weight of the pain that Gale has experienced hardly seems enough to reconcile him to his loss. The whole film is about the fallout from expressed emotions (Mary) and unexpressed emotions (Freddy), and there is little to suggest that Gale has worked through his pain and suffering and finally accepted the loss of his daughter. As a touching afterthought, Penn dedicated the film to the loss of someone he himself had cared about deeply. Just before the credits roll, a message appears on screen: 'For My Friend, Henry Charles Bukowski Jr, I Miss You, S.P.'

When he was putting the finishing touches to *The Crossing Guard,* Penn was still living in his trailer. One night in May 1995, while watching TV, Penn saw a young singer/songwriter perform a song on *The Late Show With Conan O'Brien.* Her name was Jewel. Penn was moved by her song and decided to get in touch with her to tell her so. According to Jewel biographer Mark Bego: "Penn immediately tracked Jewel down and invited her to join him at the Venice Film Festival. At the time, Sean had broken up with his live-in girlfriend Robin Wright." Bego adds that Penn and Jewel dated for "several months". Apparently, Penn also directed the promo video for Jewel's single 'You Were Meant For Me'. Earlier, he had directed a rarely seen promo video for singer/songwriter Joe Henry, who is married to a member of Madonna's family. Penn said in one interview that Jewel was "instrumental at a time when nobody believed in me".

Bego also quotes Jewel's side of the story. According to Jewel: "He saw me perform on *Conan O'Brien* and called me up to ask me to do a song for his movie *The Crossing Guard*." Jewel also complimented Penn on a personal and professional level, commenting: "He's very kind, professional and efficient and the shots in the video are beautiful." After a few months, Jewel and Penn broke up. Penn went back to Wright and Jewel (according to Bego) went back to Steve Poltz, her erstwhile boyfriend.

Penn and Wright were reunited, and this time they intended to make it last. He had clearly missed her and his children greatly during their period apart. After the reconciliation, Penn made a conscious decision to put his wild days behind him. "I knew that I had blown my relationship with this incredible woman," he reflected in 1998. "And I kept cursing the fact that I had been so stupid. But I never really gave up on the idea we could get back together. I just had to convince her . . . I had to stop being such an asshole, stop drinking so much. And behave like a responsible adult." Sean Penn had finally heard his wake-up call.

TWELVE

Time To Be Called On

Penn was just finishing *The Crossing Guard* when a script fell into his hands that was too good to pass on. The script was written by Tim Robbins and it had the working title of *Dead Man Walking*. The screenplay was adapted from the book of the same name by Sister Helen Prejean, which she intended to be an argument against the death penalty, based on her own experiences of working as a spiritual advisor to convicts on death row in Louisiana. Robbins wanted Penn to read the script with a view to playing Matthew Poncelet, a criminal awaiting execution on death row.

Robbins told *Cineaste* magazine that the film for him was "an emotional journey". He also felt that it was important to make Poncelet a human being whom audiences could feel drawn to, even if his crimes and ethics disgusted them. "You don't read a lot about executions," explained Robbins. "They're usually buried in the newspaper and the articles are usually about the crimes and the fact that the criminal was killed. You don't hear their last words, you don't hear that they have a mother or a sister or a brother, you don't hear that people wept. That side of the story is never told."

Robbins also felt that it was essential for the film not to cross over into political preaching or moralising; he wanted to keep the story human and open. "The film is directed beyond politics because I have no ambition to preach to the converted ," he stated. "It's not directed at Democrats or Republicans – it's directed at morality – which crosses political lines." The film was not only written and produced by Tim Robbins but also co-produced by Havoc Films, the production company that Robbins had founded so that he could make projects that he believed in. Havoc Films then hooked up with Polygram Filmed Entertainment and Working Title Films to raise the necessary financing. Robbins, who had written a paper opposing the death penalty on moral grounds for a philosophy class during his college days, had never previously seen the death penalty as a cause that stirred up violent emotions inside him. However, always renowned for his work as a political activist, he was entranced when he read Sister Helen's book, which his partner Susan Sarandon had introduced him to. It started him thinking about the countless perspectives that have to be taken into account when it comes to deciding whether the death penalty is right or wrong.

For Robbins, nothing was more important than securing Penn in the lead role: "I wanted the best actor I could find and he was the first name that came into my mind. I think he is the premier actor of my generation. He has a quality about him that doesn't pander to audiences. It is essential that this character doesn't try to be liked." Oddly, after Robbins asked Penn to go and spend time with Sister Helen, she called him to say that Penn eerily reminded her of Robert Lee Willie, one of the criminals on whom Robbins based Poncelet. Penn became involved with the project simply because he felt the screenplay was too powerful for him not to work on. "When I was finishing *The Crossing Guard*, Tim Robbins gave me the script of *Dead Man Walking*," he recalled. "I read this thing and my tears hit the page and I said, 'OK, time to be called on here.'"

There were tensions on set because Penn was acting opposite Sarandon in the part of Sister Helen, an actress whom he had allegedly dated during 1984. Sarandon later told *Mirabella* magazine: "I remember Tim stopped the day early once. He said, I can't watch this. It's gotten into something else. There was a big discussion of whether it was too sexual. Sean said, 'Yes it is, but that's what it is.'" She went on to add: "Sexual tension is all about connection, about two people seeing each other in a way nobody else does. And Sean and I were definitely connected." Penn threw his thoughts in too. "The feeling is mutual," he said. "I like everything about her from the top down."

Robbins was blown away by Penn's talent and talked him up as being very different to the myths and rumours that continually dog him, especially concerning Penn's 'method' approach to his roles. "In between takes, he'd break character. I'd heard stories about him, but they were totally unfounded — that bullshit about having to refer to him as his character's name. That stuff usually comes from a source that has a personal vengeance involved. I asked him about it and it came from a particular director or producer who he'd gotten into a difficult situation with. One word that I would say is the real key to understanding Sean is honesty."

The end result is a powerful film that cleverly balances social comment with the emotional relationship between Sister Helen and Matthew Poncelet. Robbins never lets us forget that Poncelet is a sick individual who participated in a horrific and senseless crime. At the point in the film when Poncelet is slowly starting to draw sympathy from the viewer, Robbins has the inmate share his white supremacist ideologies with a TV news team. We are immediately reminded why Poncelet is behind bars.

The way in which Robbins illustrates the barbaric nature of capital punishment is not dissimilar to the way in which the topic is addressed in Polish director Krzysztof Kieslowski's gruelling film about capital punishment, *A Short Film About Killing*. Kieslowski, like Robbins, keeps a strict balance between the barbarity of the criminal's crime and the equally barbaric punishment that he is in turn dealt. Both films manage to show how capital punishment is as brutal as the crimes that lead the criminals to death row.

Penn carries the film with his astonishing performance. His tattoos, facial hair and gravity-defying quiff lend him, once again, an appearance that almost makes Sean Penn the actor invisible. Robbins' story of Poncelet's journey from condemned criminal to depraved flirt to tearful penitent travels along a knife edge. The scene in which Poncelet has to say goodbye to his family makes for harrowing viewing. When his mother is forbidden to hug her son for a last time, Robbins' direction captures the brutality of the situation quite brilliantly. Poncelet's execution scene is almost unwatchable because of Penn's harrowing performance. His performance in the part would eventually earn Sean Penn an Academy Award® nomination for Best Actor. Robbins himself earned a nomination in the Best Actor category and Susan Sarandon won the Academy Award® for Best Actress. The fourth and final nomination for the film was for the Best Original Title Song, which was written and performed by Bruce Springsteen.

When *The Crossing Guard* was released in November 1995, Penn had sat back and watched all his hard work drift away into nothing.

"It seemed to come out and go away pretty quickly," he told the *Boston Globe*. "I thought *The Crossing Guard* was treated just terribly and it was the best performance that Jack Nicholson had given in years." Penn told *American GQ* magazine that he had intended *The Indian Runner* and *The Crossing Guard* to be films that should be read as "question marks". He backed this up by saying: "You change every day. You've got to give yourself time to breathe. I've been in that place where I could not move. Motivation for anything was way out of reach. Losing track of time, all of that. That's scary. A doctor had a pen on paper to give me a Prozac prescription at one point and I just wasn't going to take it. I was worried about the diminishment of highs and lows." The idea that Penn's films were left as question marks is reminiscent of a remark John Cassavetes once made: "All my life I've fought against clarity – all those stupid definitive answers. Phooey on a formula life, on slick solutions. I think it's only in the movies that it's easy. I won't call my work entertainment. It's exploring. It's asking questions of people. A good movie will ask you questions you haven't been asked before."

The reviews, like those for *The Indian Runner,* were positive on the whole and praised Penn's evolving style as a writer and director. Bruce Kirkland, reviewing *The Crossing Guard* for the *Toronto Sun* in December 1995, described the film as an "extraordinary drama about anger and forgiveness". He spoke highly of Penn's directing for not following the clichés of "straight drama" or "real action". The reviewer for *USA Today* was somewhat less generous, describing the film as the "kind of erratic left field effort that Hollywood hasn't cared to bankroll since the early '70s". On the whole, the critics paid tribute to Penn's staunchly anti-Hollywood approach. The *San Francisco Chronicle* felt that the film was "strongly reminiscent of John Cassavetes' films" and praised its "volatile, untidy quality". Angie Errigo, writing for the *Chicago Sun-Times*, managed to pick up on one aspect of the film that others had overlooked: "None of the reviews of *The Crossing Guard* that I've seen describe the Jack Nicholson character as an alcoholic but that is the key to the character and the movie." The theme of using alcohol as an escape from the problems in one's life was certainly close to home for Sean Penn.

But while many praised Penn's directorial ambition, the unrelenting grimness of the feature was widely criticised. At the time of the film's release in September 1995, *Empire's* Roger Ebert wrote: "Like Penn's directorial debut *The Indian Runner*, *The Crossing Guard* is intense, bleak stuff. His ambition to wrestle suspensefully with ethics and morality as well as revenge and redemption is admirable. But this often merely conjures a pervading air of Bruce Springsteen and proves more of a gruelling ordeal than a gripping drama." The review in *Premiere UK* was even more dismissive: "Lethargic, tedious and obtuse, it squanders its promise as a harrowing mortality drama," the writer raged, before softening a little with "Penn's intentions and sincerity are evident but messily realised."

Ana Maria Bahiana's review for *Screen International* wasn't much better either. "*The Crossing Guard* quickly loses its grip on the viewer," she wrote, "through a combination of vapid dialogue, deadly slow pacing and forced situations, including a melodramatic ending that had Venice audiences booing." She concluded that the film was a "pretentious drama". *Variety's* David Rooney found the ending "disappointingly maudlin".

But for all the criticism, there were also genuine plaudits for the film. "*The Crossing Guard* gives us the most honourable Jack Nicholson performance this decade (scintillating in its sharp turns of viciousness, although the younger Nicholson would have nailed the character more completely) and a devastating contribution from Anjelica Huston," wrote Trevor Johnston in *Sight And Sound*. He also honed in on Penn's skills as a director: "Penn's sincere understanding of the extent of the emotional carnage is actually the core of his over-egged aesthetic."

The film earned Penn a nomination for the Golden Lion category when *The Crossing Guard* was shown at the Venice Film Festival in 1995. At the 1996 Independent Spirit Awards, David Morse was nominated for the Best Supporting Male category. Anjelica Huston's beautiful performance in the film earned her a Golden Globe nomination in early 1996 for the Best Performance From A Supporting Actress In A Motion Picture. She was also nominated for the Outstanding Performance By A Female Actor In A Supporting Role Award at the Screen Actors Guild Awards in 1996.

The problem was, nobody went to see the film when it opened. According to the Imdb web-site, the film only grossed $832,910 at American box offices. Once again, Penn was left with a flop on his hands. His commercial record was now seriously tarnished as a director.

When a film that stars Jack Nicholson, Anjelica Huston and Robin Wright only grosses $800,000, something has clearly gone wrong. It's clear in retrospect that the film was simply too raw for most audiences; the harrowing subject matter just didn't gel with the popcorn-loving masses. However, the film did do well in countries such as France and Italy where serious, challenging works are generally treated with the respect they deserve.

Although his directorial efforts had not yet borne fruit, Sean Penn the actor was a highly bankable commodity again, and critically respected to boot. *Dead Man Walking*, which cost $11 million to make, opened just weeks after *The Crossing Guard* on December 29, 1995 and became hot property at box offices across the U.S., opening in most European countries during the first quarter of 1996. The film went on to gross $39 million in the U.S., giving Robbins a bona fide box-office success. Penn's hair-raising performance in the film was met with a flurry of rave reviews.

Philip Kemp, writing for *Sight And Sound*, called the film a "work of emotional honesty" and highlighted Penn's performance, commenting: "Sean Penn gives by far his finest performance to date." He gave the same compliment to Susan Sarandon, concluding that the film was "fragile but profoundly moving".

Peter Biskind, reviewing the film for *Premiere*, commented on Penn's appearance in the film "like a fitter version of *Cape Fear*'s Max Cady – heavily tattooed with swastikas and other obligatory emblems of America's death culture". *UK Premiere* saw a "steely grace" in Penn's Poncelet, noting that in the earlier parts of the film he played the "grunting hick with Rottweiler snarl to grim perfection". The reviewer also pointed out Penn's total involvement with the character: "Penn at his purest and most fearless, and he pins you to your seat – there is simply nothing between him and his character, no division or façade, no pretence. It's the least fussy performance he's ever given."

When Penn scooped the 1996 Independent Spirit Awards prize for Best Male Lead, he poked fun at his troubled past, saying: "You tolerate me, you really tolerate me," when he went up to collect his award. And the nominations kept rolling in. Susan Sarandon won the Outstanding Part By A Female Actor In A Leading Role prize at the Screen Actors Guild Awards (Penn was nominated for best actor) and Tim Robbins won the PFS Expose Award at the Political Film Society Awards.

Penn was also nominated for the Best Performance By An Actor In A Motion Picture in the 1996 Golden Globe Awards while Robbins earned a Golden Globe nomination for his screenplay.

But on the night of the 1996 Academy Awards® ceremony, Penn wasn't in the audience to see if he had won the Best Actor Award for his performance in *Dead Man Walking*. Family matters dragged him away: Robin Wright had been rushed into hospital for an emergency gall bladder operation. Penn wanted to be in the hospital for the operation and for when his partner woke up.

THIRTEEN

Love Streams

By March 1996, rumours were flying all over Los Angeles that Sean Penn was set to marry Robin Wright. After all, the couple had reunited after a lengthy separation and they had two beautiful children. When Chris Penn was interviewed by a reporter from the *Edmonton Sun* in March 1996, he was asked if it was true that his brother was planning a private wedding. Chris laughed the question off with, "I'm Sean's brother, not his manager." At the time the actor was busy enjoying the buzz garnered by his role in Lee Tamahori's *Mulholland Falls*. During the interview, Chris made some very frank comments about his background and the way in which it had unsettled his notions of a career. "Because of my family, everything was handed to me on a silver platter," confessed the youngest of the Penn brothers. "I was a good actor but I wasn't a committed actor. For me acting was the fun alternative to actually working. The fun ended when I couldn't get a job for about three years."

Producer Art Linson, who had known Sean Penn for years, first became aware of plans for the Penn-Wright wedding when the couple called by to see him one day and asked him if they could get married at his home. On asking when the big day was to be, Linson was surprised to be told that they wanted to marry in 15 days' time, though he was happy to surrender his house for the wedding. When he recounted this story to *People* magazine in January 1999, he said of the stormy on/off couple: "I think he has always been in love with Robin and Robin has always been in love with him. Everybody walks the tightrope of love in their own way."

The wedding took place on April 27, 1996 and the guests included Jack Nicholson, Dennis Hopper, Warren Beatty, Harry Dean Stanton and Marlon Brando. According to online movie site called *Mr Showbiz,* an amusing incident occurred when Jack Nicholson got up to toast the couple. "Brando reportedly unbuckled Nicholson's belt, causing his pants to fall around his ankles," relayed the online news source. "Jack proceeded with the toast anyway." From the moment that the ceremony was complete, Robin Wright changed her name to Robin Wright Penn.

Now that they were married, Wright Penn was to exert a huge calming influence on her husband. Penn would later tell a reporter that: "Robin has helped me learn not to punish myself for not living up to some impossible standard of who I should be. That kind of thing had been eating away at me for a long time and she helped me figure it out."

The couple had only been married a month when Robin Wright Penn was subjected to a terrifying ordeal, an experience that would end up being the catalyst that caused the family to leave their Los Angeles home. On May 29, 1996, at about 8 pm, she pulled into the family home driveway in her Toyota Land Cruiser; the children – five-year-old Dylan and two-year-old Hopper – were with her. She parked on the driveway and was getting out of the vehicle when two men approached her. They reportedly told Wright Penn to get out of the vehicle.

The story of what happened varies depending on which report you read. One report alleges that the men had their hands in their pockets, thereby suggesting that they were carrying weapons. Another report alleges that one man brandished a gun while the other was unarmed. Wright Penn appears to have acted instinctively and quickly, handing the keys to the vehicle to the men without resistance. "If I was alone, it would've been less harrowing," she reflected later. "It's like, 'Take the car, take the fucking house, take everything'." Her children were still locked into the back of the vehicle with seat belts on when the men approached Wright Penn, and apparently she had to sweet talk the car thieves into letting her remove the children before they got into the vehicle. As soon as the men had jumped in the vehicle and raced away, she called 911.

Wright Penn's emergency call to the police department was widely broadcast that night throughout the Los Angeles area. When asked for his comment on the attack later that night, Penn had nothing but admiration for the way in which his wife calmly and coolly handled the ordeal. "She was amazing," he said warmly. "They played it on the news and I heard her. Her voice was so calm and clear about what happened." Just minutes after she had dialled 911, police officers saw the stolen vehicle being driven along a street close by. They followed the vehicle, which was eventually abandoned by the car-jackers about three miles from the Penns' home. The police officers gave chase as the car-jackers fled the dumped Land Cruiser and managed to catch and arrest one of the men as he left the vehicle. The other man was reported to have run into an apartment complex and hidden in a large trash bin, which is where police officers found and arrested him.

Most of the news stories that followed the arrest reported that Dackery Williams, an 18-year-old Los Angeles resident, and an unnamed 16-year-old man were the two men that the police picked up and arrested. The police stated that no weapons of any description were found either on the men or in the vehicle. Williams was detained on $100,000 bail while his 16-year-old accomplice, whose name couldn't be legally released because of his age, was detained in a juvenile detention facility.

By the first week of June, news services were wiring around the developments. Apparently, Williams had pleaded not guilty to "commandeering Robin Wright Penn's car at gunpoint". On June 21, the men appeared in court. Penn and Wright Penn were apparently in the public seating area. The 16-year-old was sent to a juvenile correctional facility by the judge while Williams was held on bail pending a trial on July 2, 1996. The Penns had experienced some unbelievably bad luck with their houses. First their Malibu home had been burned to a pile of ashes by flash fires in 1993. Now, the entire family had been exposed to a situation that could have had fatal consequences. They decided that it was time to move out of the Los Angeles area and set up home somewhere safer.

Meanwhile, Penn was exploring new career possibilities. A news story that ran in the August 2 issue of *Screen International* reported that Penn had signed a deal with Mike Medavoy, the head of Phoenix Pictures. The deal gave Phoenix a "three-year, first-look deal" for all forthcoming Penn projects. The news story also referred to three projects that Penn was considering at the time. The first was a romantic thriller called *The Weight of Water* that was slated to be directed by Kathryn Bigelow. The second was a low-budget Oliver Stone film called *The Stray Dogs*, with a budget of $1.5 million. The third film, *The Thin Red*

Line, was a war film that would herald writer/director Terrence Malick's return from years of retirement. The news piece ended by saying that "Penn's outfit, Clyde Is Hungry productions, will develop films for Penn to produce, star or direct in and is in talks with Phoenix about two specific projects to kick off the deal."

Major changes were afoot both in Penn's personal life and his career; moreover, he was still clearly in love with acting. He kick-started what would turn out to be the busiest time of his entire acting career with a slight, almost light-hearted cameo role in a film called *Hugo Pool*. The film, which was shot during 1996, was written and directed by Robert Downey Sr, the father of Penn's actor buddy. The veteran director cast his son Robert Downey Jr in the film as an eccentric Dutch film director called Franz. Downey Sr had written the offbeat screenplay in collaboration with Laura Ernst, the wife of Robert Downey Sr, who died in 1994 of amyotropic lateral sclerosis aged only 36.

The film stars Alyssa Milano as Hugo, a tattooed, diabetic pool cleaner with her own pool cleaning company – the Hugo Pool Company. The film tails her during one sunny day as she cleans 44 swimming pools in the Los Angeles area. The day throws up an assortment of freaks and oddballs as Hugo goes from pool to pool. Her task is made worse by the fact that a drought is on. Additional stress comes from her father (played by Malcolm McDowell) who copes with his life as a recovering drug addict by shooting up a puppet whenever he finds the craving for drugs unbearable. On top of that, her mother (played by Cathy Moriarty, who is best known for her excellent performance in Martin Scorsese's boxing flick *Raging Bull*) is a compulsive gambler in serious debt. To clear the debt and make some money, Hugo 'hires' her for the day's work as a pool cleaning assistant.

One of Hugo's clients calls early in the morning to complain that his swimming pool is empty. Hugo explains the knock-on effect of the drought, but finally has to appease her client by telling him that she'll deliver his water by the end of the day. She borrows a tanker from a business contact and hands the keys to her father to fetch some water. However, when her father gets in the tanker, he finds a mysterious man, played by Penn (credited only as 'strange hitchhiker'), asleep on the front seat. He's wearing white socks, a blue jacket and electric blue shoes. He soon wakes up, but Hugo's father doesn't ask him why he's sleeping in the tanker and the two take off for the river together. For the rest of the film, Downey Sr intercuts scenes of Hugo's work at each client's pool with this odd couple as they drive to the river and back.

Penn's performance and character in the film are very similar to his cameo in Erin Dignam's *Loved*. He spouts strange truths like an anonymous prophet, and simply drips eccentricity. Most of the dialogue between the stranger and Hugo's father is wilfully eccentric. Hugo's father asks the stranger endlessly about his blue shoes, inferring early on that he likes them and, later on, that he wants them. The stranger tells him that there are only five pairs of shoes like his in the whole world. Whenever Hugo's father enquires about the stranger's personal life, the latter replies that he doesn't want to be asked any questions. Later, the stranger sports a red and blue hat, and looks like a low-life pimp.

When they are almost done with their mission, Hugo's father tells his mysterious passenger that they are about to meet his daughter, whereupon the stranger asks him to pull over to the side of the road. He says he doesn't want to meet any new people and hops out of the tanker – but not before leaving his blue shoes for the old man. Hugo's father follows him into a thicket and finds him cowering, head in hands, in some bushes. He gives him his puppet and the final shot we see of the stranger is of him staring at the puppet. Penn, tapping into some faraway thoughts and emotions, conjures up a powerful and wistful facial expression.

The film itself is one of those rolling multi-character Los Angeles dramas that pop up so frequently. Unfortunately, although Downey Sr may have been aiming to achieve the sort of results that make films like *Short Cuts* and *Magnolia* such powerful works, the film falls flat on its face. The bid for eccentricity degenerates into banal and predictable material and the acting – bar Penn and Alyssa Milano, who are both superb – is uniformly weak. When generally excellent actors like Robert Downey Jr and Cathy Moriarty are reduced to cringe-worthy idiots, it can only be the fault of the script and the direction. Milano does her best with a role that requires her to suffer unpleasant client scenarios (an old man offers her cash if she'll drop her underwear and give him a peep), serve as *Porky's* fodder (a man uses her scantily clad appearance as a base excuse to teach his son about the 'birds and the bees') and generally be subjected to embarrassingly lecherous camerawork.

Ultimately the film is an offbeat black comedy as well as a love story. Hugo slowly falls for one of her clients, Floyd Gaylen (played by Patrick

Dempsey), who is condemned to a wheelchair because he is dying from Lou Gerhig's Disease. Gaylen is the only person in the film with whom she connects. When she goes to see him at the end of her day, she kisses him; on returning the next day, she discovers that he has died.

After premiering at the Sundance Film Festival (which Penn attended to help support the film) *Hugo Pool* opened at only two screens on December 14, 1997 and grossed a dismal $3,620 by the time it was back in the can some weeks later. The film was savaged by the handful of critics who bothered to review it. "Although this loose farce sometimes hits a sentimental or satiric nerve," wrote Peter Keough in the *Boston Phoenix* in December 1997, "it's more self-conscious than madcap and the over-energetic exertions of its impressive cast go down the drain." He also felt that a "giddy haze of '60s culture" infested the film, eliciting unavoidable comparisons with Robert Downey Sr's 1969 cult picture *Putney Swope*. Keough also felt that Alyssa Milano's "comely proportions are ogled gratuitously" throughout – another unwelcome '60s "throwback" as far as he was concerned. "Moriarty comes across simply," wrote Thelma Adams in the *New York Times* in December 1997, "as if she's playing Gena Rowlands." For Adams, the film was a "heartfelt but inane comedy". She singled out Robert Downey Jr's performance as being particularly bad. "He earns the worst supporting actor nod," she griped, "for his excessive portrayal of a Dutch film director."

On a more positive note, Penn and his wife had finally decided on where their new home was going to be. They moved out of Los Angeles sometime during spring-summer 1997 and settled in to a new home in Marin County, just outside of San Francisco. "Los Angeles was just too violent a place to raise the children," Wright Penn told the *Edmonton Sun* in January 1998. Sean Penn was also glad to finally get out of the Los Angeles area. "The worst times of my life have been in this city," Penn admitted to one reporter. "Every time I drive by a certain corner, something happened on it that I'd prefer not to invest a lot of time undergoing déjà vu with."

Penn's next acting role was in a film called *Loved*, written and directed by Erin Dignam. Penn knew Dignam because she was one of his wife's closest friends; Dignam had also worked with Wright Penn on her 1991 debut film as a writer/director, *Loon*, in which Wright was pitted opposite Jason Patric. Penn had even given Dignam a small part in *The Crossing Guard*. When Wright Penn committed to the film, it was a perfect opportunity for her to work with a friend whom she greatly respected. She was cast opposite William Hurt who plays K.D. Dietrickson, a divorced lawyer. Penn played a small cameo role in the film, which was only added after the shoot had wrapped.

Wright Penn later said that the dialogue was one of the reasons she committed to the film. "It was Erin's writing that primarily drew me to *Loved*," she recalled. "I know her very well. In fact, she's been my best friend for ten years. Nobody writes like her and it's great to be able to speak the way people really speak. Actually Hedda (Wright Penn's character) speaks in a very out of the ordinary way but the beauty of Erin's writing is that the dialogue is so specific to each character."

The film – which is both beautifully written and superbly edited – is a clever, affecting sketch. The questions that Dignam tries to answer (in particular, how can someone love a person who abuses them?) are all underlined by the flawless atmospheric mood that runs throughout the film.

Loved is about a woman, Hedda, who is reunited temporarily with her parents and family just before Christmas. She unexpectedly receives a subpoena from the lawyer K.D. Dietrickson, requesting her presence in court as a witness. The court case concerns her abusive and dangerously manipulative ex-boyfriend who is on trial for allegedly disabling – both mentally and physically – a series of girlfriends, including Hedda herself.

The incredible dialogue (some of the best in any film of recent years) addresses the complexity of the relationship between Hedda and her troubled ex-lover. Dignam's goal is to try to present the low self-esteem and damaged ego of battered women. She gives Hedda a personality that is difficult to comprehend, but easy to sympathise with, and has K.D. Dietrickson (himself going through the aftermath of a divorce) increasingly drawn to the beaten woman.

Robin Wright Penn, whose performance in the film is remarkable, told *Empire* magazine in 1998 how her husband's cameo came about. "That was written after the film was finished," she explained. "Erin felt that the story needed a juxtaposition, something that was unconnected but relative. She just asked Sean to do it." The cameo performance by Sean Penn – as 'Man On The Hill' – comes during the first few minutes of the film. Penn appears as a random stranger in K.D. Dietrickson's life. In many ways, Penn's part reprises his work in *Hugo Pool*. Dietrickson, in headband, swigging water and mopping himself with a towel, is about to get into his car after his early morning run when Penn's character approaches him and asks him for help. Wearing a grey suit and a green shirt and sporting a bed-head mess of a haircut, his interlocutor then breaks into a despairing monologue in which he raves about the complexity of relationships and communication. Penn was probably preparing for the role of Eddie in *She's So Lovely* and his nervous, motormouth delivery in *Loved* certainly has plenty in common with his work in Nick Cassavetes' film. He stands with his hands on his hips and sways from one foot to the other as he rants and raves at Hurt, stopping once or twice to ask the bemused jogger to help him. Hurt eventually offers him money, which he accepts.

When the monologue is done, Hurt is about to get into his car when Penn asks him if he will hug him. Hurt does this and the scene is over but not before Penn has time to ask Hurt if he is an angel. This links with a scene at the end of the film when Robin Wright Penn also calls Hurt's character an angel. Hurt gets into his car just as a woman's voice can be heard calling someone – presumably Penn – up the hill for breakfast.

The film premiered at the Los Angeles International Film Festival in April 1997 and went on to amass an impressive array of award nominations at various independent film festivals. Robin Wright Penn won the Golden Space Needle Award for Best Actress at the Seattle International Film Festival in 1997. Erin Dignam was nominated for the Grand Special Prize at the Deauville Film Festival in 1997. The Independent Spirit Awards, which were held at the tail end of 1997, brought a trio of nominations for the film. Philippe Caland was nominated in the Best Feature category, Amy Madigan in the Best Supporting Female category and Robin Wright Penn in the Best Female Lead category. To finish things off, Erin Dignam was given the Someone To Watch Award.

Wright Penn discussed her role with Natasha Stroynoff from the *Toronto Sun* in September 1997 when she and her husband were in town for the Toronto International Film Festival. Both *Loved* and *She's So Lovely* were being screened at the festival. During a discussion of her role as an abused woman, Wright Penn commented, "I hope *Loved* helps women question their relationships."

The last of a trio of interesting parts for Penn came with the role of Eddie in *She's So Lovely*. It was a part that Penn had kept close to his heart from the very first day that he had read John Cassavetes' screenplay, originally titled *She's De Lovely*. In spite of Penn's countless attempts to get the film made, it was John Cassavetes' son Nick who ended up directing his late father's script, with a $16-million budget from Miramax. Nick Cassavetes left behind years of B-grade acting roles when he got the opportunity to make his debut film as a director, *Unhook The Stars*. The likeable film, which starred his mother Gena Rowlands, Marisa Tomei and France's most famous actor, Gerard Depardieu, was warmly received by the critics although it didn't perform that well at the box office.

Once Nick Cassavetes got a green light for the project, it became clear just how well-respected his late father had been. John Travolta committed to the project for what Harvey Weinstein, the head of Miramax, called a "nothing" salary. The heavyweight actor, whose career had been dramatically reborn when Quentin Tarantino cast him in *Pulp Fiction*, turned down another part, one that would have netted him a staggering $20 million, to act in the Cassavetes project. By way of explanation, Travolta told reporters at the Cannes Film Festival in 1997, "You gotta know I'm a (John) Cassavetes fan."

Penn was on board from the moment Nick Cassavetes called him about the project. For him the love story was beautiful, even if he had found most people calling it a "sick love" story. "I challenge anybody to say they have a better relationship," he enthusiastically raved. "Anybody! It doesn't get better. You might feel peaceful but there isn't much passion. You might be more healthy but you're dying in some other ways." Robin Wright Penn, who plays opposite her husband in the film, told the *Toronto Sun* about the difficulties of the shoot. "You had to remove yourself from your rationale, your reality because you find your-self asking questions and wincing," she recalled. "What? Why? You consciously had to remove yourself from that way of thinking because it would get in the way." She also found it liberating to act in a film that didn't require her to be constantly glamorous and made-up. "It was such a hoot to just be able to go with this trailer park trash," she said. "It was fun."

The original title had to be changed from 'She's De Lovely' after Cole Porter's estate refused the request for his song title to be used. Once Penn, Wright and Travolta had committed to the project, Penn also roped in his buddy Harry Dean Stanton for a small part. The film itself is a quirky, somewhat sad love story with disturbing undercurrents about the stormy relationship between violent Eddie (Penn) and his pregnant wife Maureen (Robin Wright Penn), both of whom are heavy drinkers. During one particularly manic episode Eddie, who has psychological problems, flips out and shoots a nurse. The film then fast-forwards a decade, to Eddie's release from a psychiatric hospital. When he gets out he finds that, although it is clear that she still loves him, Maureen has divorced Eddie and has started a completely new life with a new husband (Travolta).

When the film premiered at the Cannes Film Festival in summer 1997, Sean Penn's commitment to the project became apparent when he agreed to appear for a photo shoot with other members of the cast. This surprised the paparazzi, who had been on estranged terms with the actor since the late '80s.

Penn had enjoyed hearing Nick Cassavetes tell stories about his father during the shoot; Nick Cassavetes and his sister Zoe grew up in a house that was constantly doubling up as a studio and set. In 1998 he told *Neon* magazine, "Nick told us a lot of incredible personal stories about how generous his dad could be and how hard he worked to make his films. Even though he would be dead broke and mortgage his house to pay to have his film developed at the lab." He also went on to explain why the actor/director meant so much to him: "John Cassavetes lived for his art and there's no greater compliment that you can pay to him. I mean, I almost start to cry when I think of the incredible spirit of someone like that and how much he cared about his work and the people he worked with."

At the press conference for *She's So Lovely*, Nick Cassavetes outlined how he had come to direct the screenplay, which had been Penn's pet project since John Cassavetes died in 1989. "Sean had been interested in this project for a long time," Cassavetes said. "It means a lot to him. It fell away from him for a little while. So I got interested in doing the film." Penn also told his side of the story, explaining that he had been only too happy to bow out from his dream of directing the screenplay and surrender the job to John Cassavetes' son. He was anxious not to make rash comparisons between father and son, though. "Nick separates himself not only from John," he said, "but from all of us in certain ways." He then identified the main difference between father and son: "He's funnier than John."

When Nick Cassavetes was interviewed by the on-line film bible, IndieWIRE.com, he explained why he wanted to direct the film: "I liked the notion of unbridled love and it was a very politically incorrect story which appealed to my sensibilities." He also expanded a little about how he and Penn came to do the film together. "He and Dad were going to make it at one particular point," said the director. "But it didn't work out. Dad died and left the project to me. I optioned it to Sean for a couple of years."

When Penn failed to get backers for the project, the rights eventually reverted to Nick Cassavetes. He had finished *Unhook The Stars* and was looking for a follow-up project. During that what–next period, he decided to try to bring his late father's screenplay to life. "I went to Sean," he recalled, "and asked him, out of respect to him because he had loved the part originally." Penn was enthusiastic from the word go: "He said, 'Ya, I'd love to do it with Robin.' So we talked about that for a while and we talked to Robin and they were in."

Next, Cassavetes sent John Travolta the screenplay. "John had always been a big fan of Dad's work," recalled Cassavetes. "So I thought maybe we'd have a chance to get him. He read the script and loved it." He didn't have to wait for Travolta to become free either: "He became available and we were in production." He also talked about one magical day when he caught himself looking around at the set: "My mother is in the film, three wonderful actors and a script of my Dad's. It doesn't get a whole lot better than that." He was also full of praise for Sean and Robin as the husband and wife team, both on and off the set. "The foremost thing I would say about working with Robin and Sean," said the director, "is that they were devoted to this project and devoted to their characters."

Richard Corliss, writing for *Time*, quoted Nick Cassavetes who called Eddie and Maureen "mentally and emotionally retarded" lovers before adding: "They have one talent, they can love each other really good." Corliss enjoyed a certain 'symmetry' that he found in the film. "A Cassavetes directing a beautiful blonde with serious acting chops (not Rowlands but Wright)," he mused. "And her gifted 'difficult' actor/director husband (not John but Sean)." Corliss got a Travolta quotation about why he committed to the role of Joey. "Joey was a tribute to all the male characters in Cassavetes films," explained the actor. "I was Ben Gazzara, Peter Falk and Cassavetes all wrapped into one." Corliss also heard a nice story from Nick about growing up around his film-mad parents: "I would wake up in the middle of the night and find a piece of film in my bed that showed my mother scratching her nose." Nick's directorial approach towards his star cast, as revealed to Corliss, was amusingly simple: "Put actors into a situation, talk to them about what you feel until they're ready to scream, then turn on the camera."

Not that it was plain sailing for all concerned. Robin Wright Penn had a lot of problems when it was time to shoot a scene that falls at the beginning of the film in which her character is raped by her sleazy neighbour. "You rip your soul apart," she recalled, "and lay it on the table. Then you go home and be a mom." Corliss also reported on a certain amount of tension between Penn and his director. Apparently, Penn wouldn't shoot extra scenes that Nick wanted. He also apparently "fiddled with the director's cut" and "put different music on the soundtrack". Miramax boss Harvey Weinstein passed comment on this. "Here's Sean's method of negotiating," said Weinstein. "He says 'My way.' He can be a rascal but then who isn't?"

Whatever behind-the-scenes shenanigans there may have been, the interplay between Penn and Wright Penn in front of the camera is wonderful to behold. When Eddie stands in the pouring rain and tells Maureen how beautiful he thinks she is, the viewer can't help wondering how much of Penn and Wright Penn's own relationship is being revealed up there on the screen. The same can be said of the scene in which Eddie takes Maureen dancing. The love between the two actors (and characters) simply screams out as they goof about on the dance floor.

Although it revolves around a serious examination of a troubled relationship, the film is also very funny at times. Eddie's bizarre monologue about Maureen's body, and in particular his rant about 'where hair comes from', is hilarious. The same kind of manic ranting and raving also dominates his performance in the film version of *Hurlyburly*, while the wonderful, offbeat dialogue is typical of John Cassavetes' poetic, idiosyncratic take on life.

The film premiered at the Cannes Film Festival on May 15, 1997, and was reviewed in late May 1997 by a reporter from *Screen International*. Allan Hunter described the film as "a quirky comic valentine to a love that cannot be denied." However, he went on to say that although the film boasted Penn's Cannes prize-winning performance and Travolta's extremely bankable name, he felt that it was ultimately "too overblown and eccentric" to break through to mainstream cinema audiences.

Hunter applauded the way that Cassavetes Jr kept his focus "between whiny, pregnant Maureen and her adoring volatile husband" in the first half of the piece. For Hunter, this created the necessary spark, and he paid tribute to "the raw power and heartfelt performances that became the trademark of his father's best work". However, he felt that the second half of the film was let down by a looser, less linear narrative and by the number of issues left unresolved.

Most importantly for Penn's career, the screening at the Cannes Film Festival resulted in tangible praise: he was awarded the festival's Best Actor Award for his performance in the film. This was only one of the film's awards or near-awards. Thierry Arbogast shared the Technical Grand Prize with Luc Besson's *The Fifth Element* and Nick Cassavetes was nominated for the Golden Palm Award. Arbogast was also nominated for the Golden Frog Award at the Camerimage Festival. Robin Wright Penn was also nominated for the Outstanding Performance By A Female Actor In A Leading Role Award at the Screen Actors Guild Awards in 1998.

Even though the awards and nominations suggested a lot of attention for the film, its box-office performance was less than dazzling. The film opened at 800-plus cinemas across the U.S. in August 1997 and took roughly $3 million in the first weekend. Thereafter, the admissions took a nose-dive and the film only ended up grossing $7 million when its American run came to a close, though it fared well in France and most other European countries where John Cassavetes has long been a cult figure. The film was screened at the 1997 London Film Festival, but that proved to be the first and last time that it played on a British cinema screen. Robin Wright Penn was present at the festival and took to the stage before the film was screened to give a brief introduction. British audiences had to wait until October 1998 for *She's So Lovely* to go to video before they could see the film.

The reviews that greeted the film's U.S. opening were mixed. Barbara Shulgasser, writing for the *San Francisco Examiner*, had her own take on the film. "*She's So Lovely* is a movie that pretends to be about love, but is actually about alcoholism and mental illness," she mused. "I bring this up not because alcoholism and mental illness aren't worthy subjects for movie-making but because these issues are more or less ignored here which makes everything that happens in the movie read wrong or at least misleadingly." Shulgasser contextualised this theory within the myth surrounding John Cassavetes, observing both that he had made some striking and brave films and that he himself had struggled with alcohol.

The critic honed in on Robin Wright Penn's performance, comparing it with Jennifer Jason Leigh's performance as Dorothy Parker in *Mrs Parker And The Vicious Circle*. She criticised the finished product for not acknowledging the part that drinking played in the relationship between Maureen and Eddie. However, in spite of these criticisms, Shulgasser couldn't fault Penn's passionate performance: "Penn, who won the big award at Cannes this year, makes the most of Eddie's personality swings. He is an actor who has a special ability to summon and communicate what seems to be real emotion and it's awe-inspiring to see."

Mick LaSalle, reviewing the film for the *San Francisco Chronicle*, summarised the film as having a "harsh lyricism about it" as well as a "vague unreality". He felt that the film had an odd structure, but paid tribute to the way that its "desperate, emotional characters" were put on the screen "not only without judgement" but also "with love". He also felt that Nick Cassavetes had played it safe and never once taken liberties with the script. In this respect, LaSalle saw a clear distinction between father and son: "John who loved to follow his impulses and let his actors experiment on the set, almost certainly would have made a much different film." LaSalle also shared Barbara Shulgasser's theory about alcoholism threading the story together. He describes Wright Penn's Maureen for the first part of the film as a "pregnant alcoholic with bleached, unwashed hair and the fidgety gestures of a drug addict" and found a boyishness in Penn's portrayal of the character of Eddie. He concluded by saying that "those of a romantic disposition may view *She's So Lovely* as a movie about the power of love. Those of a more practical bent may see it as a sad depiction of a woman unable to escape completely the lure of sex and self-abuse."

There were many who found fault with the film, however. Gary Kamiya, reviewing the film for Salon.com, singled out the plot ("dumb ass, non tracking" and "morally repugnant") and the screenplay (a "bottom drawer effort" that "basically aspires to make a Bukowski-like plot into a Hallmark card") for particularly acerbic criticism. He also personally attacked Penn's performance, primarily for what he saw as the actor's tendency to go for type as "Sensitive Vinnie, complete with pimp spread collar, what the fuck you talkin' about diction and orthodox New Jersey pompadour. Enough already Sean – we're bored with this grifter shit."

"Though I'll defend much of John Cassavetes work against charges of aimless incoherence, the rap is all too appropriate here," Russell Smith complained in the *Austin Chronicle*. In common with other reviewers, Smith highlighted discrepancies between the two parts of the feature. "The disparity between the disturbing, crazy electricity of the first half and the farcical drawing room comedy of the second is impossible to resolve," he wrote. He paid tribute to Penn's performance, however, commenting that the actor "comes closest to locking onto Cassavetes' quavery frequency, using all his craft and unimpeachable emotional integrity to salvage bathetic situations and contrived, florid dialogue." The Travolta and Dean Stanton cameos were downplayed as "sly and ingratiating"; Smith felt that they became lost in a confused and unsatis-fying narrative.

Other reviews were, at best, mixed. For Janet Maslin, the *New York Times'* film critic, the film was a "go for broke tribute to John Cassavetes' free spirit". Rita Kempley of the *Washington Times*, saw it as a "badly mixed cocktail". Like the *Austin Chronicle's* Russell Smith, Carrie Rickey, writing for the *Philadelphia Enquirer*, summed the best elements of the film up as "Sean Penn's performance" which she described as "alternately endearing and frightening". More compliments for Penn, though such personal praise would not have been likely to cheer him, given the general roasting that the film as a whole received.

One thing was clear, though: Sean Penn's decision in 1990 to retire from acting now appeared to be history. His performances as an actor were now receiving more consistently favourable reviews than ever before. Now that Penn had cleared his debt to John Cassavetes, he delved into another trio of high-profile films.

FOURTEEN

Playing The Game

The next project that Sean Penn committed to was *The Game*, a film directed by David Fincher, who had scored a big hit with *Seven* in 1995. The big name attached to the project was Michael Douglas who had the lead role, playing Sean Penn's older brother, Nicholas Van Orton. Van Orton is a corporate control freak, living a life of controlled routine. The plot revolves around an unusual birthday gift that his wild younger brother Conrad – played by Penn – gives his older brother. To shake up Nicholas's regimented lifestyle, Conrad gives him the Game. The latter is an adult adventure which, when activated by the participant, becomes a roller-coaster of unsettling proportions. People force their way into the player's life, dangerous situations are instigated and make-believe plots become all too real. What starts out as a mysterious gift and challenge from the 'black sheep' to his corporate-success-story sibling soon turns into a chilling nightmare that won't stop.

Fincher told *Uncut* magazine that he started getting involved with the project before *Seven* came along. "It was written by the guys who later wrote *The Net* but I dicked around with it a lot," he revealed. Penn's interest in the screenplay was fairly obvious. It was another film about the troubled relationship between two brothers – his pet topic. Therefore, although it was a major budget movie, it did fit in thematically with many Penn films, from *At Close Range* through to *The Indian Runner*. Penn also already knew Fincher because he had directed a Madonna video back in the '80s. The idea of working behind the camera remained uppermost in Penn's mind, however. He commented at the time, "I like to consider acting jobs as going to directing school."

159

"He (Michael Douglas' character) takes this kind of *Mission Impossible* 12 Step program and has his nose rubbed in his worst fears, to the point where he embraces them to survive," Fincher explained in *Uncut*. In this respect the plot was not a dissimilar subject to Fincher's next film, *Fight Club*, which Penn was initially interested in but eventually went cold on. Michael Douglas described the film as a "Scrooge parable".

The film initially started out as a very different story and Fincher and his editing team had a hard time settling on the right ending to the film. "We did shoot a couple of endings," Fincher told *Uncut*. "But the others seemed trite – there was no movement between Michael's and Sean's characters. Part of the hero's awakening and rehabilitation is his under-standing that he doesn't hold all the controls. He'd been trapped by his sense of entitlement, by how he'd felt people should deal with him. Then he sees how alone he is. As far as I'm concerned he's dead on page one, dead on page 119, alive on page 120. That's a character arc."

In the original screenplay, the film wasn't about the relationship between two troubled brothers, but rather about the relationship between a brother and a sister. According to a news report on the film in *Empire* magazine in November 1997, Jodie Foster was slated to play the role of the sister and Michael Douglas was to play her brother. The film's producer Steve Golin had orally wooed Foster to the project and in the contract that was initially drawn up, he had assigned script and character approval to the actress. However, the deal was done on the basis that she would play the sister of Douglas' character. Problems began when Foster allegedly approached Golin with the idea of making her character Nicholas Van Orton's daughter instead of his sister. Golin talked the idea over with Douglas, but the 52-year-old actor said that he felt that he and Foster wouldn't really make a cred-ible father-daughter team for audiences. She told Polygram, who were financing the project, that she thought that this would make for a more dynamic film. However, Polygram disliked the idea, feeling that the original idea of a brother-sister relationship tussle would make for a better story. According to *Empire*'s piece, when Foster said she would only commit if the part was for the daughter, Polygram removed her involvement in the project.

Polygram had the screenplay rewritten and in a new draft, the role of the sister became that of a younger brother. This was when Penn became interested in the film, no doubt enticed by the theme of strained fraternal relations. Penn initially had reservations about being able to accommodate the preparation for his new role. "Sean was shooting *She's So Lovely* at the time," recalled David Fincher. "And he said, 'I don't have a lot of time to devote to coming up with this character.'" Fincher replied: "Sean, this is a guy who's charming and kind of fucked up. It's you. You just have to show up."

The Game opened at cinemas in the U.S. on Friday September 12, 1997. The review in *Empire* magazine was less than glowing. "This is a major disappointment," wrote Adam Smith. "There are a couple of nice sequences, Sean Penn (in a tragically underdeveloped role) is as fine as he always seems to be these days." The review that ran in *Uncut* magazine was far more positive. "*The Game* is gleefully unsettling," wrote Allan Jones. "Toying wickedly and relentlessly with its audience and their expectations. As the plot unravels as fast as Van Orton's life and mind, we are as unsure as he is about everything that's happening. Like him, we don't know who to believe, who to trust." Jones also responded to the way in which the familiar was made unfamiliar, even dangerous, in the film.

Michael Penn also resurfaced in 1997 after a lengthy five-year sabbatical, and had himself a good year. His album *Resigned* was released and was well received by the songwriter's existing fan base, although it failed to break any new ground. More successfully, he collaborated with a film director and screenwriter called Paul Thomas Anderson who was busy putting the finishing touches on his debut film *Hard Eight*. Released in late 1997, the film featured a score written by Michael. The two worked well together and when Anderson quickly launched his second feature, *Boogie Nights*, which received widespread critical acclaim and proved to be a major box-office draw, he once again called on the oldest of the three Penn sons to score the music. Michael Penn even had a tiny cameo in the film, playing a record producer. To finish off a successful year, he married his partner, the singer-songwriter Aimee Mann. The latter had found only limited success as the frontwoman of Los Angeles based band Til Tuesday, and was a solo singer-songwriter by the time she and Penn started dating.

Meanwhile, Oliver Stone was looking around Hollywood to cast his new film, *U Turn*. The film – part tribute, part send-up of Westerns and film noir classics of yesteryear – derived from a novel called *Stray Dogs* that Stone had optioned earlier, written by a comedian called John Ridley. Stone hawked the script around a number of producers before

Mike Medavoy, head of Phoenix Pictures, finally gave the project the green light.

Stone's reputation won him a cast who were content to work for far less money than they would usually command. Nick Nolte, Jennifer Lopez, Claire Danes and Jon Voight were all signed up for the film, which was mostly shot in the Arizona desert, and wrapped in 38 days, just before Christmas 1996. The part that Penn ended up playing was offered to him early on in the project's evolution but at the time he anticipated being too busy working on the film *Hurlyburly* to fit the work into his schedule. Consequently Stone cast Bill Paxton – then riding high after the success of the blockbuster *Twister* – in the lead role of Bobby Cooper.

However, a week before shooting began, Paxton dropped out of the project and Stone was suddenly trapped in a nightmare position. Paxton later commented, rather vaguely, "I had become uncomfortable with the role." Other figures on the set suggested that he was freaked out about how to follow up the success of *Twister*. Stone called Mike Medavoy and got him to ask Penn again if he had time to pick up the role. Fortunately, the latter was now available, as the shoot for *Hurlyburly* had been pushed back due to unforeseen delays. Penn apparently put the phone down after the call from Medavoy, hastily packed a bag and jumped straight into his car. He drove from Los Angeles to Superior, Arizona in one manic stretch, a drive that took an entire night. After he arrived on set, he applied himself to the role with his customary gusto, working solidly six days a week for six weeks. He was cast opposite actress-singer Lopez, Stone's second choice after Sharon Stone.

The part required Penn to get knocked around a lot as his character is forced to spend time in the dusty one-horse town of Superior, in the Arizona desert, after his car breaks down. Bobby Cooper is forced to leave his car in the hands of Darrel the mechanic – Billy Bob Thornton – a man who works at his own snail's pace; Thornton put on 40 pounds for the role. Penn's character is left with nothing to do except to explore the small town where he gets drawn into all manner of noirish goings-on. Stone describes the range of oddballs that Penn's character encounters as "scorpions in a bucket".

Penn's female co-star and femme fatale-ish love interest in *U Turn* is played by Jennifer Lopez, the Bronx-born actress who was still only 27 when she committed to Stone's film. Lopez was fresh from shooting three films back to back: *Blood and Wine, Anaconda* and *Selena*. In *U Turn* she plays Nick Nolte's adulterous, double-crossing wife Grace. "There is a lot of sex and violence in *U Turn* but it is all justified by the plot," Lopez told the *Calgary Sun* at the time of the film's release in October 1997. "I knew I'd be doing several sex scenes but Oliver Stone said there would be no nudity." This was good news for Lopez who says she usually tells her family if there's any nudity or violence in any film she appears in so they know what to expect.

However, Stone took Lopez aside one day and said that he did need her to do a nude scene. "When I objected," Lopez told the *Calgary Sun*, "Oliver reminded me that I'd done a nude scene for *Blood and Wine* but I reminded him it got cut out." The matter didn't end there. "We talked for a long while before I agreed to do the nudity," explained Lopez. "Jennifer the actress has nothing against nudity but Jennifer the person really hates it. The actress always wins out by reminding me this is what I'm paid to do."

Just before the film opened across the U.S. on Friday, October 3, 1997, Lopez spoke to Bob Thompson of the *Toronto Sun* about her role as, in Thompson's words, "a sexy small-town manipulator who plots her escape from an abusive marriage". When asked how she found acting out the sex scenes Lopez was less than glad to dredge up the memories. "I hope I never have to do it again," she told Thompson. When asked if she had been warned about Stone's personality before setting foot on the set, Lopez laughed it off saying: "I thought to myself, Hell, he'll like me. I come in prepared and that gains respect."

When she was interviewed by Eonline, she talked about how she and Stone had crossed paths before. "I met Oliver Stone first and he loved me," recalled the actress. "Then I went off to film *Anaconda* and research *Selena*. Sharon Stone got interested in the part and I thought, That doesn't work, the role's an Apache Indian. I figured they'd just change it for her and I was much too busy to care. But they couldn't agree on a price, so Oliver called me back." She also dismissed any problems she may have had with Stone. "He's not crazy," she argued. "He's a genius. I love Oliver, I loved working with him. He was totally great to me – a real actor's director."

Lopez and Stone had crossed paths before, when she auditioned for his never-made Manuel Noriega film. Lopez turned up and read for a four-page scene only to find that Stone ignored her and instead busied himself arranging the office furniture. She told Movieline that she told her agent after the reading: "I've never been treated like this and I never want to work for Oliver Stone." It was while she was on the *Anaconda* shoot in Brazil and preparing herself for the role in *Selena* that she'd just bagged, that Lopez's agent called to say that Stone wanted her to audition for *U Turn*. Still angry, Lopez reiterated to her agent that she didn't want to work with Stone.

When she returned from Brazil, Stone called again. Perhaps impressed by his persistence, Lopez did at least agree to meet with the director. This time the two got along well and when Lopez got home from the audition, her agent called to say that Stone had offered her the part. (Somewhat cryptically, he had also told her agent that she was "like a tall drink of cocoa".) No sooner had this happened, than Sharon Stone told Oliver Stone she was interested in the part and Lopez had to wait for the two Stones to quibble about salaries before she could finally begin work on the film.

When Movieline asked her what it was like working with Penn, Lopez didn't hold back. "He has a lot of strength and we got along great actually," said the actress. "He could tell right away I wasn't intimidated to be there with him and Oliver. I remember asking him, 'Why do we always see pictures of you looking like you're ready to hit somebody?' and he goes, 'Because in those pictures, I'm never with my friends.'" Movieline also asked Lopez which of her various co-stars she would – in a parallel universe – have a 'thing' with. She replied: "In a parallel universe, Sean. I was engaged when we were shooting *U Turn* and one day he said, 'If I wasn't married and you weren't engaged, would this have been a very different movie?' And I go, 'Yeah! Very different.' So we kind of . . . well, we both had our own lives so that made a real difference."

Penn told *Premiere* magazine that the film was the "fastest thing" he'd ever done. He also let slip a few revealing asides about the art of acting. "Once you read a script," he explained, "you start working on it. It's in your head. When it comes time to act, a lot of little things that germinate through your subconscious are there." Penn's commitment to the role was absolute. He saw *U Turn* as a classic film noir piece and was excited to be working with such a legendary director.

Interestingly, Penn's reputation on set was the cause for some trouble. It was a small, stripped-down, functional shoot with none of the usual luxuries afforded a star of Penn's stature. Moreover, both Penn and Stone are strong characters – it would hardly be surprising if they failed to see eye-to-eye on everything. Producer Clayton Townsend told *Premiere* that he thought there was a battle of wills going on. "Oliver's a power-ful guy," he told the magazine. "I don't know how much Sean likes it." The on-set report that *Premiere* ran contained a story about a tussle between Penn and a producer's son. Apparently, the boy was handing out snacks and when he failed to serve Penn's assistant fast enough, Penn "grabbed the kid's food service tray, shoved him with it and had him kicked off the set". *Premiere* was also told by a teamster driver that the crew's feelings towards Penn were "not warm".

Stone himself dismissed this kind of on-set gossip. "Not everyone hated Sean," he commented, rather wryly. "Not across the board. People respected him. Sean is excellent on performance. No matter how tired or wasted he was, it fit the role."

In an article about *U Turn* in the *New York Post*, Stephen Schaefer summed the movie up as "Oliver Stone's all-star send-up of the film noir, westerns and black comedy starring Sean Penn, Nick Nolte and Jennifer Lopez". The article mostly concerned Stone's casting of Billy Bob Thornton, the writer/director of the film *Sling Blade*, which won an Academy Award® for its screenplay.

The review in *Neon* magazine described the film as a "grim black comedy, a cameo-packed film noir". The reviewer felt that the film owed a "major debt to pulp writer Jim Thompson". Penn's perform-ance was praised, the actor lauded for being at his "seedy best". Overall though, Stone took a knocking. "A fine cast shows Stone can still be original," pondered the reviewer, "but his Wagnerian style leaves no room for subtlety." Allan Jones, who interviewed Stone for *Uncut*, tagged the film as a "ferocious desert noir . . . the best thing of its kind since Peckinpah's *Bring Me The Head Of Alfredo Garcia*". In the inter-view, Stone revealed that the film had bombed in the U.S. "The movie died over here," lamented the director. "It was killed by indifference and critical stupidity. The box office was terrible. People said it was a film about nothing, that it was violent, meaningless and nihilistic. It's five weeks since it was released, and you can't see it anywhere. You can't even find it at a drive-in." That said, Stone himself acknowledged that the lack of sympathetic characters alienated many movie-goers. "What it's about is lust. Murder. Betrayal. Money. Jealousy. Sex. And what

U Turn says about life is this: no one gets out alive. Basically, it's my vulture movie. Everybody's got to make a vulture movie once in their lives. You take a detour into the darkness, where the vultures live and the greed rages. It's my *Treasure Of The Sierra Madre*. It's in some ways deeply pessimistic about life. Very film noir. A very bleak, black film in that regard. In those old noir classics, the hero often died. That was the deal. No one gets out alive, right?"

Stone also told Jones that he himself wasn't sure what the theme of the film was, although he thought it might be 'self-delusion'. "All the characters, apart from Voight's Indian and Darrel the mechanic, are clearly self-deluding," he reflected. "And that self-delusion is very much in line with some of the themata I've been dealing with for years. *U Turn* in its way is a political film but not so much about national politics as domestic politics." Stone also expressed anger at the way the film had been primarily appraised as a work of violence rather than a discrete critique of American society on a grand scale. "With *U Turn*, the violence was picked out and it hurt the film," Stone commented. "The violence became an issue."

Meanwhile, back in Marin County, Robin Wright Penn improved the size of the family bank balance by starring opposite Kevin Costner in a big Warner Brothers-backed film called *Message In A Bottle*. The film grossed $20 million during its first weekend at American cinemas and was Wright Penn's first big-budget film since she starred opposite Tom Hanks in *Forrest Gump*. Clearly, such a money-spinner was exactly the kind of project that her husband would deliberately avoid. Wright Penn was upfront about her involvement in the film: "Sometimes you gotta do big movies because you gotta pay the rent," she commented simply.

The director Luis Mandoki, sensed Wright Penn's wariness when they initially met. "My sense was that she felt I was maybe catering to some commercial studio kind of agenda," admitted Mandoki later. "But I don't direct from that place." For her part, once she had finished work on the film, Wright Penn freely admitted that it was very different to working on *She's So Lovely*. The film also featured old-timer Paul Newman as Costner's father. The veteran actor generously described Wright Penn as a "dynamite lady and first-class actress".

Meanwhile, in November 1997 Penn made an unlikely TV appearance on the *Ellen* show alongside Emma Thompson in which they poke fun at Ellen Degeneres' recent coming out as a lesbian by both proclaiming themselves to be gay (even though in real life, Thompson, like Penn, is not gay). Thompson jokingly outs herself to Ellen after the latter catches her kissing her girlfriend. Penn – sending up his reputation as a tough guy – comes out via satellite during an awards ceremony. Thompson's character plans a high-profile 'outing' of herself at the same awards ceremony but Penn gets there first. His willingness to appear on this show suggests that the allegations made during his marriage to Madonna – namely that he wasn't too friendly towards her gay friends – were either untrue or long since behind him. The appearance also showed a more light-hearted side to Penn and provided an interesting antidote to his long-held public image as a hell-raiser and rebel. Not only was Penn sending himself up, he was also offering yet more evidence that his somewhat icy relationship with the public was something that he wanted to thaw out and reconsider.

FIFTEEN

Give Me A Dollar And Point The Way

Anthony Drazan is quoted on the official *Hurlyburly* site as saying that he was drawn to David Rabe's play because of the language, the humour and what he describes as the "hyper real tone". When Anthony Drazan decided to adapt *Hurlyburly* for the big screen, it took him two years to get the project off the ground. He started things off by getting in touch with David Rabe. Once Rabe expressed an interest in his idea, Drazan moved to Connecticut (where Rabe was living at the time) so that the two could work together on the screenplay. Drazan says that after he and Rabe met, the two of them spent two whole days and nights talking incessantly about how to adapt the play without diluting any of its crackling energy or charm.

As the two men talked, a clear plan came together. They decided that the most important thing to maintain was the audience's sense of being on a 'roller-coaster ride', something that had been a key factor in the play's success. Drazan felt that the screenplay must maintain the play's intensity without compromising an ounce of the play's "wickedly funny" nature. He also told Rabe that for all of this to work, it would be necessary to shift the focus away from Mickey and onto Eddie (both are Hollywood 'players'). Drazan is quoted on the web-site as saying: "We turned the story into Eddie's quasi-heroic journey towards redemption and the slightest intimations of love."

The play had been set in Malibu. Drazan and Rabe decided to set the film in the Hollywood Hills. Once the screenplay was finished, they set about casting. Rabe had obviously discussed the writing as it progressed with Penn and the actor felt that – although he wasn't necessarily des-perate to reprise the role again – the part was somehow his. He told

Drazan and Rabe that he wanted to do it primarily because he didn't want anyone else to play Eddie. "I was just attached to the character," he commented at the time of the film's completion.

Drazan and Rabe found themselves with an amazing cast once Penn committed to the project. Firstly Robin Wright Penn became involved. Drazan then got Kevin Spacey, Chazz Palminteri, Meg Ryan and TV superstar Garry Shandling (of *Larry Sanders* fame) to commit to the film. Anthony Drazan talked to *Newsweek* in 1998 about how impressed he was with Penn. "His preparation is extraordinary," said the director. "He gets past his fear to expose the emotion. It's very courageous and raw."

In January 1998 Robin Wright Penn talked to Louis B. Hobson from the *Edmonton Sun* about the *Hurlyburly* project while it was in production. Meanwhile, the film was relocated once again. Although the play had originally been set in the Los Angeles area, Drazan had worked with Rabe to get the location shifted to the Hollywood Hills. Finally, they had to recreate the Hollywood Hills in the San Francisco area because it was the only way that Penn and Wright Penn would commit. "It's near enough home that we can be with the children at night," Wright Penn explained to the *Edmonton Sun*. Instead, the film was shot in the Oakland Hills. "We shot a lot at night," Penn told the *San Francisco Chronicle*. "So I would sometimes sleep the day away at the Claremont Hotel and the kids would come there. Then I'd go to work." Wright Penn also revealed that the couple had "made a pact" that regardless of how exciting a project sounded, one of them would always be around to hang out with the children at night and to see them off to bed.

The film's total budget was in the region of $40 million – substantially less than the average Hollywood blockbuster. One of the key issues on Anthony Drazan's mind when he approved the casting choices was the fact that Penn had performed in the play of *Hurlyburly* in 1988 in Los Angeles and Kevin Spacey had performed in a stage play version in New York. This, to Drazan, created a solid foundation for the film.

Spacey told the *Toronto Sun* that he was 100 per cent committed from the moment Drazan got in touch with his agent. He was thrilled that the play was even getting adapted for the big screen: "There will always be filmmakers and there will always be people to raise money about ideas, to do films that are dialogue driven." Initially, Drazan found it extremely hard to get backing from the studios: "It was just too much of a talkie film, too centred around drugs and dysfunctional lifestyles, too '80s." Even though the 'action' centres around a bunch of Holly-wood people, Rabe told the newspaper that he didn't see it as a Hollywood critique or satire. "I don't feel it's about the business," said Rabe. "I think it's about this certain group male thing that can happen. They're all divorced. They've all been flung out of their first attempt to organise and domesticate themselves. It hasn't worked so there is a lot of resentment free-floating."

When the film premiered at the 1998 Venice Film Festival, *Screen International* was there to cover it. "Sean Penn, Kevin Spacey, Chazz Palminteri and (in a lower key) Meg Ryan act their hearts out," wrote Lee Marshall in his review. "In this dark, claustrophobic LA comedy about a group of male film biz friends and their problems." He singled out Penn's performance in particular, calling it "mesmerising". He also drew comparisons with the work that the couple did together in *She's So Lovely*, although he felt that the film was "less tightly constructed and unlikely to attract quite such a large indie audience".

Penn won the Best Actor Award at the Venice Film Festival for his superb performance in the film. The award followed on nicely from the Best Actor Award that he won at Cannes the year before for his performance in *She's So Lovely*. "The film is raw, ugly, anxiety provoking, terrifically funny and fabulous," wrote Liz Braun when she reviewed the film for the *Toronto Sun* in 1999. She described the central theme as being about the "war between men and women" and argued that the film's mostly male viewpoint made "misogyny just one more pathetic misinterpretation of the world as these guys think they know it". She rated Penn, though: "The strength of his and the other performances carry the picture".

Once Penn had shaken off yet another ghost from his past, it was time to deliver on an old promise. This time the debt was to cult director Terrence Malick. Word spread that the maverick director was thinking of making a comeback after almost two decades spent in a reclusive haze, and no one was surprised when Sean Penn committed to the project. As a young actor Penn had once walked into a Texas bar, only to realise that one of his favourite directors – the man behind *Badlands* and *Days Of Heaven* – was sitting in there. Penn approached his hero and the two got talking. Later, over a few beers, Penn told Malick that if he ever got around to making another film, all he had to do was give Penn a dollar and show him the way. Penn, who has always enjoyed driving around the U.S., subsequently took to calling in on Malick whenever one of his epic road trips led him to Austin, Texas, where the director lived.

When word spread that Malick was planning to come out of his self-imposed exile, he cashed in Penn's earlier pledge. Malick's return to filmmaking generated a great deal of excitement. The so-called JD Salinger of cinema was reported to have spent the past two decades in Paris, Nepal, Greece, India and Nova Scotia indulging his passions for bird-watching and Buddhism. For his comeback film, he adapted James Jones' war novel, *The Thin Red Line*, himself. The film, which is centred around the battle over Guadalcanal between American and Japanese armies in 1942, attracted actors including Nick Nolte, John Travolta, Woody Harrelson, Elias Koteas, John Cusack and Jared Leto as well as Penn. Malick, who hadn't been interviewed since 1974, remained completely anonymous during both the production of the film and its promotion.

The project was brought to life by Mike Medavoy, the Chairman of Fox's producing partner, Phoenix Pictures who had known Malick since 1967. Medavoy countered Malick's reputation as a recluse saying: "He is anything but a dark and reclusive personality." He added that Malick was "somebody who feels deeply about humanity, deeply about religion, deeply about life". The cast were equally in awe of Malick. "His mind is extremely wide and diverse," enthused Nick Nolte. "He's just a lovely, lovely man," offered Ben Chaplin.

The film was shot on various locations in Australia and the Solomon Islands between June and October 1997. Penn flew out to Australia in July. Happy to be working with another of his heroes, he also took advantage of the location to go diving at the Great Barrier Reef on days off. Dash Mihok, who plays one of the many grunts (extras) in the film, told the *Calgary Sun*'s Louis B. Hobson what it was like to work alongside Penn: "(He) is a real conundrum. He's many, many things, one of which is a real regular guy. He hung out with all us extras and was good-natured when he became the brunt of our jokes. We had this real life-like snake that we put on him one day when he was napping. I can't really elaborate except to say he didn't get mad – but he sure got even."

The Australian shoot lasted for 100 days; then a further 24-day shoot took place in the Solomon Islands. When Malick first cut the film in the editing suite, it was over five hours long. The finished work weighs in at nearly three hours and is epic in its ambitions, although perhaps a little too serene and idiosyncratic to really hit home. Malick's reverence for nature lends the film undercurrents of a deeply spiritual nature. There is no 'story' as such. Malick chooses instead to work with atmospheres and mood. If there's any judgement going on in the film, it has less to do with which side is right and more to do with 'man' running amok in nature. The cinematography is often beautiful – perhaps too beautiful, if that's possible – and at times it feels as though Malick is primarily interested in the aesthetics of his picture. Penn's role is fairly standard fare. His character – like nearly all the characters – is impressionistic. There's no meat on the role, no substance and in some respects, a talent such as Penn's is wasted by being used in such a way.

Just before *The Thin Red Line* opened at cinemas across the country, the critics started debates about the film's merits via a series of reviews. Janet Maslin, writing for the *New York Times* called Malick's towering reputation into question. "Intermittently brilliant as it is," she pondered, "*The Thin Red Line* shows why being a great film director and directing a great film are not the same." Rod Dreher, reviewing the film for the *New York Post*, described it as a "pretentious mess". Not content to stop there, he wrote: "Sticking with a three-hour film in which the beautifully billowing grass is the most captivating element is an onerous task." Kenneth Turan, writing for the *Los Angeles Times*, felt that the film was a "stubbornly personal film, an artwork that only one person will understand and appreciate completely".

Richard Corliss, writing about the film for *Time* magazine, felt that *The Thin Red Line* was the continuation of themes that Malick had explored earlier in *Badlands* and *Days of Heaven*. "Each film is a tragedy of small folks with too grand goals, each is narrated by a hick with a dreamy touch of the poetic, each sets its tiny humans against nature in ferocious rhapsody," argued Corliss. He went on to hone in on what he saw as Malick's intentions, to express "emotional truth, the heart's search for saving wisdom".

When he was finished with the shoot for *The Thin Red Line*, Penn returned to California. It was strongly rumoured that he was planning to direct an adaptation of Gabriel Garcia Marquez's novel *The Autumn Of The Patriarch*. The rumours were put on hold when Penn – who rarely seemed to stop working at this point in his career – signed up to work on Philip Haas' film *Up At The Villa*. The film was shot on location in Florence and Sienna in Italy during late summer 1998, on a modest budget of $11 million. It is based on a 1940 novel by Somerset Maugham and was adapted for the screen by the director's wife, Belinda Haas. Philip Haas, whose debut film as a director was an adaptation of Paul Auster's novel *The Music of Chance*, had made a second film – an adaptation of A.S. Byatt's novel, *Angels And Insects* – before starting work on *Up At The Villa*.

The film is set in Tuscany in 1938, just as World War II starts to loom on the horizon and the fascists are beginning to overrun Italy. The story revolves around Mary Panton (played by Kristin Scott Thomas), a recently widowed and penniless Englishwoman who is passing time at a friend's villa in Tuscany. A dignified and aristocratic Englishman, Edgar Swift (James Fox) proposes to her and then goes away on a three-day trip, intending to return to find out if she will accept his proposal.

During this time, her friend, Princess San Ferdinando (Anne Bancroft), a gossip-obsessed queen bee at the centre of the expatriate circle, advises Mary to accept the marriage proposal but to take lovers if she finds herself bored. The princess introduces Mary to Rowley Flint (Sean Penn), a smooth-talking, married American man with a reputation as a promiscuous playboy. The rest of the film brings Mary and Rowley together, via a web of suicide, corruption, sex and deception.

Philip Haas described the film as an intense drama. "A woman gets entangled with several men. Yet the action is reflected by what's going on in history. The personal and historical dilemmas reverberate." Belinda Haas also talked about her screenplay in similar terms: "The key for us was the context. Taking the main event and filling around it."

Penn's performance in what was for him an atypical part drew praise from his director. "One of the pleasures of *Up At The Villa* is to see Sean Penn reinvent himself as a 1930s movie actor," Haas commented. "Women who have seen the film find him incredibly attractive. But in fact, I think what's appealing about Sean is the way he acts, not just the way he looks." He went on to say: "Rowley is smooth and rough in equal measure. Sean has usually played more energised, working-class characters. I think part of the fun is that he's unexpected in this kind of role." Philip Haas also loved casting Penn opposite Scott Thomas. "They're a fantastic pairing," he enthused. "She with her English reserve and spikiness, he with his American intensity. They're two supreme actors with very different traits. Sean brought extreme charm and attractiveness to the role."

The role of Karl Richter, a servant and refugee who ends up killing himself after a one-night stand with Mary, was played by Jeremy Davies. It was Sean Penn who suggested Davies to Philip Haas, having been hugely impressed by the actor's work in the independent feature *Spanking The Monkey* and the blockbuster *Saving Private Ryan*. After Davies had been cast, it became apparent that he was a massive Sean Penn fan. "It's one of the most flattering things that's ever happened to me," said the actor when Haas explained that he was going to cast him on Sean Penn's recommendation.

When Penn finished *Up At The Villa*, he returned to his home in Marin County and took some time off to get back to work on shaping up his next project as a director. He was also busy negotiating his involvement in a new Woody Allen project called *Sweet and Lowdown*. Penn was also asked to contribute a split-second cameo role to a wacky and truly original film called *Being John Malkovich*, directed by Spike Jonze. Penn appears in the film for a matter of seconds and talks about John Malkovich while sitting in front of a framed poster that was used to promote *The Crossing Guard* in France. The film also featured a cameo by Penn's childhood buddy, Charlie Sheen.

In January 1999, Penn told the online magazine Salon.com how he had come to star in *Sweet and Lowdown*, explaining first that he had been approached by Allen on numerous occasions but that his schedules never seemed to fit in with Allen's production timelines. When Allen had a copy of the *Sweet and Lowdown* screenplay sent to Penn, the actor felt straight away that he was being offered a "great part". Woody Allen had earmarked the lead role – that of Emmet Ray, a jazz guitarist in the 1930s – for Penn, who saw a "marriage of tragedy and comedy" in the character's life.

It was no great surprise that Penn ended up working with Woody Allen. When Penn was busy promoting *The Crossing Guard* in 1995, he told *Interview* magazine that he admired Allen. "I'm a huge Woody Allen fan," gushed the star. "Good movie, bad movie, it doesn't matter – I just like his movies." He also drew an unexpected comparison between Allen and another of his directorial heroes: "What John (Cassavetes) and Woody have in common is almost a resentment for the camera."

175

The shoot started in late summer/early autumn in New York. The time was a harrowing one for Penn because his father had fallen sick and was diagnosed as suffering from lung cancer. The actor, by then committed to the Allen film, had to juggle the shoot with seeing his sick father, which meant continuous flights from New York to Los Angeles and back again.

All did not run smoothly during filming. There were plenty of allegations made during the shoot that suggested Penn had fallen out with Allen and the producers. Some allegations were made that Penn had been calling in sick on a regular basis and that the no-show situation held up the production and drained the budget. Penn's publicity team never confirmed any of these rumours or allegations, although it was true that Penn suffered a bad case of flu during the shoot. When Penn talked to Sam Whiting from the *New York Daily News* in December 1998, the reporter addressed the rumours: "Word on the set was that Penn called in sick so many times, a lawsuit was threatened. Penn's publicist says there is no basis for the lawsuit but Penn admits he hates being away from his wife Robin Wright, their daughter Dylan, seven, son Hopper, five, and their new hometown of Ross, California."

Mr Showbiz ran a news story during the shoot that quoted a 'high-level source' who had talked about the on-set problems. The source alleged: "Sean's been playing sick because he's P.O.'d at the way Woody works." The source went on to say that the producers threatened to sue Penn if he took any more time off: "They basically said, 'We'll cancel the rest of the shoot and sue you for the cost of the whole movie.'" The news story claimed that Penn's sick days had put the film's production schedule back a whole month.

In his defence, Penn was distracted and understandably worried about his father's health at the time. The more Penn raced to and from Los Angeles, the more exhausted he became. When Leo Penn finally died on Saturday September 5, 1998, Penn was devastated. His father, who was 77, had always been a strong presence in his life.

Clearly Penn was having to go through some major readjustments in his life. During his period working on *Sweet and Lowdown* he admitted to the *New York Times*: "I like Woody but I am desperate to finish this project. You have to ask yourself, are you stopping your life to do your work? You try really hard and the audience is so limited. That's a very disappointing thing." The problems between Penn and Allen continued into 1999. When Woody Allen wanted to re-shoot various scenes in early 1999, it was alleged that Penn didn't want to go and help Allen out. He was fed up with acting again and only went when it became clear that he had no choice.

Penn had quit acting before because the high hopes and emotional investment that he put into each new part had so often been frustrated by the film's reception. In a December 1998 interview with the *San Francisco Chronicle*, during which he revealed that he was in the process of remodelling the new family home in California, Penn confided that he wanted out of acting in films. Instead, he said that he was planning to put together a theatre group in or near San Francisco dedicated to 'real' acting, to be funded under the Clyde Is Hungry banner.

The Thin Red Line and *Hurlyburly* both opened on December 25, 1998. On November 19 – according to a *Mr Showbiz* news story – there was a celebrity-filled screening of *Hurlyburly*. There was a party afterwards full of names including Tim Robbins, Susan Sarandon, Robert De Niro, Nicolas Cage, Eddie Vedder, Denis Leary, Stephen Dorff and Patricia Arquette. Penn then went on to a bar with Vedder, Cage and Arquette, where he celebrated getting the Actors Studio Lifetime Achievement Award on the Monday night – an award also given to De Niro, Pacino and Brando. To be in such illustrious company was clearly an honour, and Penn's youth compared with that of the other recipients made the award even more of an achievement.

By mid-December 1998, the New York Film Critics Circle had awarded Terrence Malick the Best Director Award for *The Thin Red Line*. Much head-scratching went on when it turned out that the Best Picture Award had gone to fellow war movie *Saving Private Ryan*.

The Thin Red Line took $11 million during its opening weekend. It had opened in most countries by April 1999 and went on to take approximately $80 million worldwide. Although this doesn't compare with most commercial blockbusters, it was considered a financial success even though its final budget was in the region of $52 million. Most films see their box-office performance go through the roof after a flurry of Academy Award® nominations, but oddly *The Thin Red Line* took a nosedive after the nominations were published. The IMDB web-site on February 24, 1999, quoted Tom Sherak from 20th Century Fox as saying: "I have a feeling that because of the kind of movie it was –

more of an art movie that went really wide – the people who had wanted to see it went to see it."

When the Academy Award® nominations were released, the categories were listed on the IMDB website on February 9, 1999. *Shakespeare In Love* was nominated for 13 awards, *The Thin Red Line* was nominated for 7 awards and *Saving Private Ryan* – *The Thin Red Line*'s key competitor – was nominated for 11 awards. *The Thin Red Line* received nominations for John Toll in the Best Cinematography category, Leslie Jones (along with Saar Klein and Billy Weber) for the Best Film Editing category and Terrence Malick in the Best Director category. Hans Zimmer was nominated for the Best Dramatic Score category, while Anna Behlmer (along with Paul Brincat and Andy Nelson) was nominated for the Best Sound category and Robert Michael Geisler (along with Grant Hill and John Roberdeau) received a nomination for Best Picture. Finally, Malick was nominated for the Best Writing of A Screenplay Based on Material from Another Medium category.

The film's numerous nominations surprised many people. It had been completely overlooked in the Golden Globe nominations, which had favoured *Shakespeare In Love*, *The Truman Show* and *Saving Private Ryan*. Malick's tour de force was passed over in every single category.

Advance hype for the film kicked in when *The Thin Red Line* won the Golden Bear Award at the Berlin International Film Festival in 1998. Sean Penn and Nick Nolte both flew to Berlin to accept the award and promote the film. Apparently, the announcement of the award met with a mixed reception because the critics' favourite for the prize had been *Shakespeare In Love*.

Many other festivals and panels lauded *The Thin Red Line* with awards and award nominations. Plaudits from the American Cinema Editors, the American Society Of Cinematographers, the Australian Film Institute, the Australian Screen Sound Guild, the Directors Guild Of America, the Motion Picture Sound Editors, the New York Film Critics Circle Awards and the Political Film Society among others indicated just how revered Terrence Malick was across the film industry.

It's hard to know whether Penn was happy with the finished film or not. "I haven't seen it," he quipped when he was asked what he thought of the film by *Newsweek*'s Karen Schoemer in December 1998. "Until I put down my $7 and see it like everyone else, I'm reluctant to comment." He also suggested that his work had as usual been re-shaped in the editing suite. "Terry (Malick) makes movies in an unusual way," Penn said of the enigmatic director. "You do half the job and he does the other half. It has to do with the acting being solid and neutral, so that he can adapt your character in the editing."

Penn and Brando were also in the news because there was talk of the two of them producing a film based on the life of Geronimo Pratt, the Black Panthers' defence minister. They had apparently met with Eriq La Salle (who plays the *ER* character Dr Benton) and offered him the director's chair. Although Penn would have put his Clyde Is Hungry production company behind the project, Brando was the key to its success because he knew Pratt, who had served 25 years in jail, person-ally. However, as exciting as it sounded, the project was never realised. Penn was also rumoured to be signing up as director of a film called 'Monsters Ball', a film about a prison guard who works on death row. The subject, of course, reprised Penn's work in *Dead Man Walking* and took him back to the issue of capital punishment. The film was rumoured to be a collaboration between the production companies Clyde Is Hungry Productions and Fine Line, and Penn was reputed to be attempting to persuade Robert De Niro to commit to the project. Penn had also signed a "first look deal" between Clyde Is Hungry and October Films.

Now showing a greater interest in interviews than he had done in recent years, Penn was talking to a whole host of magazines and news-papers about his plans. Two interviews he gave contained controversial critiques of his long-term friend, Nicolas Cage. In one interview with *Newsweek* in December 1998, Penn attacked big, deliberately commer-cial films, in particular those that starred talented actors who – in his opinion – were selling out their talents. When he attacked *Snake Eyes*, a film that had just opened starring Nicolas Cage, he was bound to court controversy. "I saw *Snake Eyes* last night," Penn told *Newsweek*. "It's not just that movie, it's most movies. As damaged as I am, as reckless as I've been, I never murdered my own voice." He didn't stop there. "I think actors shit on their profession all the time," continued Penn. "They can't do a pure movie again because they carry so much baggage." Seemingly not content just to bash Cage in *Newsweek*, Penn also laid into his friend and fellow actor in another interview with the *New York Times* in December. This time he was even more direct: "Nic Cage is not an actor. He could be again but now he's more like a performer."

It was no surprise that a hurt Nicolas Cage responded with the same public candour. "I was particularly upset," Cage revealed, after reading the first of Penn's interviews, "because the day before he made his hurtful remarks Sean visited me and my wife on the set of our new movie *Bringing Out The Dead*." Cage was clearly stung by Penn's comments, and was brutal in his response: "The door to our friendship is now closed. In this business you get enough negativity from the press without having your friends dump on you in public." He also explained that when Penn visited him and his wife Patricia Arquette on the set of the Martin Scorsese/Paul Schrader project, he had seemed as friendly as usual. Cage revealed that he and Arquette later went out for dinner and drinks with Penn, a fact that made his comments to *Newsweek* all the stranger. "He kept calling us his family," complained the *Snake Eyes* star. "Then the next day he stabs me in the back." Penn, when asked about this odd episode on a live internet chat on AOL LIVE commented: "I don't see anything disparaging about the things I said about Nic Cage. I think they were fairly accurate and one of the things I said referred to his tremendous acting talent."

Penn also told the *New York Times* in December 1998 that he was through with acting once more. "This is it," he told the newspaper's magazine. "I'm not going to act in movies again." The decision came hot on the heels of *Hurlyburly* being slated by critics as self-indulgent and dull. Famous friends quoted shortly after his declaration sought to put Penn's vow into some kind of perspective. "He won't quit," said Jack Nicholson. "What Sean means is that he would like to give up the thought of making the brand of picture that opens big on a Friday night," added Warren Beatty.

Penn, who has revealed that his agent was approached with a view to him starring in blockbusters including *Armageddon* and *Independence Day*, was still lashing out at big movies in January 1999. He outlined his problems with these kind of films by saying: "That's what I avoid – that feeling of going through life making money and being famous."

In an interview with the *Boston Globe*, also in December 1998, Penn talked about how important his family life was: "I have a sense of home now. My son likes everything outdoors. He's an outdoors guy. My daughter is more of an indoors person." Penn revealed that he liked to hang out on the beach with his children or take them camping, adding that mostly he liked to "sit around and cuddle them". This was a far cry from the

Sean Penn of the 1980s, and he looked back on that troubled chapter of his life too during the interview. "Frankly some of the things I was despised for I take complete credit for," Penn confessed. "There were other times when, through arrogance, you take pride in getting away with things like abusing alcohol." He was still angry, though, about the paparazzi: "A lot of the things I got in trouble for, all it took was one pretty Princess getting killed in a tunnel and everybody's feeling about it was different." Penn was alluding to the global backlash against the paparazzi in the aftermath of Princess Diana's death in 1997; he knew exactly how she felt when the photographers pursued her wherever she went.

When Penn spoke to Salon in January 1999, he was asked about his unexpected return to acting and replied that the flurry of acting jobs had come out of commitments made much earlier on. "I got on a kind of spin that I didn't intend which had to do with two movies that I had been involved with a long, long time ago," he explained. "One was John Cassavetes' screenplay for *She's So Lovely*, the other was *The Thin Red Line*. I had had an agreement with Terry Malick some years before where I'd said, 'You give me a dollar and point the way.'" He also said that his involvement with *Hurlyburly* stemmed from a similar place; as he had acted in the play in 1988, he felt an affinity with the piece and an obligation to act in the film. Interestingly, Penn told Salon that these acting jobs were more about a spring-cleaning of earlier commitments than a sign of renewed passion for the profession. He reaffirmed that he was "trying to get rid of all of them" (the roles he had committed to) because he was through with acting. "I do want to stop," he said. "Hopefully that will be soon."

When he spoke to Salon in January 1999, Penn enthusiastically discussed his hunger to return to writing and directing, commenting that he was planning to start shooting his third feature, which he had already written. He added that he also had a few other possible films that he wanted to direct, although none of the screenplays were written by him. Penn also talked about how he had tried to adapt Jim Thompson's novel *The Killer Inside Me* and also Harry Crews' novel *The Knockout Artist* (Penn had cast Harry Crews in a small part in *The Indian Runner* and had been a friend of his for years). Although Penn worked on both adaptations for almost two years, neither ever shaped up the way he wanted them to. After a while, it seemed that he felt he had to write his own stories for them to properly float.

Another film that Penn was apparently planning to start shooting in spring 1999 was slated to star Eddie Vedder, the lead singer with Seattle-based grunge band Pearl Jam. Penn even discussed teaming up with Vedder in an interview with the *San Francisco Chronicle*, although the singer had not made any public statements that he was involved in the project. By March 1999, it appeared that the Penn-Vedder collaboration was off. In July 1999, the *Halifax Herald* reported that Penn was going to star in *The Weight of Water,* which would start shooting in Nova Scotia in September 1999, contrary to his previous claims that he was abandoning acting again. Penn did indeed commit to the project and spent the last quarter of 1999 on location shooting the film with director Kathryn Bigelow.

A news story in *Variety* in September 1999 stated that Sean Penn was slated to star in a film called *The Assassination of Richard Nixon*. The independent feature, which had previously had a working title of *Killing Dick*, was based around the story of would-be assassin Samuel Byck, a salesman who deluded himself that Nixon was a figurehead of all the problems in the world. The film was set to be directed by a first-timer called Niels Mueller who also co-wrote the screenplay. However, according to *Variety* the project was having problems finding financing. Oliver Stone's *Nixon* had only grossed $13.5 million, and producers were wary about committing to another film based around the president. This was just one of several roles that Penn was rumoured to be committing to at the time. He was also rumoured to be going to star opposite Meg Ryan in a film called *This Man, This Woman,* a film about the troubled relationship between a married couple and the lengths they go to in order to stop their relationship from falling apart. Penn was also alleged to have ditched the Eddie Vedder project in favour of directing a biopic about the life of Irish King Brian Boru. News stories that circulated about the film said that Robin Wright Penn was going to have a major role in her husband's film. Penn's name was also connected with David Fincher's follow-up to *The Game, Fight Club*. Finally, Penn turned down a part in *Million Dollar Hotel*, a film written by U2 star Bono and slated to be directed by Wim Wenders. He had been rumoured to be starring opposite supermodel-actress-musician Milla Jovovich but Mel Gibson had filled his shoes after Penn pulled out.

Sweet and Lowdown premiered at the Venice Film Festival in September 1999. Merissa Marr, reviewing the film for Reuters wire service, revealed that the script was an old one that Allen had written years before and had recently revived. Marr quoted Allen's written press notes for the premiere: "We take the character through a series of hilarious and harrowing events. As he clashes with lovers, musicians and gangsters in a comic and touching farce of his own crazy making." The critic at *Film Comment* was rather lukewarm in his praise of Penn's performance in the film. "Playing a cartoon hipster – the sort of hot-headed, pencil moustached musician who would fit right in on the bandstand of an early Thirties Warner Brothers speakeasy – Sean Penn is quite entertaining as Emmett Ray, a pioneering, wholly fictional swing guitarist." Other reviewers were more effusive. "Penn is a marvel as Ray," wrote Louis B. Hobson in the *Calgary Sun* in January 2000. "He gives shading to the man, even if the script doesn't. He has scenes which are truly poignant, yet he also finds great humour in Ray's personal and professional follies." Lou Lumenick, writing for the *New York Post*, was uncertain as to whether *Sweet and Lowdown* was a rip-off or a homage. He also felt that the film bore too much resemblance to one of Fellini's classics: "The Woodman's latest bears a decided resemblance to Federico Fellini's 1954 film *La Strada* which featured Anthony Quinn as a womanising circus strongman who victimises the woman who loves him, waifish Giulietta Masina."

In November 1999, the *Calgary Sun* reported that Penn was out and about in British Columbia looking for potential locations for his third effort as a director, *The Pledge*. The news story confirmed that Jack Nicholson would indeed be the picture's star – his first acting job since *As Good As It Gets*.

Sean Penn was back in the news at the end of January 2000 because of comments he made about the Oscars® and the Golden Globes – two long-standing Hollywood institutions – to a French journalist. "The Globes and the Oscars® are nothing but a fix. The whole thing is ridiculous," the actor seethed. Penn, who was nominated for a Golden Globe for his performance in *Sweet and Lowdown,* let rip with his strong opinions at a time when it seemed that he was not only seriously acting again, despite his vows to the contrary, but (in light of taking parts in big-budget films such as *The Game*) apparently happy to work within the Hollywood system. Although he didn't win the Golden Globe for Best Actor, Penn's work was at least recognised, even if he saw such recognition as "a fix". He was also nominated for the Best Actor Award for

his performance in *Sweet and Lowdown* when the Academy Award®
nominations were announced in February 2000.

One film that did notch up plenty of Academy Award® nominations,
as well as furthering the Penn family's reputation, was *Magnolia*, a film
about a series of Los Angeles residents whose paths cross via moments
of chance and coincidence. Once again, as with *Hard Eight* and *Boogie
Nights*, Michael Penn's wife Aimee Mann wrote a series of moody songs
that director/writer Paul Thomas Anderson used to accentuate the
emotional terrains of his dark, powerful film. Penn's mother Eileen
Ryan also had a small part in the film.

Sean Penn branched out in quite an unexpected way when he went
into partnership with John Malkovich, Simply Red singer Mick
Hucknall and Johnny Depp to fund and open a restaurant in Paris called
Man Ray. It was named after the legendary photographer artist. When the
restaurant opened in 1999, the opening night party was attended by
guests such as Bono, Kate Moss, Michael Keaton and Stella McCartney.
The restaurant, which is situated on Rue Marbeuf just off the Champs
Elysées in the heart of Paris, swiftly became a trendy hot-spot full of the
city's rich and beautiful. The decoration is Eastern in style, complete with
exotic sculptures, while the walls are covered in framed black-and-white
photographs. The menu is a mix of Thai, Japanese and French cuisine; a
brief biography of Man Ray's life is printed on each menu.

The year 2000 finds Penn busy with two projects. Once *The Weight of
Water* was wrapped up, he prepared himself to start work on his third
film in the director's chair – *The Pledge*. The cast is rumoured to include
Jack Nicholson, Benicio Del Toro, Sam Shepard, Mickey Rourke,
Harry Dean Stanton, Vanessa Redgrave and Robin Wright Penn.

Sean Penn's renaissance as an actor is now complete. All he has to do
now is direct a film that performs at the box office and his status as one
of the film industry's key players will be assured. If this does happen, it's
hard to imagine what Penn might do next. Maybe he'll only work as
writer, producer and director. Although he has once again vowed to
stop acting, it seems unlikely that this is a promise set in stone. There
will always be another project that Penn has to get involved in, another
role that only he can bring to life.

Sean Penn Career Awards

1995: Berlin Film Festival
Category: Best Actor
Film: *Dead Man Walking*

1995: Independent Spirit Awards
Category: Best Actor
Film: *Dead Man Walking*

1997: Cannes Film Festival
Category: Best Actor
Film: *She's So Lovely*

1998: Venice Film Festival
Category: Best Actor
Film: *Hurlyburly*

SEAN PENN: FILMOGRAPHY

Director Filmography

The Indian Runner (1991)
Directed by Sean Penn
Written by Sean Penn
Starring: David Morse, Viggo Mortensen, Valeria Golino, Patricia Arquette, Charles Bronson, Sandy Dennis, Dennis Hopper, Jordan Rhodes, Eileen Ryan, Harry Crews
Running Time: 121 minutes

The Crossing Guard (1995)
Directed by Sean Penn
Written by Sean Penn
Starring: Jack Nicholson, Anjelica Huston, Robin Wright, Robbie Robertson, David Morse
Running Time: 114 minutes

The Pledge (2000)
Directed by Sean Penn
Written by Mary Olson, Jerzy Kromolowski, Sean Penn
Starring: TBC
Running Time: TBC

Producer Filmography

The Indian Runner (1991)
The Crossing Guard (1995)
Loved (1997)
She's So Lovely (1997)
The Pledge (2000)

Actor: Theatre

Earthworms, Los Angeles Group Repertory Theater (1979)
The Girl On The Via Flaminia, Gene Dynarksi Theater, Los Angeles (1979)
Terrible Jim Fitch, Los Angeles Group Repertory Theater (1980)
Heartland, Century Theater, New York City (1981)
Slab Boys, Playhouse Theater, New York City (1983)
Goose And Tom-Tom, Lincoln Center, New York City (1986)
Hurlyburly, Westwood Playhouse, Los Angeles (1988)

Documentary Appearances

Dear America: Letters Home From Vietnam (1987)
Schneeweissrosenrot (1991)
The Last Party (1993)
The American Film Institute Salute To Jack Nicholson (1994)
Robbie Robertson: Going Home (1995)
Charles Bukowski (1995)
Inside The Actors Studio: Sean Penn (1998)

Made-for-TV films

Hellinger's Law (1981)
Directed by Leo Penn
Sean Penn plays 'uncredited'

Co-starring: Thomas Christopher, Melinda Dillon
Running Time: 92 minutes

The Killing Of Randy Webster (1981)
Directed by Sam Wanamaker
Sean Penn plays 'Don'
Co-starring: Hal Holbrook, Anthony Edwards, Sondra Blake, Jennifer
    Jason Leigh
Running Time: 100 minutes

Film Appearances

Taps (1981)
Directed by Harold Becker
Sean Penn plays 'Alex Dwyer'
Co-starring: George C. Scott, Timothy Hutton, Ronny Cox, Tom
    Cruise, Brendan Ward
Running Time: 126 minutes

Fast Times At Ridgemont High (1982)
Directed by Amy Heckerling
Sean Penn plays 'Jeff Spicoli'
Co-starring: Jennifer Jason Leigh, Judge Reinhold, Phoebe Cates,
    Brian Backer
Running Time: 92 minutes

Bad Boys (1983)
Directed by Rick Rosenthal
Sean Penn plays 'Rick O'Brien'
Co-starring: Reni Santoni, Jim Moody, Eric Gurry, Esai Morales,
    Ally Sheedy
Time: 123 minutes

Crackers (1983)
Directed by Louis Malle
Sean Penn plays 'Dillard'
Co-starring: Donald Sutherland, Jack Warden, Wallace Shawn, Larry
    Riley, Trinidad Silva
Running Time: 91 minutes

Summerspell (1983)
Directed by Lina Shanklin
Sean Penn plays 'Buddy'
Co-starring: Louis Davis, Edna Wisdom
Running Time: 100 minutes

Racing With The Moon (1984)
Directed by Richard Benjamin
Sean Penn plays 'Henry "Hopper" Nash'
Co-starring: Elizabeth McGovern, Nicolas Cage, John Karlen,
    Rutanya Alda, Max Showalter, Crispin Glover
Running Time: 108 minutes

The Falcon And The Snowman (1985)
Directed by John Schlesinger
Sean Penn plays 'Andrew Daulton Lee'
Co-starring: Timothy Hutton, Pat Hingle, Joyce Van Patten, David
    Suchet, Lori Singer, Richard Dysart
Running Time: 131 minutes

At Close Range (1985)
Directed by James Foley
Sean Penn plays 'Brad Whitewood Jr'
Co-starring: Christopher Walken, Mary Stuart Masterson,
    Christopher Penn, Millie Perkins, Eileen Ryan
Running Time: 115 minutes

Shanghai Surprise (1986)
Directed by Jim Goddard
Sean Penn plays 'Glendon Wasey'
Co-starring: Madonna, Paul Freeman, Richard Griffiths, Philip Sayer,
    Clyde Kusatu, Kay Tong Lim, Michael Aldridge
Running Time: 97 minutes

Colors (1988)
Directed by Dennis Hopper
Sean Penn plays 'Danny McGavin'

Co-starring: Robert Duvall, Maria Conchita Alonso, Randy Brooks,
 Grand Bush, Don Cheadle, Gerardo Mejia, Glenn Plummer, Sy
 Richardson, Trinidad Silva
Running Time: 121 minutes

Judgment In Berlin (1988)
Directed by Leo Penn
Sean Penn plays 'Guenther X'
Co-starring: Martin Sheen, Sam Wanamaker, Max Gail, Jurgen
 Heinrich, Heinz Hoening, Carl Lumbly, Max Volkert Martens,
 Christine Rose, Marie-Louise Sinclair, Joshua Sinclair, Jutta
 Speidel, Harris Yulin
Running Time: 96 minutes

Cool Blue (1988)
Directed by Mark Mullin, Richard Shepard
Sean Penn plays 'Phil The Plumber'
Co-starring: Woody Harrelson
Running Time: 121 minutes

Casualties of War (1989)
Directed by Brian De Palma
Sean Penn plays 'Sergeant Meserve'
Co-starring: Michael J. Fox, Don Harvey, John C. Reilly, John
 Leguizamo, Thuy Thuy Lee, Erik King
Running Time: 113 minutes

We're No Angels (1989)
Directed by Neil Jordan
Sean Penn plays 'Jim'
Co-starring: Robert De Niro, Demi Moore, Hoyt Axton, Bruno
 Kirby, Ray McAnally, James Russo, Wallace Shawn
Running Time: 110 minutes

State of Grace (1990)
Directed by Phil Joanou
Sean Penn plays 'Terry Noonan'
Co-starring: Ed Harris, Gary Oldman, Robin Wright, John Turturro,
 John C. Reilly, RD Call, Joe Vitorelli, Burgess Meredith
Running Time: 134 minutes

Carlito's Way (1993)
Directed by Brian De Palma
Sean Penn plays 'David Kleinfeld'
Co-starring: Al Pacino, Penelope Ann Miller, John Leguizamo,
    Ingrid Rogers, Luis Guzman, James Rebhorn, Joseph Siravo,
    Viggo Mortensen
Running Time: 145 minutes

Dead Man Walking (1995)
Directed by Tim Robbins
Sean Penn plays 'Matthew Poncelet'
Co-starring: Susan Sarandon
Running Time: 122 minutes

Hugo Pool (1997)
Directed by Robert Downey Sr
Sean Penn plays 'Strange Hitchhiker'
Co-starring: Alyssa Milano, Mark Boone Jr, Malcolm McDowell,
    Robert Downey Jr, Cathy Moriarty
Running Time: 93 minutes

Loved (1997)
Directed by Erin Dignam
Sean Penn plays 'Man on the Hill'
Co-starring: William Hurt, Robin Wright Penn, Amy Madigan,
    Lucinda Jenney, Joanna Cassidy
Running Time: 102 minutes

She's So Lovely (1997)
Directed by Nick Cassavetes
Sean Penn plays 'Eddie Quinn'
Co-starring: Robin Wright Penn, Harry Dean Stanton, John Travolta,
    Gena Rowlands, James Gandolfino, Susan Traylor, Debi Mazar
Running Time: 96 minutes

The Game (1997)
Directed by David Fincher
Sean Penn plays 'Conrad Van Orton'

Co-starring: Michael Douglas, Deborah Unger, James Rebhorn,
    Peter Donat
Running Time: 128 minutes

U Turn (1997)
Directed by Oliver Stone
Sean Penn plays 'Bobby Cooper'
Co-starring: Jennifer Lopez, Clare Danes, Jon Voight
Running Time: 125 minutes

Hurlyburly (1998)
Directed by Anthony Drazan
Sean Penn plays 'Eddie'
Co-starring: Kevin Spacey, Meg Ryan, Chazz Palminteri,
    Robin Wright Penn
Running Time: 126 minutes

The Thin Red Line (1998)
Directed by Terrence Malick
Sean Penn plays 'First Sergeant Edward Welsh'
Co-starring: Adrien Brody, James Caviezel, Ben Chaplin,
    George Clooney, John Cusack, Woody Harrelson, Elias Koteas,
    Jared Leto, John Savage, John Travolta, Nick Nolte
Running Time: 170 minutes

Being John Malkovich (1999)
Directed by Spike Jonze
Sean Penn plays himself
Co-starring: John Malkovich, John Cusack, Cameron Diaz
Running Time: 112 minutes

Up At The Villa (1999)
Directed by Philip Haas
Sean Penn plays 'Roley'
Co-starring: Kristin Scott Thomas, Anne Bancroft, James Fox,
    Derek Jacobi
Running Time: 115 minutes

Sweet and Lowdown (1999)
Directed by Woody Allen
Sean Penn plays 'Emmett Ray'

Co-starring: Samantha Morton
Running Time: 95 minutes

The Weight of Water (2000)
Directed by Kathryn Bigelow
Sean Penn plays 'Thomas James'
Co-starring: Elizabeth Hurley
Running Time: TBC

Robin Wright Filmography

Santa Barbara (TV series: Kelly Capwell 1984–88)
Hollywood Vice Squad (1986)
The Princess Bride (1987)
State of Grace (1990)
Loon (1991)
The Playboys (1992)
Toys (1992)
Forrest Gump (1994)
The Crossing Guard (1995)
Moll Flanders (1996)
She's So Lovely (1997)
Loved (1997)
Hurlyburly (1998)
Message In A Bottle (1999)
The Pledge (2000)
Just To Be Together (2000)

SOURCES

Periodicals

– Amy Heckerling, *Films in Review*, October 1982
– An Interview With Amy Heckerling by Kenneth Chanko, *Films in Review*, October 1982
– An Interview With Nick Cassavetes by Tom Cunha, IndieWiIRE.com, February 2000
– Anjelica Huston by Sofia Coppola, *Interview*, 1994
– Appetite For Destruction, *Uncut*, October 1998

– Art Linson, *People*, January 1999
– At Close Range on– set report by Margy Rochlin, *American Film*, 1985
– At Close Range review by David McGillivray, *Films & Filming*, September 1986
– At Close Range review by Richard Combs, *Monthly Film Bulletin*, August 1986
– At Close Range review, *Variety*, February 1986
– Bad Boys by Anne Thompson, *Premiere* (U.S. edition), October 1997
– Bad Boys review by Steve Jenkins, *Monthly Film Bulletin*, May 1983
– Bad Boys review, *Variety*, March 1983
– Bad Girl by Harry Dean Stanton, *Time Out*, 1986
– Bukowksi by Sean Penn, *Interview*, 1987
– Carlito's Way by Roger Ebert, *Chicago Sun-Times*, 1994
– Carlito's Way review by John Harkness, *Sight And Sound*, February 1994
– Carlito's Way review by Kim Newman, *Empire*, February 1994
– Carlito's Way review by Roger Ebert, *Chicago Sun-Times*, December 1993
– Carlito's Way review, *Empire*, 1994
– Casualties of War review by Gavin Smith, *Film Comment*, July/August 1989
– Casualties of War review by John Pym, *Monthly Film Bulletin*, February 1990
– Casualties of War review by Terrence Rafferty, *Sight And Sound*, Winter 1989/90
– Casualties of War review, by Lloyd Bradley, *Empire*, February 1990
– Chris Penn, *Edmonton Sun*, March 1996
– Chris Penn, Nice Guy by Jeff Dawson, *Empire*, September 1996
– Chris Penn, *Premiere*, October 1993
– Colors review by George Robert Kimball, *Films & Filming*, November/December 1988
– Colors review by Steve Jenkins, *Monthly Film Bulletin*, November 1988
– Cool Jerk, Sean Penn by Chris Mundy, *Rolling Stone* magazine, April 1996
– Crackers review by Tom Milne, *Monthly Film Bulletin*, January 1985

– Crackers review, *Variety*, January 1984
– Dead Man Walking review by Peter Biskind, *Premiere*, April 1996
– Dead Man Walking review by Philip Kemp, *Sight And Sound*, April 1996
– Dead Man Walking review by Ryan Gilbey, *Premiere*, April 1996
– Dear American review by Richard Combs, *Monthly Film Bulletin*, November 1989
– Downeys' Inanities Sink Pool by Thelma Adams, *New York Post*, December 1997
– Fast Times At Ridgemont High review by Marjorie Bilbow, *Screen International*, October 1982
– Fast Times At Ridgemont High review by Paul Taylor, *Monthly Film Bulletin*, November 1982
– Fast Times At Ridgemont High review, *Variety*, August 1982
– Friendship's Toast by Louis B. Hobson, *Calgary Sun*, March 1999
– Gang Slam by Kevin Wilson, *Sky*, October 1988
– Gang Wars: Dennis Hopper by Bill Kelley, *Sky*, October 1988
– Girl Talk With Loved Ones by Natasha Stoynoff, *Toronto Sun*, September 1997
– Hollywood Star Brands Oscars As Nothing But A Fix: *Daily Mail*, January 27, 2000
– Hugo Pool review by Peter Keough, *Boston Phoenix*, December 1997
– Hugo Pool review by Thelma Adams, *New York Times*, December 1997
– Hurlyburly review by Lee Marshall, *Screen International*, October 1998
– Hurlyburly review by Liz Braun, *Toronto Sun*, December 1998
– Hurlyburly: A Bumpy Ride by Bruce Kirkland, *Toronto Sun*, January 1999
– In His Prime by Richard Corliss, *Time*, August 1997
– Irish Eyes, Neil Jordan by Marlaine Glicksman, *Film Comment*, January/February 1990
– Is Woody A Rip-Off Artist? by Lou Lumenick, *New York Post*, 1999
– Jennifer Lopez Stays Humble by Bob Thompson, *Toronto Sun*, October 1997
– Jennifer Lopez, Eonline, 1997

– Jennifer Lopez, Movieline, 1997
– John Schlesinger by Marjorie Bilbow, *Screen International*, May 1985
– Judgment In Berlin review, *Monthly Film Bulletin*, April 1990
– Judgment In Berlin video review, *Empire*, April 1990
– Just A Dash Of Awe by Louis B. Hobson, *Calgary Sun*, January 1999
– Lopez Takes The Heat by Louis B. Hobson, *Calgary Sun*, October 1997
– Loved review by Jessica Mellor, *Empire*, November 1998
– Made For Each Other by Bruce Kirkland, *Toronto Sun*, August 1997
– Madonna by Harry Dean Stanton, *Interview*, December 1985
– New Directions For Sean Penn by Kristine McKenna, *Los Angeles Times*, August 1991
– News column, *Screen International,* August 2 1996
– News piece by Leonard Klady, *Screen International*, April 1990
– Oliver Stone by Allan Jones, *Uncut*, 1998
– Oliver Stone by Ben Mitchell, *Neon*, May 1998
– Patricia Arquette by Kendell Crowstrom, *Interview*, February 1992
– Penn and the Art by Louis B. Hobson, *Edmonton Sun*, April 1999
– Penn And Wright Wedding, *Mr Showbiz*, April 1996
– Penn Behaving Badly by Rupert Howe, *Neon*, May 1998
– Penn by Paul Sherman, Salon, January 1999
– Penn by Scott Raab, *GQ* (U.S. edition), September 1998
– Penn Eyes British Columbia by Louis B. Hobson, *Calgary Sun*, November 1999
– Penn online chat, AOL Live, 1999
– Penn Pals With Paparazzi by Bruce Kirkland, *Toronto Sun*, May 1997
– Penn Signs For Killer Picture by Chris Petrikin, *Variety*, September 1999
– Penn's Crossing by Wilder Penfield, *Toronto Sun*, November 1995
– Phil Joanou by Randy Sue Coburn, *Interview*, October 1990
– Phillipe Rousselot, *American Cinematographer*, 1990
– Racing With The Moon review by Geoff Brown, *Monthly Film Bulletin*, August 1984
– Racing With The Moon review by John Kobal, *Films & Filming*, July 1984
– Rebelution: Dennis Hopper by Sean Penn, *Interview*, October 1994

— Reticent Penn Opens Up by Sam Whiting, *San Francisco Chronicle*, December 1998
— Robin Wright Now by Michael Kaplan, *Interview*, April 1992
— Robin Wright Penn by Simon Braund, *Empire*, November 1998
— Sean Penn At Close Range by Gavin Smith, *Film Comment*, September/October 1991
— Sean Penn Bites Back by Christopher Connelly, *Premiere* (U.S. edition), 1991
— Sean Penn by Graham Fuller, *Interview*, October 1995
— Sean Penn by Jay Carr, *Boston Globe*, December 1998
— Sean Penn by Julian Schnabel, *Interview*, 1991
— Sean Penn In A U Turn news story, *Mr Showbiz*, 1996
— Sean Penn May Star In Nova Scotia Shot Film, *Halifax Herald*, July 1999
— Sean Penn the Wild One by Christopher Hemblade, *Empire*, October 1997
— Sean Penn, The Human Tempest by Bruce Weber, *New York Times*, September 1991
— Sean To Run, by Roger Ebert, *Sky*, October 1988
— Shanghai Surprise review by Richard Combs, *Monthly Film Bulletin*, November 1986
— Shanghai Surprise review by Sally Rowland, *Films & Filming*, December 1986
— Shanghai Surprise review, *Variety*, September 1986
— She's So Lovely review by Allan Hunter, *Screen International*, May 1997
— She's So Lovely review by Barbara Shulgasser, *San Francisco Examiner*, 1997
— She's So Lovely review by Carrie Ridley, *Philadelphia Enquirer*, 1997
— She's So Lovely review by Gary Kamiya, Salon, 1997
— She's So Lovely review by Janet Maslin, *New York Times*, 1997
— She's So Lovely review by Mick La Salle, *San Francisco Chronicle*, 1997
— She's So Lovely review by Rita Kempley, *Washington Times*, 1997
— She's So Lovely review by Russell Smith, *Austin Chronicle*, 1997
— She's So Lovely video review, *Empire*, 1998
— State of Grace review by Tom Charity, *Sight And Sound*, June 1991
— State of Grace review, *Variety*, September 10, 1990

- Summerspell by Arthur Lazere, *Culture Vulture*, 1999
- Susan Sarandon, *Mirabelle*, 1996
- Sweet and Lowdown review by Dave Kehr, *Film Comment*, October/November 1999
- Sweet and Lowdown review by Louis B. Hobson, *Calgary Sun*, January 2000
- Taps review, *Monthly Film Bulletin*, March 1982
- Taps review, *Variety*, December 1981
- The Crossing Guard by Ana Maria Bahiana, *Screen International*, 1995
- The Crossing Guard by Angie Errigo, *Empire*, 1996
- The Crossing Guard by David Rooney, *Variety*, 1995
- The Crossing Guard by Janet Maslin, *New York Times*, November 1995
- The Crossing Guard by Roger Ebert, *Chicago Sun-Times*, 1995
- The Crossing Guard by Trevor Johnston, *Sight And Sound*, 1996
- The Crossing Guard review by Bruce Kirkland, *Toronto Sun*, December 1995
- The Crossing Guard, *Premiere*, 1996
- The Crossing Guard, *San Francisco Chronicle*, 1995
- The Dark Stuff, David Fincher by Chris Roberts, *Uncut*, November 1997
- The Falcon And The Snowman review by David Anson, *Newsweek*, 1985
- The Falcon And The Snowman review by Kim Newman, *Monthly Film Bulletin*, April 1985
- The Falcon And The Snowman review by Vincent Canby, *New York Times*, 1985
- The Falcon And The Snowman review, *Variety*, January 1985
- The Game by Allan Jones, *Uncut*, November 1997
- The Game news story by Caroline Westbrook, *Empire*, November 1997
- The Game news story, *Mr Showbiz*, 1996
- The Game review by Adam Smith, *Empire*, November 1997
- The Indian Runner review by Janet Maslin, *New York Times*, September 1991
- The Indian Runner review by Mark Kermode, *Sight And Sound*, 1991
- The Master Malick returns by Bruce Kirkland, *Toronto Sun*, December 1998

- The Thin Red Line by Louis B. Hobson, *Calgary Sun*, January 1999
- The Thin Red Line review by Janet Maslin, *New York Times*, December 1998
- The Thin Red Line review by Kenneth Turan, *Los Angeles Times*, December 1998
- The Thin Red Line review by Richard Corliss, *Time*, December 1998
- The Thin Red Line review by Rod Dreher, *New York Post*, December 1998
- The Wow by Stephen Rebello, Movieline, February 1998
- The Wright Project by Louis B. Hobson, *Edmonton Sun*, January 1998
- The Wright Stuff by Garth Pearce, *Empire*, July 1992
- Tim Robbins by Roy Grundman and Cynthia Lucia, *Cineaste*, 1996/97
- Timothy Hutton, *Interview*, 1983
- Tough Guy Talking by Karen Schoemer, *Newsweek*, December 1998
- U Turn by Stephen Schaefer, *New York Post*, 1997
- U Turn review by Gareth Grundy, *Neon*, May 1998
- We're No Angels by Robin Brunet, *American Cinematographer*, February 1990
- We're No Angels review by Pam Cook, *Monthly Film Bulletin*, June 1990
- We're No Angels review by Rob Beattie, *Empire*, June 1990
- Who Is Sean Penn? by Scott Haller, James Grant, Pamela Lansden, Mary Norbon, Frank Sanello, *People*, February 1985
- Woody Allen's Latest Jazzes Up Venice Film Festival by Merissa Marr, Reuters, September 1999
- Workman by Dan Yakir, *Film Comment*, 1986
- Wright Track by Kyle Smith, Elizabeth Leonard, Julie Jordan, Michael Sommers, Sue Miller, *People*, January 1999
- Wright Track by Kyle Smith, Elizabeth Leonard, Julie Jordan, Sue Miller, Michael Sommers, *People*, January 1999

Books

Andersen, Christopher: *Madonna Unauthorized* (Simon & Schuster, 1991)

Biskind, Peter: *Easy Riders, Raging Bulls* (Bloomsbury, 1998)

Carney, Ray: *The Films Of John Cassavetes* (Cambridge, 1994)

Duncan, Patricia: *Jennifer Lopez Unauthorized* (St Martins, 1999)

French, Philip: *Malle On Malle* (Faber & Faber, 1993)

Hirsch, Foster: *A Method To Their Madness* (Da Capo Press, 1984)

St Michael, Mick: *Madonna In Her Own Words* (Omnibus Press, 1990)

Thompson, Douglas: *Like A Virgin, Madonna Revealed* (Smith Gryphon, 1991)

Voller, Debbi: *Madonna The Style Book* (Omnibus Press, 1992)

Websites

All box-office gross figures are stated as cited on the us.imdb website.

Career awards as stated on the website us.imbd and in BFI London library.

Information about Leo Penn and Eileen Ryan's careers as displayed on the us.imdb website and in BFI London library.

The only mention that Sean Penn's middle name is Justin is on the unauthorised Indian Runner homepage.